PENGUIN BOOKS

THE SHAPE OF THE BEAST

Arundhati Roy is the author of *The God of Small Things* which won the Booker Prize in 1997. Two volumes of her non-fiction writing, *The Algebra of Infinite Justice* and *An Ordinary Person's Guide to Empire*, were published by Penguin India in 2001 and 2005 respectively. She lives in New Delhi.

The Shape of the Beast

conversations with

Arundhati Roy

PENGUIN BOOKS

PENGUIN
Published by the Penguin Group
Penguin Books India Pvt. Ltd, 11 Community Centre, Panchsheel Park, New Delhi 110 017, India
Penguin Group (USA) Inc., 375 Hudson Street, New York, New York 10014, USA
Penguin Group (Canada), 90 Eglinton Avenue East, Suite 700, Toronto, Ontario, M4P 2Y3, Canada (a division of Pearson Penguin Canada Inc.)
Penguin Books Ltd, 80 Strand, London WC2R 0RL, England
Penguin Ireland, 25 St Stephen's Green, Dublin 2, Ireland (a division of Penguin Books Ltd)
Penguin Group (Australia), 250 Camberwell Road, Camberwell, Victoria 3124, Australia (a division of Pearson Australia Group Pty Ltd)
Penguin Group (NZ), 67 Apollo Drive, Rosedale, North Shore 0632, New Zealand (a division of Pearson New Zealand Ltd)
Penguin Group (South Africa) (Pty) Ltd, 24 Sturdee Avenue, Rosebank, Johannesburg 2196, South Africa

Penguin Books Ltd, Registered Offices: 80 Strand, London WC2R 0RL, England

Published in Penguin by Penguin Books India 2009

10 9 8 7 6 5 4 3 2 1

ISBN 9780143066545

For sale in the Indian Subcontinent only.

Typeset in Bembo by Mantra Virtual Services, New Delhi
Printed at Gopsons Papers Ltd, Noida

CONTENTS

PREFACE

It's been a while since I wrote *The God of Small Things*. These last ten years have been years of intensely public political engagement, at once dream and nightmare for a writer of fiction. It was, of course, the decade of the War on Terror and India's debut on the world's stage as an economic and nuclear power. To some these years have brought undreamt of wealth and prosperity, to others such penury, such starvation, such despair as to render them barely human. To the Muslims of Gujarat they brought genocide. To the Muslims of India the spectre of Hindu fascism. To more than a hundred thousand farmers they brought suicide. To corporations, prospecting for profits, they brought unimaginable returns on investment. To the adivasis of Dantewada they brought enforced displacement and a brutal, government-sponsored civil war. To people in Kashmir, Manipur, Nagaland they brought continued military occupation elaborately dressed up as 'normality'.

Radical change has also brought new ways of doing things, creating things, communicating. Above all, there has been the excitement of witnessing the dawn of a new era of people's resistance.

The older, non-violent Gandhian movements have been reduced to functioning like advocacy groups and NGOs. Desperately trying to hold on to what little democratic space remains, most of them have buried their structural, political critiques under reformist enterprises and legal battles, bravely striving to extract some purchase for the poor from a marauding corporate-driven state. The grandest of them all, the struggle in the Narmada valley (whose critique of that great capitalist enterprise called 'development' has become the anthem of most resistance movements), has been all but crushed in excruciating slow motion, humiliated in full public view by every democratic institution it appealed to.

In the meantime, a range of more militant struggles have loomed into view. They have (as they should) asked profound questions of the current practice of non violent resistance. They ask how the hungry can go on hunger strikes, how people with no incomes can refuse to pay taxes, how those with no possessions can boycott foreign goods. They ask whether these are not tactics only available to middle class people and are meaningless to truly radical struggles. They believe that the threat of offering themselves up for harm (a practice fundamental to the principles of Satyagraha) cannot prevail over an Indian state that would be only too happy to see millions of poor people annihilate themselves.

Every day, every week, every month, more and more people are rising up in myriad ways, massing into a colossal wave of resistance—all kinds of resistance, violent, non violent, revolutionary and criminal—that threatens to engulf the country, fill the prisons, and for better or for worse shatter the almost pornographic contentment of India Shining.

The government's reaction has been to meet this uprising with police firings, arrests, with threats to call out the army, and if necessary, the air force. New laws have been pushed through. They make every kind of dissent—including non violent dissent—a criminal offence punishable by long years of imprisonment. In our trickle down economy, the only thing that seems to have trickled down, pretty effectively, is bullets and widespread state repression. In this way, before our very eyes, our hollow to begin with democracy has begun to devolve into an elaborately administered tyranny.

This is the backdrop against which I have lived and worked as a writer. This is the backdrop (which has quite often turned into a frontdrop) against which the conversations in this book have taken place. Some of them are straightforward interviews recorded in a single sitting. Others went on for days, back and forth on email, on the phone, while I was travelling. Four interviews in the section with David Barsamian called 'The Chequebook and the Cruise Missile' were done with the specific intention of compiling them in a book (*The Checkbook and the Cruise Missile*, 2004, South End Press).

I found myself enjoying these semi formal conversations because they were a flexible way of thinking aloud, of exploring ideas, personal as well as political, without having to nail them down with an artificially structured cohesion and fit them into an unassailable grand thesis. *The Shape of the Beast* was born and raised in that amorphous, liminal space—somewhere between the spoken and the written word.

It's probably not wise to attempt to re package in a preface something which exists only because it wasn't amenable to packaging in the first place. So I'll leave the reader to wander through these ideas in the way I did—not aimlessly, but not aimfully either.

Let me simply say that it takes more than one person to have a good conversation (though I admit I've had a few good ones with myself). So I take this opportunity to express my gratitude to my co conversationalists—N. Ram, David Barsamian, Anthony Arnove, S. Anand, Amit Sengupta, P.G. Rasool and Shoma Chaudhury.

Only the very young or the very naïve believe that injustice will disappear just as soon as it has been pointed out. But sometimes it helps to outline the shape of the beast in order to bring it down.

New Delhi
February 2008

Arundhati Roy

Scimitars in the Sun

'Deep at the heart of the horror of what's going on lies the caste system: this layered, horizontally divided society with no vertical bolts, no glue, no intermarriage, no social mingling; no human—*humane*—interaction that holds the layers together. So when the bottom half of society simply shears off and falls away, it happens silently. It doesn't create the torsion, the upheaval, the blowout, the sheer structural damage that it might, had there been the equivalent of vertical bolts.'

SCIMITARS IN THE SUN

IN CONVERSATION WITH N. RAM, JANUARY 2001.

Arundhati Roy, the Supreme Court judgement is unambiguous in its support for the Sardar Sarovar dam.[1] Is it all over? Are you, as the saying goes, running on empty?

There are troubled times ahead, and yes, I think we—when I say 'we', I don't mean to speak on behalf of the NBA, I just generally mean people who share their point of view—yes, I think we are up against it. We do have our backs to the wall ... but then, as another saying goes, 'It ain't over till the fat lady sings' [smiles]. Remember, there are a total of thirty Big Dams planned in the Narmada valley. Upstream from the Sardar Sarovar, the people fighting the Maheshwar dam are winning victory after victory. Protests in the Nimad region have forced several foreign investors—Bayernwerk, Pacgen, Siemens—to pull out. Recently, they managed to make Ogden Energy Group, an American company, withdraw from the project.[2] There's a full-blown civil disobedience movement on there.

But yes, the Supreme Court judgement on the Sardar Sarovar is a tremendous blow—the aftershocks will be felt not just in the Narmada valley, but all over the country. Wise men—L.C. Jain,[3] Ramaswamy Iyer[4]—have done brilliant analyses of the judgement. The worrying thing is not just that the Court has allowed construction of the dam to proceed, but the manner in which it disregarded the evidence placed before it. It ignored the fact that conditional environmental clearance for the project was given before a *single* comprehensive study of the project was done. It ignored the

'Scimitars in the Sun' first appeared in Frontline.

government of Madhya Pradesh's affidavit that it has no land to resettle the oustees, that in all these years MP has not produced a *single* hectare of agricultural land for its oustees. It ignored the fact that *not one* village has been resettled according to the directives of the Narmada Water Disputes Tribunal Award,[5] the fact that thirteen years after the project was given conditional clearance, *not a single* condition has been fulfilled, that there isn't even a rehabilitation Master Plan—let alone proper rehabilitation. Most importantly, most urgently, it allowed construction to proceed to ninety metres despite the fact that the Court was fully aware that families displaced at the current height of the dam have not yet been rehabilitated—some of them haven't even had their land *acquired* yet! It has in effect *ordered* the violation of the Tribunal Award, it has indirectly endorsed the violation of human rights to life and livelihood. There will be mayhem in the Narmada valley this monsoon if it rains—and of course, mayhem if it doesn't, because then there'll be drought. Either way the people are trapped—between the Rain Gods and the Supreme Court Gods.

For the Supreme Court of India to sanction what amounts to submergence without rehabilitation is an extraordinary thing. Think of the implications—today, the India country study done for the World Commission on Dams (WCD) says that Big Dams could have displaced up to *56 million people* in this country in the last fifty years![6] So far there has been, if nothing else, at least a pretence, that rehabilitation has been carried out, even though we know that lakhs of people displaced half a century ago by the famous Bhakra Nangal dam have still not been resettled. But now it looks as though we're going to drop even the charade of rehabilitation.

But the most worrying thing in the Sardar Sarovar judgement is the part where it says that once the government begins work on a project, after it has incurred costs, the Court ought to have no further role to play. This, after the very same Court found enough cause in 1994 to hold up construction work for six whole years ... With this single statement, the Supreme Court of India is abdicating its supreme responsibility. If the Court has no role to play in arbitrating between the state and its citizens in the matter of violations of human rights, then what is it here for? If justice isn't a court's business, then what *is*?

Why do you think things have come to this pass? This figure you have spoken of several times—between 33 million and 56 million people displaced by big dams in the last fifty years—it is hard to imagine something of this magnitude happening in another country without it being somehow taken into serious account ...

Without it being taken into account, without it giving pause for thought, without it affecting the nature of our country's decision-making process. The government doesn't even have a record of displaced people, they don't even count as statistics, it's chilling. Terrifying. After everything that has been written, said and done, the Indian government continues to turn a deaf ear to the protests. Six hundred and ninety-five big dams—40 per cent of all the big dams being built in the world—are being built in India as we speak. Yet India is the *only* country in the world that refused to allow the World Commission on Dams to hold a public hearing here. The Gujarat government banned its entry into Gujarat and threatened its representatives with arrest![7] The World Commission on Dams was an independent commission set up to study the impact of large dams. There were twelve commissioners, some of them representatives of the international dam industry, some were middle-of-the-roaders and some were campaigners *against* dams. It was the first comprehensive study of its kind ever done. The report was released in London in November by Nelson Mandela. It's valuable because it's a negotiated document, negotiated between two warring camps and signed by all the commissioners. I don't agree with everything that the WCD Report says, not by a long shot—but compared to the Supreme Court judgement that eulogizes the virtues of big dams based on *no evidence whatsoever*, the WCD Report is positively enlightened.[8] It's as though the two were written in different centuries. One in the Dark Ages, one now. But it makes no difference here. There was a tiny ripple of interest in the news for a couple of days. Even that's died down. We're back to business as usual. As they say in the army—'Bash on regardless'. Literally!

You must have an explanation, a personal theory perhaps, of why the government is so implacable, so unwilling to listen?

Part of the explanation—the relatively innocent part, I'd say—has to do with the fact that belief in Big Dams has become a reflex article of faith. Some people—particularly older planners and engineers—have internalized the Nehruvian thing about Big Dams being the Temples of Modern India. Dams have become India's secular gods—faith in them is impervious to argument. Another important part of the explanation has to do with the simple matter of corruption. Big Dams are gold mines for politicians, bureaucrats, the construction industry ... But the really sad, ugly part has less to do with the government than with the way our society is structured. More than 60 per cent of the millions of people displaced by dams are Dalit and adivasi. But adivasis account for only 8 per cent and Dalits about 15 per cent of our population. So you see what's happening here—a vast majority of displaced people don't even weigh in as real people.

And another thing—what percentage of the people who plan these mammoth projects are Dalit, adivasi or even rural? Zero. There is no egalitarian social contact *whatsoever* between the two worlds. Deep at the heart of the horror of what's going on lies the caste system: this layered, horizontally divided society with no vertical bolts, no glue, no intermarriage, no social mingling; no human—*humane*—interaction that holds the layers together. So when the bottom half of society simply shears off and falls away, it happens silently. It doesn't create the torsion, the upheaval, the blowout, the sheer structural damage that it might, had there been the equivalent of vertical bolts. This works perfectly for the supporters of these projects.

But even those of us who do understand and sympathize with the issue, even if we feel concern, scholarly concern, writerly concern, journalistic concern—the press has done a reasonably persistent job of keeping it in the news—still, for the most part, there's no real empathy with those who pay the price. Empathy would lead to passion, to incandescent anger, to wild indignation, to action. Concern, on the other hand, leads to articles, books, PhDs, fellowships. Of course, it is dispassionate inquiry that has created the pile-up of incriminating evidence against Big Dams. But now that the evidence *is* available and is in the public domain, it's time to do something about it.

Instead, what's happening now is that the relationship between concern and empathy is becoming oppositional, confrontational. When concern turns on empathy and says 'this town isn't big enough for the two of us', then we're in trouble, big trouble. It means something ugly is afoot. It means concern has become a professional enterprise, a profitable business that's protecting its interests like any other. People have set up shop, they don't want the furniture disturbed. That's when this politics becomes murky, dangerous and manipulative. This is exactly what's happening now—any display of feeling, of sentiment, is being frowned upon by some worthy keepers of the flame. Every emotion must be stifled, must appear at the high table dressed for dinner. Nobody's allowed to violate the dress code or, god forbid, appear naked. The guests must not be embarrassed. The feast must go on ...

But to come back to your question: as long as the protest remains civil and well-mannered, as long as we, the self-appointed opinion-makers, all continue to behave in respectable ways, as long as we continue to mindlessly defer to institutions that have themselves begun to cynically drop any pretence of being moral, just or respectable, why should the government listen? It's doing just fine.

Speaking of embarrassment, you have been criticized for embarrassing the NBA, for being tactless in your comments about the Supreme Court, for calling India a Banana Republic, for comparing the Supreme Court judgement to the NATO bombing of Yugoslavia ...

I'm being arraigned for bad behaviour [laughs]. I wear that criticism as a badge of honour. If 'tactless' was all I was about that judgement, then I'm guilty of an extreme form of moderation. As for embarrassing the NBA—the NBA has said and done far more radical things than I have. After the judgement, Baba Amte said—let me read this out—'the judiciary at times wearing the cloak of priesthood, suffocates the human rights of the poor. Corruption and capital are given legitimacy instead of adhering to the rule of law ...' Its leader Medha Patkar was arrested for picketing the gates of the Supreme Court.

Anybody who thinks that I have been intemperate has their ear very far from the ground. They have no idea how people in the valley reacted to the judgement. Days after it came out, a spontaneous procession of youngsters buried it in a filthy public gutter in Badwani. I was there. I saw it happen—the rallying slogan was 'Supreme Court ne kya kiya? Nyaya ka satyanaash kiya!'—(What has the Supreme Court done? It has destroyed justice!)

But I want to make it quite clear that I am an independent citizen. I don't have a party line. I stated my opinion. Not carelessly, I might add, I said what I thought. If that embarrassed anybody, it's a pity, but it's too bad. But perhaps my critics should check back with the NBA before voicing their touching concern.

But in the time-honoured tradition of our worst politicians, may I clarify what I *actually* said? I was talking to the press about the fact that the Supreme Court judgement had made things worse for the NBA than they were before it went to court. The Court ordered that the final arbiter of any dispute would be the prime minister. This is clearly in contravention of the directives laid down by the Narmada Water Disputes Tribunal Award. I said that a country in which it is left to the prime minister to clear a large dam project without any scientific studies being done, in which it is left to the prime minister to decide the final height of a dam regardless of how much water there is in the river, in which it is left to the prime minister to decide whether or not there is land available for resettlement—sounds very much like a Banana Republic to me. What is the point of committees and ministries and authorities if it's all up to Big Daddy in the end?

As for the business about the NATO bombing—I was talking to

a not-very-bright journalist, it turns out. I said that when the developed countries were industrializing, most of them had colonies which they cannibalized on their way up. We, on the other hand, have no colonies, so we turn upon ourselves and begin to gnaw at the edges of our own societies. I said it reminded me of the tiger in the Belgrade zoo which, driven insane with fear by the NATO bombing, began to eat its own limbs. This was twisted into the absurd statement that was eventually published. But it's my fault. I should have known better than to try and explain this to a disinterested journalist.

What next? Where does the struggle go from here?

I don't know, really. It has to move into a different gear. All our eyes are on the NBA, waiting for its next move. It will take some time to evolve a strategy. But they are extraordinary people—brilliant. I have never met a group of people with their range of skills—their mobilization abilities, their intellectual rigour, their political acumen. Their ability to move effortlessly from a dharna in Jaisindhi to arguing a subtle legal point in the Supreme Court, to making a presentation about the situation in the valley which leaves the World Bank no option but to pull out. The monsoon will be a terrible time for them—if it rains, people will need help on an emergency footing. The whole adivasi belt will go under.

You see, while the rest of us sit around arguing about how much we ought to respect the Supreme Court judgement, the people in the valley have no option. They can hardly be expected to respectfully accept their own dispossession. They will fight—how, is the question, and a very important one. The judgement, apart from what it says about the Sardar Sarovar, has sent out another very grave signal. After all, the fifteen-year-old struggle in the valley has so far been a spectacularly non-violent one. Now if that has come to naught, yielded nothing, I fear to think about what must be going through peoples' heads. They watch as the world around them gets more and more violent—as kidnappings, hijackings and the events that unfold in another valley further north grab the attention of the government and yield instant results. Already extremist groups have taken up position in parts of Madhya Pradesh. I'm sure they're watching the Narmada valley with great interest. I don't know what would happen if the NBA were to lose ground. I worry. I really do ...

It's something the government must think very seriously about. A fifteen-year-old non-violent people's movement is an extraordinary, magnificent thing. If it is dismissed in this contemptuous fashion, if violence is the only thing that forces the government to the negotiating table, then anarchy lurks around the corner.

Meanwhile in Gujarat, interesting, predictable things are happening. The false propaganda, the deliberate misinformation about the Sardar Sarovar is all coming home to roost. As long as the project was stalled, as long as it was a *potential* dam, it was easy to sell to voters as a miracle dam—the Sardar Sarovar will mend your bad knee, will produce your daughter's dowry, will serve you breakfast in bed. But major disputes over the water have already begun. People in Kutch and Saurashtra are waking up to the Big Con. The Kutch and Saurashtra branch of the BJP boycotted the inauguration-of-construction ceremony at the dam site. You know what happened there—three BJP ministers had their official Cielos burnt by an irate BJP mob, one minister was hurt and had to be airlifted out. The Kutch Jal Sankat Nivaran Samiti has a case against the government in court asking for construction to be stayed until Kutch is given its fair share of water. But a most interesting development is that the spokesperson of the Sardar Sarovar dam, the public face of the pro-dam lobby—Narmada Minister Jai Narain Vyas—was unceremoniously sacked recently. In the long run, it's probably good for Vyas—he'll be associated with the 'victory', but not with the murky politics of who gets the water. You can see it happening before your eyes: consensus in Gujarat is quickly coming unstuck.

Still, the honest answer to your question is: I don't really know what next. The answer will come, should come, from the people of the Narmada valley.

Have you read Ramachandra Guha's tirade against you in *The Hindu*?

[Smiles] Tirades. Plural. Yes, yes, of course I have. He's become like a stalker who shows up at my doorstep every other Sunday. Some days he comes alone. Some days he brings his friends and family, they all chant and stamp ... It's an angry little cottage industry that seems to have sprung up around me. Like a bunch of keening god-squadders, they link hands to keep their courage up and egg each other on—Aunt Slushy the novelist who's hated me for years, Uncle Defence Ministry who loves big dams, Little Miss Muffet who thinks I should watch my mouth. Actually, I've grown quite fond of them and I'll miss them when they're gone. It's funny, when I wrote *The God of Small Things*,[9] I was attacked by the Left—when I wrote 'The End of Imagination', by the Right.[10] Now I'm accused by Guha and his Ra-Ra Club of being—simultaneously—extreme Left, extreme Right, extreme Green, RSS, Swadeshi Jagran Manch *and*, by some devilish sleight of hand, on Guha's side too! Goodness, he's skidding on his own tail!

I don't know what it is with me and these academics-cum-cricket statisticians—Guha's the third one that I seem to have sent into an incensed orbit. Could it be my bad bowling action ...? [laughs]

Why have you chosen not to respond to Guha? Do you, as many others seem to, dismiss it as just a bad case of envy?

No, no, not at all. That would be too convenient, too easy. One could end up saying that about everybody who was critical. No, I think that would be unfair. I'd say it's far more complex and interesting than that. Guha's outburst is dressed up as an attack on my 'style'—but it's not really that at all.[11] If you part the invective, you'll see that our differences are serious, and seriously political. Chittaroopa Palit of the NBA has done a wonderful dissection of Guha's politics in her article, 'The Historian as Gatekeeper'.[12]

My language, my style, is not something superficial, like a coat that I wear when I go out. My style is me—even when I'm at home. It's the way I think. My style *is* my politics. Guha claims that we—he and I—are 'objectively' on the same side. I completely disagree. We are worlds apart, our politics, our arguments. I'm inclined to put as great a distance as possible between the Guhas of the world and myself.

Take his book—his biography of Verrier Elwin. It's competent and cleanly written. But our political differences begin with his choice of subject—personally, I think we've had enough, come on, *enough* stories about white men, however interesting they are, and their adventures in the heart of darkness. As a subject for a biography, frankly, I'm much more interested in Kosi Elwin, his Gond wife.

And the title of his book!—*Savaging the Civilized: Verrier Elwin, His Tribals, and India.*[13] *His* tribals! *His* tribals? For heaven's sake! Did he own them? Did he buy them? There's a bog, a marsh, a whole political swampland stretching between us right here. But it's his other work, his history books—he calls himself an ecological historian, you know that, don't you?

Yes, I believe so ...

Well, he's co-authored two books. One claims to be *An Ecological History of India*,[14] nothing less, the other he calls *Ecology and Equity*. The subtitle is *The Use and Abuse of Nature in Contemporary India* and it was published as recently as 1995.[15] In his ecological history, big dams don't merit *so much as a mention*. The other one has a thumbnail sketch of the struggle against big dams, and a cursory, superficial account of the struggle in the Narmada valley. For someone who sets himself up as a chronicler of the ecological history of a country that is the third-largest builder of big dams in the world, that has 3,600 big dams which have displaced maybe up to 56 million people, that have submerged *millions* of acres of prime forest land, that have led to the waterlogging and salinization of vast areas, that have destroyed estuarine ecosystems and drastically altered the ecology of almost every river in this country—wouldn't you say that the man has missed a wee thing or two! For goodness' sake—today, big dams are *the* staging ground for the most contentious debates on ecology, equity, social justice, bureaucratic and political intrigue, international finance and corruption on an unimaginable scale. Why does *none* of this merit attention from this ecological historian?

I'll tell you why: no amount of research, however painstaking, can make up for political vacuousness. If you don't ask the right questions, you don't get the right answers. If your politics is clear, if you had your ear to the ground, you wouldn't, you couldn't possibly, miss your mark so completely.

Look at the work of people like Ashish Kothari, Ramesh Billorey, Claude Alvarez, Himanshu Thakkar, Shripad Dharmadhikary, and further afield, Edward Goldsmith, Nicholas Hildeyard, Patrick McCully—McCully's book, *Silenced Rivers*, is a dazzling analysis of the ecology and politics of big dams.[16] Even someone like Anil Agarwal, though his views on the subject differ from those of the NBA—at least he engages with the issue. Their work is out there, it's vital stuff, it occupies centre stage in the debate—but let's face it, all of this puts Mr Guha in an extremely embarrassing position. He's like one of the creatures that didn't make it on to the ark. An ecological historian who missed the boat completely.

Does he have anything substantial to say? Apart from insulting me personally, deliberately, wilfully, maliciously, Guha has no argument against my argument, nothing to say about my facts. So he tries to legislate on how I ought to *feel* about them. Never was there a more passionate indictment of passion, a more hysterical denunciation of hysteria—he's right, I *am* hysterical. I am screaming from the bloody rooftops. And he is going *Shhhh ... you'll wake the neighbours!* But I *want* to wake the neighbours, that's my whole point. I want everybody to open their eyes.

Anyway, as far as I am concerned, it's not his insults I find as corny as the rest of it—his pronouncements about what's good for the environmental movement and what's not—the quintessence of which is that *he's* good for the movement and I'm not. His pronouncements on what constitutes good writing. His does. Mine doesn't. His unsolicited advice—advice to the NBA to disengage from me, advice to me to stop writing political essays and go back to literature. I mean apart from being someone with the Jurassic notion that politics and literature are mutually exclusive, who *is* he—the headboy? Cupboard captain? What's next? Is he going to put me on a diet? Choose my wardrobe? Sentence me to mustard bell-bottoms for a whole month?

Why have you not responded to Guha's charges?

Well, for one because I thought that four Sundays in a row (he's already used up three) discussing Arundhati Roy's work would be a bit much for readers ... and anyway, how does one respond to a Punch and Judy show?

Guha hasn't really read my work—he's ransacked it, wearing lenses so thick with animus that they blur his vision. He's virtually imagined the essays he wishes I'd written in order for him to demolish with his piercing wit and intellect, while his friends and colleagues nod and grin. Any response from me would end up sounding like—oh, I didn't say this, I didn't mean that ... But if he can't be bothered to read my work carefully, why bother with a response?

Let me give you an example of what I mean: Guha tries to ridicule me for comparing big dams to nuclear bombs. But my essay says ... here's exactly what it says [reads]:[17]

> Big Dams are to a nation's 'development' what nuclear bombs are to its military arsenal. They are both weapons of mass destruction, both weapons governments use to control their own people, both twentieth-century emblems that mark a point in time when human intelligence has outstripped its own instinct for survival ...

Surely Guha ought to know that this, in the English language, is what's called a relative analogy. In a relative analogy, one is comparing two relationships. I'm saying that big dams and nuclear bombs are both political instruments, extremely undemocratic political instruments. But I'm not saying bombs are dams. I'm not saying that dams are radioactive when they explode or that nuclear bombs irrigate agricultural land. If I say Amitabh Bachchan is to film stars what Coke is to fizzy drinks, I'm not comparing Amitabh Bachchan to a Coke or saying that film stars are fizzy drinks. In algebra, if I say x:y what w:r, it doesn't mean I'm saying x=w.

This is just one small example, there are other more sinister ones.

For instance, he picks out one sentence from my new essay 'Power Politics' that was published in *Outlook*.[18] It says:

> When the history of India's miraculous leap to the forefront of the Information Revolution is written, let it be said that 56 million Indians (and their children and their children's children) paid for it with everything they ever had.

It's not the horror of 56 million displaced people that bothers Guha. It's my reference to the Information Revolution, which was used to compare the meteoric development of one sector of the Indian economy with the horrific dispossession of another. Guha gratuitously makes out that I'm attacking—not just attacking—being 'grossly slanderous' to the IT giants, Tata, Wipro and I forget who else—he actually names particular companies ... *I don't!*[19] Having invented the insult, our intrepid knight in shining armour rallies to their defence. Is he real? Is he looking for friends in high places?

Talking about your essay 'The Greater Common Good', critics like Guha and B.G. Verghese say that it's sentimental without being factual, that it romanticizes adivasi lifestyles ...

Sentimental without being factual? Look, just because I don't wave my footnotes in people's faces and don't do the academic heavy breathing stuff doesn't mean I haven't studied the subject in depth. I don't believe that there's a single fact or argument—social, ecological, economic or political—about the Sardar Sarovar dam that's missing, or that has not been addressed, in my essay. For this I have to thank the NBA for making available to me every document at its disposal—and all the people who've published wonderful work on this issue over the years. I'm talking of Himanshu Thakkar, L.C. Jain, the FMG Report, Ramaswamy Iyer, Shripad Dharmadhikary, the Morse Committee Report, Rahul Ram's booklet *Muddy Waters*,[20] Ashish Kothari ... I owe a lot to long, sparky conversations with brilliant people in the valley, to *Kaise Jeebo Re,* Jharana Jhaveri and Anurag

Singh's documentary film, which first sent me on my travels in the Narmada valley ... It's a long, long list, and it's been more vital and insightful and instructive than doing years of research in a library.

As for the charge of romanticizing adivasi lifestyles—I thought the time when that sort of thing sent a frisson of excitement through the academic community had come and gone. I mean, come on—even the good old Gujarat government feeds at that foetid trough. When I was writing 'The Greater Common Good' I was acutely aware of two things: one, that I was not going to write on 'behalf' of anyone but myself because I think that's the most honest thing to do—in our society particularly, the politics of 'representation' is complicated and fraught with danger and dishonesty. Two, I was not writing an anthropological account of the lifestyles of people that I knew very little about. I was writing about social justice, about the politics of involuntary displacement, about what happens to people who are forcibly uprooted from an environment they know well and dumped in a world they know nothing about—a world in which, instead of a forest and a river and farmlands, they have unemployment and a tin shack. It's an unfair, unequal bargain for anybody—adivasi or Aggarwal. At no point in my essay have I even attempted to describe adivasi lifestyle, let alone romanticize it. Here's an early passage from 'The Greater Common Good' [reads]:

> Let me say at the outset that I'm not a city-basher. I've done my time in a village. I've had first-hand experience of the isolation, the inequity and the potential savagery of it. I'm not an anti-development junkie or a proselytiser for the eternal upholding of custom and tradition ...

Does that sound particularly romantic? The fact is I grew up in a village—not an adivasi village, but a village nevertheless. As a child, all I ever dreamed of was escaping. I don't need to do 'research' or 'fieldwork' or write a PhD to figure out what goes on. Anyone who's read *The God of Small Things* could work that out. If I do romanticize anything, it's the freedom, the anonymity of urban life ...

I'm sorry to go on about this, but Guha also denounces your work as self-indulgent and unoriginal. A serious charge against a fiction writer, wouldn't you say?

Self-indulgence is not the kind of charge that one can refute. If I *am* self-indulgent then ... what can I say? I'll stand in the corner and hang my head in shame [laughs]! But I think that the accusation has really to do with the fact that I often write in the first person. Like I said, I do that deliberately. I guess academics and journalists are trained to believe that saying 'I' is somehow anathema—because they're supposed to come across as objective. Of course that's nonsense—a person who conceals his or her identity is no more objective than a person who reveals it. Any clued-in anthropologist should know that. For an artist, a painter, a writer, a singer, introspection—contemplating the self, placing yourself in the picture to see where you fit—is often what art is all about. For a writer, to use the first person is a common narrative device. It's not just crudity, it's a fallacy, to equate this with self-indulgence. Mind you, this is not the only time that Guha shows a reflexive hostility towards writers and an opacity to literature.

There's a fine but important difference between self-indulgence and self-awareness. Self-awareness, in this case, is being aware—when you write—that you are complicit, that you are a beneficiary of the terrible politics of the society in which you live. When you reveal who you are and how you have benefited. Self-indulgence is when, masquerading as a concerned academic, you fill the Sunday papers with personal invective against somebody you don't like, and follow that up by selectively publishing your friends' personal letters of support, and then your rejoinder that supports their support ... and so on.

As for the charge of being unoriginal—when one is writing to advocate a political position, or in support of a people's movement that has been yelling its lungs out for the last fifteen years, one is not trying to be original, one is adding one's voice to theirs in order for *them* to be heard. Almost by definition, one is reiterating what they are saying. My essays are not about me or my brilliance or my originality or lack of it. They're not meant to be a career move—they're about re-stating the issue, they're about saying the *same* things over and over again ...

You actually do say something about this in your essays ...

Yes, I'm flattered that you remember. Here, from 'The End of Imagination' [reads]:[21]

> There can be nothing more humiliating for a writer of fiction to have to do than to re-state a case that has, over the years, already been made by other people... and made passionately, eloquently and knowledgeably. But I am prepared to grovel. To humiliate myself abjectly, because in the circumstances, silence would be indefensible ...

And again, in 'The Cost of Living', my Nehru Lecture on Big Dams:[22]

> If you're a writer, you tend to keep those aching eyes open ... Every day you are reminded that there is no such thing as innocence. And every day you have to think of new ways of saying old and obvious things. Things about love and greed. Things about politics and governance. About power and powerlessness ... things that must be said over and over again ...

You see, once again Guha is guilty of flabby conclusions drawn from sloppy reading. Frankly, between his suspect politics and slapdash scholarship, a woman's spoiled for choice. Does anyone have the right to defame someone in such careless, wanton fashion?

What about the charge that you simplify things, express them in black and white?

I don't simplify things. I try and explain complicated things in simple language. That's an entirely different enterprise. I find it offensive, this notion that things are too complicated to explain to an ordinary reader—again, this coterie, this club mentality. I write about things that vitally affect people's lives. To say that things are too complicated to explain is just not good enough. They must be explained. Experts love to hijack various aspects of an issue—displacement, rehabilitation, drainage, hydrology—and carry them off to their lairs where they guard them against the curiosity of the interested layperson. But eventually it's not rocket science. It's about our daily lives. All these things must be understood, connected up and explained—simply and cogently. It's not enough to accuse me of simplifying things—how? What? Where? Be specific. I can handle it. Everybody needs to know and understand what's going on. Not just the headboy and cupboard captain or the people who went to good schools. Not explaining something is a way of wresting power and holding on to it. It's a way of making yourself seem important, of trying to sound cleverer than you are. Of course I understand, there are jobs and there is money in that. But beyond a point, it becomes vulgar ...

As for my monochromatic vision, things *are* more black and white than we like to admit. The subtlety is seeping out of our lives at a pretty nifty pace.

One of the more persistent criticisms of the NBA and you is that you are negativists, naysayers ...

Ah yes, that's the 'Has Medha Patkar ever made a gobar gas plant?' school of thought. I just don't understand it. Big Dams wreak havoc. They have displaced millions of people, destroyed rivers and estuaries, submerged forests. The Narmada valley project alone will submerge 4,000 square kilometres of forest. How does the fight to save this count as negativity? If there's a forest fire raging and someone's trying to put it out, is it negativism or is it conservation? If everything is destroyed there'll be nothing left to conserve! The NBA has been an inspiration to people's movements all over the world—how can you knock this? Any *one* of its activists is worth more national pride than all the Miss Worlds and Miss Universes put together a thousand times over. There are amazing people doing the most wonderful work in water-harvesting and water management all over India. Premjibhai Patel of Upleta, Manubhai Mehta of Savarkundla, the Tarun Bharat

Sangh in Alwar and hundreds of others dotted across the country. But the firefighters and the water harvesters are *both* part of the alternative solution. Neither would be much good without the other. One makes space for the other. The NBA is like an ice-breaker—a ship that clears the way through cliffs of ice for other ships to sail through. There's no need for Medha Patkar to prove herself by designing a gobar gas plant, or for Rajinder Singh of the Tarun Bharat Sangh to prove himself by leading a dharna. They *both* do what they do wonderfully well. Pitting them against each other is small-minded, and it's destructive.

In his attack on your new essay 'Power Politics' published in *Outlook*, Guha says—and I quote: '... instead of turning on globalization ... we should come to terms with it, bend it as best we can to our interests—if we want to hold our own against foreign capital, we must encourage innovation by our technologists and entrepreneurs, not mock them as Roy does.'[23] Your comment?

I'm getting a bit tired of this bloke. You know, I think he must have read someone else's essay. Because I haven't yet—at least not that I'm aware of—written an essay on globalization. 'Power Politics', for anyone who's prepared to read it and not just the blurb on the cover of *Outlook*, is an essay that argues specifically against the privatization and corporatization of *essential infrastructure*. The word 'globalization' is not mentioned in the entire essay, not *once*. However, if and when I do write about globalization, I can assure you that my views on the subject will be very different from Guha's.

But to answer his charge that I have mocked our technologists—take a look at this, it's a passage from 'Power Politics':

> The First World needs to sell, the Third World needs to buy—it ought to be a reasonable business proposition. But it isn't. For many years, India has been more or less self-sufficient in power equipment. The Indian public sector company, Bharat Heavy Electricals Ltd (BHEL), manufactured and even exported world-class power equipment. All that's

> changed now. Over the years, our own government has starved it of orders, cut off funds for research and development and more or less edged it out of a dignified existence. Today BHEL is no more than a sweatshop. It is being forced into 'joint ventures' (one with GE, one with Siemens) where its only role is to provide cheap labour while they provide the equipment and the technology. Why? Why does more expensive, imported foreign equipment suit our bureaucrats and politicians better? We all know why. Because graft is factored into the deal. Buying equipment from your local store is just not the same thing.'

Does this sound like I'm mocking our technologists? Seriously, are we talking about the same essay? Is there some other Arundhati Roy? Arundhati Rao? Aradhana Roy? Does she write essays for *Outlook* and *Frontline*? And this man lectures me about intellectual probity?

The globalization debate has a very interesting spin on it—all its admirers, from Bill Clinton, Kofi Annan, A.B. Vajpayee to the cheering brokers in the stalls, all of them say the same lofty things: if we have the right institutions of governance in place—effective courts, good laws, honest politicians, participative democracy, a transparent administration that respects human rights and gives people a say in decisions that affect their lives—*then* the globalization project will work for the poor as well.

My point is that if all this were in place, then almost anything would succeed: socialism, communism, you name it. Everything works in paradise, even a poor old Banana Republic! But in an imperfect world, is it globalization that's going to bring us all this bounty? Is that what's happening here now that India is on the fast track to the free market? Does any *one* thing on that lofty list apply to the Narmada issue? Has the Supreme Court been just and accountable? State institutions transparent? Have people had a say, have they even been informed of decisions that vitally affect their lives? The answer is no, no, no ... And strange to say, in this beleaguered democracy, is it the votaries of globalization who are out there on the streets demanding accountability and responsible government? Of course not! And when someone else does—the NBA, or another people's movement, or an unfortunate private citizen, and has to contend with the police or, worse, academics with dubious politics—do these guys spring to their defence?

People have said that your essay 'Power Politics' is self-contradictory because it is an argument against the market and globalization by one who is placed at the heart of the global market for celebrity-hood.

People have said? [chuckles] It's the old boy again, isn't it—what's his thesis this time? That *all* celebrities *must* support globalization? Or that all writers who sell more than a certain number of copies of a book must support globalization? What's the cut-off? 30,000 copies? Do language editions count? Audio books? Braille?

I learned that *The God of Small Things* has sold six million copies in some forty languages. Your agent, David Godwin, also tells me that you've turned down offers for film rights from all over the world, including Hollywood. Are you waiting for the right director? Can we ever expect to see a film version of your novel?

No ... it's not about the right director. I don't think my book would make a good film. Besides, I don't think cinema *has* to be the last stop for literature, for novels. I had written two feature screenplays before I started writing *The God of Small Things*. I was feeling a little confined by the 'externality' of cinema. I wanted to be free to write from *within*, from *inside* people's hearts and heads. I wanted to feel free to write a whole page describing the moon and the trees in the river, not just have to write *Scene 21. Ext. Night. River.* Perhaps *because* I was a screenwriter, I set out to write a stubbornly visual but unfilmable book. And I did. The most visual things about *The God of Small Things* are the *feelings*. How would you film lonely, frightened little Rahel communing with a kangaroo-shaped waste bin in Cochin airport? I don't see cinema capturing the magic whisper, the helicopter kisses, the secret breathing of a cement kangaroo. Not unless you were making the Walt Disney version.

Also, I think that each reader of *The God of Small Things* has his or her own version of the film running inside their heads—there are six million different versions of the film. It would be a pity, don't you think, to let a single film-maker extinguish and appropriate all those versions, and force-fit them into a single, definitive one. This decentralized democracy is fine by me [smiles].

And this may sound silly, but I couldn't bear the idea of seeing actors play Estha, Rahel, Velutha, Ammu, Chacko ... it would kill me. I love them too much. I always will.

It's interesting that Prime Minister Vajpayee has been vacationing in a resort in Kerala made internationally famous by *The God of Small Things*. The media have been full of this connection ...

[Smiles] ... Yes. 'The History House. Whose doors were locked and windows open. With cool stone floors and dim walls and billowing ship-shaped shadows on the walls. Where plump, translucent lizards lived behind old pictures and waxy, crumbling ancestors with tough toe-nails and breath that smelled of yellow maps gossiped in sibilant, papery whispers ... '[24] I know that bit by heart. When I was a child it was an old, abandoned, crumbling house that filled my imagination. It's odd, when the prime minister goes vacationing in the setting of your worst, most private, childhood terrors. But wasn't it Toni Morrison who said something like 'literature is a very private thing, fashioned for public consumption'? It's funny how my terrors have become a tourist paradise ... but it's okay. I'm a big girl now [laughs].

Coming back to the issue of celebrity-hood—what's your relationship with it? How does it affect your writing? How do you deal with it?

Celebrity-hood—I hate that word. How do I deal with it? When Rock Hudson's career was on the skids, if he heard of a friend or colleague who was doing well, he'd say, 'Damn him, I hope he dies.'

That's a bit how I feel about my celebrity-hood. When I see a picture of myself in the papers, I feel hostile towards my public self and say, 'Damn her, I hope she dies ... [smiles].'

But actually, it's a very, very difficult thing for a person to come to terms with. For a while I thought it would drive me clean crazy. But I think I'm beginning to get the hang of it now. I worked it out from first principles—I'm a writer first and a celebrity next. I'm a writer who happens to have become, for the moment, a celebrity. As a matter of principle, I never do anything because I'm a celebrity. I don't inaugurate things, I don't appear as a chief guest anywhere, I don't grace occasions, I don't do chat shows, I don't do interviews, unless, of course, I'm rubbishing ecological historians or have something very specific to say.

But I also don't not do the things I want to do. I live, I love, I bum around, but above all, I write. And I support what I write. The celebrity part just trails along behind me making a heck of a noise—like a tin can attached to a cat's tail. I can't take it off, but it'll fall off on its own sooner or later. For now, I try to ignore it. Of course, it's not that simple. Every time I show up at an NBA dharna—and whether or not I show up is always a collective decision taken with them—the press invariably reports that I 'led' it along with Medha. Now that's ridiculous! Ridiculous to equate us in any way, ridiculous to imply that I lead anything, leave alone the NBA. Fortunately, both Medha and I are aware of the double-edged nature of media attention. As I keep saying, she's the good one, I'm the bad one, and the bad news is that we're friends!

How does all this affect your writing? It's given you a lot of space to say what you want to say. Does that put any pressure on you? Do you run the risk of becoming a ragbag of good causes?

Make no mistake, it's not the tin can, not celebrity-hood, that's given the space. It's my writing. I'm very clear on that one. I'm a celebrity because I'm a writer, not the other way around. After all, you or Vinod Mehta of *Outlook*—you're not running a soup kitchen, are you? You give me the space because it's worth it to you, because you know that I am read.

But if you're asking whether the fact that I know the space is available puts pressure on me—it does. At times. Because for me, to say nothing is as political an act as to say what I *do* say. There are these two voices virtually at war within me—one that wants me to dive underground and work on another book, another that refuses to let me look away, that drags me deep into the heart of what's going on around me. As for becoming a ragbag of good causes—you're right, the pressure is tremendous. Simply because horror lurks around every corner and it's hard to listen to an account of it and then say that you can do nothing to help. But, you know, for me to become an ambassador of good causes would do injustice to the causes and a great violence to my writing self—and that's something that I will not sacrifice. At any cost. A singer sings, a painter paints, a writer writes. For some it's a profession. For others it's a calling. One does it because one must.

It sounds like a lonely place that you work from. What do you find most difficult about being who you are and doing what you do?

Well, every writer—good, bad, successful or not—who's sitting at a desk looking at a blank piece of paper, is lonely. It's probably the loneliest work in the world. But once the work is done, it's different. I'm not lonely at all—I'm the opposite of lonely. How can I, of all people, complain? I like to think that if by chance I were to become completely destitute, I could spend the rest of my life walking into people's homes and saying, 'I wrote *The God of Small Things*, will you give me lunch?' It's a wonderful feeling. When I go to the Narmada valley, I see my essay being read in Hindi, in Gujarati, in Marathi—even translated orally into Bhilali. I see parts of it being performed as a play. What more could a writer ask for? How much less lonely can I be?

It's true that I write about contentious things. Closer to home, there's some hostility. Each time I step out I hear the snicker-snack of knives being sharpened, I catch the glint of scimitars in the sun.

But that's good. It keeps me sharp—fit, alert, it focuses my thought, hones my argument, makes me very careful about what I say and how I say it. On the whole, it isn't a bad university to go to. I don't have the luxury of carelessness that some of my critics do.

Well, even Ramachandra Guha applauds you for your courage and the NBA for its loyalty to you.

Courage and loyalty? They sound like kind words for a good horse. D'you think that's what he meant when he called us 'neigh-sayers'? [laughs helplessly] ... Sorry about that, Ram!

A woman stands in front of a temple submerged by the dam on the Narmada.
Photo © Karen Robinson.

‘My language, my style, is not something superficial, like a coat that I wear when I go out. My style is me—even when I’m at home. It’s the way I think. My style *is* my politics.’

The Chequebook and the Cruise Missile

'Once you've seen certain things, you can't un-see them, and saying nothing is as political an act as speaking out ... There's no innocence and there isn't any sense in which any of us is perfect or not invested in the system. If I put money in a bank it's going to fund the bombs and the dams. When I pay tax, I'm investing in projects I disagree with. I'm not a completely blameless person campaigning for the good of mankind. But from that un-pristine position, is it better to say nothing or to say something?'

THE COLONIZATION OF KNOWLEDGE

IN CONVERSATION WITH DAVID BARSAMIAN, FEBRUARY 2001.

Tell me about Kerala where you grew up. It's a singular place in India for many reasons. It's multi-religious, has a high rate of literacy and has been reasonably free from the kinds of sectarian violence that plague other parts of the country.

Kerala is a place where great religions coincide. You have Christianity, Hinduism, Islam and Marxism [laughs]. They all rub each other down and metamorphize into something new. Politically Kerala is quite volatile. This might mean a clash between the Marxists and the right-wing Hindu nationalist Rashtriya Swayamsevak Sangh [RSS] or between different communist parties, though it's relatively free of the kind of caste killing that you have in states like Bihar or Uttar Pradesh.[1] When I first came to north India, it was almost like visiting a different century. Still, Kerala is a complex society because it's progressive and parochial simultaneously. Even among the Syrian Christians—who are the oldest, most orthodox Christians in India—you have caste issues. If you look at the communist parties, most of their leaders are from the upper castes. When they fight elections, candidates are carefully chosen to represent the dominant caste of their respective 'vote bank'—an example of how communism will harness the traditional caste system in its quest for power in a 'representative' democracy. Kerala is known for its high literacy rate, but the quality of the education itself is execrable. Kerala University is among the worst universities in India.

An earlier version of 'The Colonization of Knowledge' appeared in The Progressive, *April 2001.*

I don't think that something like the Narmada valley development project could easily happen in Kerala.[2] That kind of mass injustice—the eviction of hundreds of thousands of people—might be hard to pull off. On the other hand, the first thing E.M.S. Namboodiripad did when he came to power as head of the first democratically elected communist government in the world, was to get Birla, the big industrial group, to set up a huge rayon factory in Calicut.[3]

In the last thirty years that factory has denuded the bamboo forest, poisoned the Chaliyar river and polluted the air. There is a high incidence of cancer among the local people and the factory workers. The factory is Kerala's biggest private industry and Kerala, being Kerala, has thirteen trade unions. In the name of employing 3,000 people it destroyed the livelihood of hundreds of thousands who lived on these natural resources: fishermen, bamboo workers, sand quarriers. (They don't qualify as 'workers' in the communist dictionary.) The government and courts did nothing about it. Eventually the factory closed down on its own because it had finished off all the raw material there and wanted to move elsewhere.

Because Kerala is so riven with internecine politics, everybody disagrees with everybody else. There are hundreds of factions, and eventually everything remains frozen in a sort of political rigor mortis.

What's the status of women generally in Kerala? Is it different from the rest of India given the high levels of education?

I know that people say that fertility rates have dropped in Kerala because of literacy.[4] It's probably true. But you have only to watch Malayalam cinema to feel sick to your stomach at the way women are treated and the way women behave. When I was a child, every film I saw had the heroine being raped. Until I was about fifteen, I believed that every woman gets raped. It was just a question of waiting for yours to happen. That was the kind of terror that was inculcated in young girls.

My mother is very well known in Kerala because in 1986 she

won a public interest litigation case. She challenged the Syrian Christian inheritance law that said that a woman can inherit one-fourth of her father's property or Rs 5,000, whichever is less. The Supreme Court ruling in her case gave women equal inheritance with retrospective effect from 1956. But actually no women go to court to claim this right. Everyone said, 'You can't have it going back to 1956 because the courts will be flooded with complaints.' It didn't happen. The churches had will-making classes. They taught fathers how to disinherit their daughters. It's a very strange kind of oppression that happens there. Women from Kerala work all over India and all over the world. Many of the world's nuns and nurses are from Kerala. They send all the money they earn back home to support their families. And yet the nurses, who earn comparatively huge salaries, will get married, pay a dowry and end up having the most bizarrely subservient relationships with their husbands.

Growing up in a little village in Kerala was a nightmare for me. All I wanted to do was to escape, to get out, to never have to marry somebody there. Not that people were queuing to marry me [laughs]. I was the worst thing a girl could be: thin, black and clever. No looks, no dowry, no good.

Your mother, Mary, also broke the unofficial love laws.

She married a Bengali Hindu and then, what's worse, divorced him, which meant that everyone was confirmed in their opinion that it was a terrible thing to marry for love—outside the community.

What was it like growing up without a father at home?

In Kerala everyone has what is called a *tharavaad*, your ancestral home. If you don't have a father, you don't have a *tharavaad*. You're a person without an address. 'No address', that's what they call you. I grew up in Ayemenem, the village in which *The God of Small Things* is set.[5] Given the way things have turned out, it's easy for me to say that I thank god that I had none of the conditioning that a normal middle-class Indian girl would have. I had no father, no presence of this man 'looking after' us and beating or humiliating our mother occasionally in exchange. I had no caste, no religion, no supervision.

It was made very clear to me early on by everyone around me that I would not be given the protection that other children around me had. Anything could have happened to me. I could have gone under. But because I didn't, I have a vantage point from which to watch what's going on now. I'm not rural, not urban, not completely 'traditional' nor wholeheartedly 'modern'. I grew up in a village. I saw rural India at work. And yet I had the advantage of having an education. It's like being at the top of the bottom of the heap—without the blinkered single-mindedness of the completely oppressed nor the flabby self-indulgence of the well-to-do. There must be very few girls in India whose mothers say, 'Whatever you do, don't get married. And don't sleep with a man until you're financially independent.' It was sound advice—not that I listened [laughs]. When I see brides all dressed up for the sacrifice, it gives me a rash. I find them ghoulish, almost. I find what that whole thing means in India so frightening—to see this decorated, bejewelled creature willingly, happily entering a life of permanent subjugation.

You're close to your mother today?

I left home when I was sixteen, for all sorts of reasons, and didn't see her for many years. Like many mothers and daughters, we had a complicated relationship—nothing to do with our politics, though. My mother is like someone who strayed off the set of a Fellini film. But to have been brought up by a woman who never made it her mission in life to find another partner to entwine herself around is a wonderful thing.

My mother runs a school in the town of Kottayam. It's phenomenally successful. People try to book their children into it before they are even born. Yet folks in town don't know quite what to make of her. Or me. The problem is that we are both women who are unconventional. The least we could have done was to be unhappy. But we aren't. That's what bothers people: the fact that you can make these choices and be happy—like a pair of witches.

My mother's school is very unconventional. She started it with five or six students when I was about four or five. She managed to persuade the Rotary Club of Kottayam to rent us their premises in the daytime. In the morning we would put up tables and be taught how to read and write. In the evening the men would meet and smoke and leave their cigarette butts and teacups and whisky glasses all over. Middle-class Indian men leave their rubbish everywhere for others to clean up. The next morning we would clean it all up and then it would be the school. I used to call it a sliding, folding school. People know that the education children get from my mother's school is invaluable. And yet it makes them uncomfortable because she's not amenable to all the rules and regulations of their society.

Now it's complicated even further by what has happened to me since *The God of Small Things* was published. I was the first student from her school. In a way she's vindicated—it's like a B-grade film script. Suffering, belief and hard work, then beautiful retribution. You can't imagine that something like this could happen: the way we were treated by that town, the way things were when I was a child, compared to now. Even the book, people don't know how to deal with it. They want to embrace me and to say that this is 'our woman', and yet they don't want to address what the book is about, which is their society and its intrinsic, callous brutality. They have to find ways of filtering out the parts they don't want to address. They have to say it's a book about children, something like that.

You were the target of a criminal case in Kerala because someone said *The God of Small Things* was obscene.

I was charged with corrupting public morality [laughs]. As though public morality was pure until I came along. I was at the high court in Cochin a year or two ago. I had appealed to have the case quashed, saying that for a number of reasons it wasn't legally valid. The lawyers of both sides were ready to argue but the judge came on and said, 'I don't want to hear this case. Every time it comes up before me I get chest pains.' [laughs] He postponed the hearings, and the case still sits there in court.

Since you wrote your novel, you've produced some remarkable political essays. What was that transition like, from writing in the world of fiction and imagination to writing about concrete things, like dams, people being displaced in the Narmada valley, globalization and Enron?

It's only to other people that it appears to be a transition. When I was in fourth year in architecture school, I already knew that I would never practice architecture because it involves being a part of a chain of such ugly exploitation. I couldn't do it. I was very interested in urbanization and town planning, in how a city comes to be, what it is and what it does to those who live in it.

I've been doing this kind of work since I was twenty-one. It's only to the outside world, those who came to know me after *The God of Small Things*, that it seems like a transition. I wrote political essays before I wrote the novel. I wrote three essays called 'The Great Indian Rape Trick' (in two parts) and 'The Naughty Lady of Shady Lane' about the way the film *Bandit Queen* exploited Phoolan Devi and whether or not somebody should have the right to re-stage the rape of a living woman without her consent.[6]

I don't see a great difference between *The God of Small Things* and my non-fiction. In fact, I keep saying, fiction is the truest thing there ever was. Today's world of specialization is bizarre. Specialists and experts end up severing the links between things, isolating them, actually creating barriers that prevent ordinary people from understanding what's happening to them. I try to do the opposite: to create links, to join the dots, to tell politics like a story, to communicate it, to make it real. To make the connection between a man with his child telling you about life in the village he lived in before it was submerged by a reservoir, and the WTO, the IMF, and the World Bank. *The God of Small Things* is a book which connects the very smallest things to the very biggest. Whether it's the dent that a baby spider makes on the surface of water in a pond or the quality of the moonlight on a river or how history and politics intrude into your life, your house, your bedroom, your bed, into the most intimate relationships between people—parents and children, siblings and so on.

If you lose these connections, everything becomes noise, meaningless, a career plan to be on track for tenure. It's a bit like the difference between allopathy and homeopathy or any other form of indigenous medicine. You don't just treat the symptoms. You don't just say, 'Oh, you've got a patch on your skin, so let me give you some steroids.' You ask, 'Why do you have it? How has it come there? What does it mean? What are you thinking about today? Are you happy? Why has your body produced this?' You can't just be a skin expert. You must understand the human body and the human mind.

You've talked about the colonization of knowledge and its control and a Brahmin-like caste that builds walls around it. What do you think the relationship should be between knowledge and power and politics?

All over the world today people are fighting for a right to information. The organizations that control the world today—the WTO, the IMF, the World Bank—operate in complete secrecy. Contracts that goverments sign with multinationals, which affect people's lives so intimately, are secret documents. For example, I think that the contract between Enron, the giant Houston-based energy corporation, and the government of Maharashtra should be a public document. It is the biggest contract ever signed by the Indian government. It guarantees this one corporation profits that add up to more than 60 per cent of India's rural development budget.[7] Why is it a secret document? Who is the government to sign away its public buildings as collateral? The government holds everything, whether it's the natural resources or the Rashtrapati Bhavan, the President's residence in New Delhi, in trust for the people that it represents. It cannot sign these things away. That contract must be a public document. That's one aspect of the relationship between knowledge and power.

But there is a more insidious aspect. It isn't a coincidence that 400 million Indian people are illiterate. When I say 'illiterate', I don't want to imply that the kind of education that is being imparted is literacy. Education sometimes makes people float even further away from things they ought to know about. It seems to actually obscure their vision. The kind of ignorance that people with PhDs display is unbelievable. When the Supreme Court judgement about the Narmada valley came out in October 2000, I wrote an analysis of what it meant.[8] Then I went to the valley. People were marching. They were so angry, they desecrated a copy of the judgement and buried it. There was a public meeting at which many adivasis and farmers spoke. A friend of mine said, 'Isn't it amazing that there isn't a single point that you have brought up that they're not already talking about with the same sophistication?' I said, 'No, we're the ones who have to make the leap of faith. For them, it's their lives.'

The Supreme Court judgement transforms their lives. It's not an intellectual exercise. It's not research. If you see how far away people who are educated and have become consultants or experts or whatever have floated from what's happening, I think you'll see the entire 'development' debate is a scam. The biggest problem is that what they say in their project reports and what actually happens are two completely different things. They've perfected the art of getting it right on paper, but that has nothing to do with what is happening on the ground.

The distance between power and powerlessness, between those who take decisions and those who have to suffer those decisions, has increased enormously. It's a perilous journey for the poor—it's a pitfall filled to overflowing with lies, brutality and injustice. Sitting in Washington or Geneva in the offices of the World Bank or the WTO, bureaucrats have the power to decide the fate of millions. It's not only their decisions that we are contesting. It's the fact that they have the power to make those decisions. No one elected them. No one said they could control our lives. Even if they made great decisions, it's politically unacceptable.

Those men in pin-striped suits addressing the peasants of India and other poor countries all over again—assuring them that they're being robbed for their own good, like long ago they were colonized for their own good—what's the difference? What's changed? The further and further away, geographically, decisions are taken, the more scope you have for incredible injustice. That is the primary issue.

The power of the World Bank is not only its money, but its ability to accumulate and manipulate knowledge. It probably employs more PhDs than any university in the world. It funds studies that suit its purpose. Then it disseminates them and produces a particular kind of world view that is supposedly based on neutral facts. But it's not. It's not at all. How do you deal with that? What is the difference between that and the Vishwa Hindu Parishad (VHP) or the Bharatiya Janata Party (BJP) openly rewriting history texts and saying that we will now give you the Hindu version of history?[9] The World Bank version of development is the same thing.

The Narmada valley project envisions the construction of something like 3,000 large and medium dams along the course of the Narmada river and its tributaries. It covers three states, Maharashtra, Gujarat and Madhya Pradesh. There's been a resistance movement to what was originally a World Bank scheme. The World Bank has now withdrawn from the project and the government of India has taken it over. Tell me about the Narmada Bachao Andolan (NBA), the Save the Narmada Movement.

The remarkable thing about the NBA is that it is a cross-section of India. It is the adivasis, the upper-caste big farmers, the Dalits, and the urban middle class. It's a forging of links between the urban and the rural, between farmers, fishermen, writers, painters and lawyers. That's what gives it such phenomenal strength.

When dam proponents in India say, 'You know, these middle-class people, they are against development and they're exploiting illiterate farmers and adivasis,' it makes me furious. After all, the whole Narmada valley development project was dreamed up by the middle-class mind. Middle-class urban engineers designed it. You can't expect the critique to be just rural or adivasi. People try to delegitimize the involvement of the middle class, saying, 'How can you speak on behalf of these people?' No one is speaking on behalf of anyone. The criticism of middle-class dam opponents is an attempt to isolate the adivasis, the farmers and then crush them. After all, government policy documents aren't in Hindi or Bhilali, and the Indian Supreme Court doesn't work in Hindi or Bhilali.

The NBA is a fantastic example of a resistance movement in which people link hands across caste and class. It is India's biggest, finest, most magnificent resistance movement since the independence struggle succeeded in the 1940s. There are other resistance movements in India. It's a miracle that they exist. But I fear for their future.

When you travel from India to the west, you see that the western notion of 'development' has to do with a lack of imagination. A taming of the wilderness, of the human soul. An inability to understand that there is another way to live. In India, the anarchy and the wilderness still exist (though they're under the hammer). But still, how are you going to persuade a Naga sadhu—whose life mission has been to stand naked on one leg for twenty years or to tow a car with his penis—that he can't live without Coca-Cola? It's an uphill task.

Estha, one of the characters in your novel, walks 'along the banks of the river that smelled of shit and pesticides bought with World Bank loans'.[10]

When I first met activists from the NBA, they told me, 'We knew that you would be against big dams and the World Bank when we read *The God of Small Things*.' I've never had that kind of a reading before [laughs].

In India, the whole pesticide issue is just unbelievable. The Green Revolution, bringing canal irrigation, borewells, and chemical pesticides and fertilizer, has now led to serious problems. After a point, the productivity of the land begins to diminish. That has started happening in places like Andhra Pradesh, where farmers have been forced to abandon traditional farming and grow cash crops. Now that move has backfired because of the import of foodgrains under new WTO rules. Hundreds of farmers in Punjab and Andhra

Pradesh are committing suicide because of their growing debt. They have to invest more and more in pesticides and fertilizers. Pests have grown resistant to the chemicals. The farmers have to make large capital investments to force a little bit of productivity out of these dead lands. They end up killing themselves by drinking pesticide.

Arrogant interventions in ecosystems that you don't understand can be ruinous. In the Northeast of India, some states started exporting frog legs to France. It became a big earner of foreign exchange. As the frogs began to disappear, the pests they used to eat began to destroy crops. The states started having to buy pesticides (with World Bank loans), which eventually cost more than the money they made by exporting frog legs.

I think it was in Tanzania that farmers began to shoot hippos because they were raiding and destroying the crops. When the hippos disappeared, so did the fish in the river. Later they discovered that these fish used to lay their eggs in the shit of the hippos. When human beings don't respect something that they don't understand, they end up with consequences that you cannot possibly foretell.

The western notion of thinking that you must understand everything can also be destructive. Why can't we just be satisfied with not understanding something? It's all right. It's wonderful to not understand something. To respect and revere the earth's secrets.

There was a particular mountain in the Himalayas that hadn't ever been climbed. Some climbers wanted to climb it. I had a friend who led a campaign to allow that one peak to remain unclimbed. There's a kind of humility in that. I don't mean to take an extreme position and say that science is bad. But there ought to be a balance between curiosity, grace, humility and letting things be. Must everything be poked at and prodded and intervened in and understood?

Proponents of the Narmada valley project say that it will bring water to the thirsty and crops to the parched land of three states. What's wrong with that?

I've written about this extensively in my essay 'The Greater

Common Good'.[11] They say the Sardar Sarovar dam is going to take water to Kutch and Saurashtra, the regions of Gujarat which were the hardest hit by the earthquake in January 2001. They have a terrible drought in these areas. But if you look at the government's own plans, you'll see there is no possibility that the water will get to these regions, even if everything that they say were to work. For example, they arbitrarily assume an irrigation efficiency of 60 per cent. No irrigation project has ever been more than 35 per cent efficient in India. Kutch and Saurashtra are right at the tail end of this big canal system, but all the politically powerful areas are right up at the head of the canal. They will take away all the water. Already big sugar factories have been licenced before the dam has been built. According to the project, sugar was not going to be allowed to be planted. Huge five-star hotels and golf courses have been built.

Even if all this hadn't happened, according to the Gujarat government's own plan, the Sardar Sarovar dam will irrigate 1.2 per cent of the cultivable area of Kutch and 9 per cent of Saurashtra. That's forgetting about the irrigation efficiency and the sugar factories, about the fact that rivers close to Kutch and Saurashtra are being dammed and the water is being taken to central Gujarat.

In fact, when the Supreme Court judgement came and the Gujarat BJP government had a huge ceremony to inaugurate the beginning of the construction of the dam, Kutch and Saurashtra boycotted it. They said, 'You are just using us to mop up 85 per cent of Gujarat's irrigation budget—and in the process not leaving any money for local water harvesting or for more local solutions to this problem.'

That's one thing. The second is that they don't even ask, 'Why is there a drought in Kutch and Saurashtra?' The reason is that the government has systematically cut down all the mangrove forests. They have mined groundwater indiscriminately and so there's an ingress of seawater from the coast. They have big industrial complexes that poison whatever groundwater remains. The Gujarat government will do nothing, nothing at all to control this kind of thing.

If they want to take water from the Narmada to Kutch just to make a political statement, of course they can, but it will be as a circus—an economically unviable political circus—like taking red wine or champagne to Kutch. Narmada is so far away from Kutch and Saurashtra that it's a joke to take all that water all the way up through Gujarat. For the price of the Sardar Sarovar dam, you could finance local water-harvesting schemes in every single village in the state of Gujarat.[12]

What prompted the World Bank to pull out of the project?

The people's resistance movement in 1993 and 1994. The World Bank was forced to set up an independent review. They sent out a committee under a man named Bradford Morse. The Morse Report, which is now a kind of landmark, said in no uncertain terms that the Bank should pull out. Of course the Bank tried to cover up the report. It sent another committee, the Pamela Cox Committee, which tried to say everything's fine. But Morse had agreed that he would do this study only provided it was an independent report. Finally the World Bank was forced to pull out.[13] This is unprecedented in the murky history of the World Bank.

The government of India seems to be determined to complete the Narmada project. What's driving it?

First of all, you must understand that in India the myth of big dams is sold to us from the time we're three years old. In every school textbook, we learn that Pandit Nehru said 'dams are the temples of modern India'.[14] Criticizing dams is equated with being anti-national.

The thing about dams and the struggle against them is that people have to understand that they're just monuments to corruption and they are undemocratic. They centralize natural resources, snatch them away from people, and then redistribute them to a favoured few.

The first dam built on the Narmada was in Madhya Pradesh, the Bargi dam, which was completed in 1990. They said it would displace 70,000 people and submerge 101 villages. One day they just filled the reservoir. 114,000 people, almost twice the government's projection, were displaced and 162 villages were submerged. They were just driven from their homes when the waters rose. They had to run up the hill with the cattle and children. Ten years later, that dam irrigates 5 per cent of the land that they said it would. It irrigates less land than it submerged.

In Gujarat, the Sardar Sarovar dam has been used by every political party as a campaign issue for years. The amount of disinformation about this dam is extraordinary. For contractors and politicians, just the building of the dam makes them a lot of money.

Forty per cent of the big dams that are being built in the world today are in India. Tens of millions of Indians have already been displaced by many of the dam projects.[15] What happens to these people? What kind of resettlement or compensation is provided by the government?

Nobody knows. When I was writing 'The Greater Common Good', what shocked me more than the figures that do exist and are thrown around and fought over by pro-dam and anti-dam activists are the figures that don't exist. The Indian government does not have any estimate of how many people have been displaced by big dams. I think that's not just a failure of the state, but a failure of the intellectual community. The reason that these figures don't exist is that most of the displaced are the non-people, the adivasis and the Dalits.

I did a sanity check based on a study of fifty-four dams done by the Indian Institute of Public Administration. According to that study, the number of reservoir-displaced, which is only one kind of displacement, came to an average of something like 44,000 people per dam. I said, 'Let's assume that these fifty-four dams are the bigger of the big dams. Let's *quarter* this average and say each dam displaced 10,000 people. We know that India has built 3,300 big dams in the last fifty years. So just a sanity check says that it's 33 million people displaced.' At the time I wrote this, people mocked this figure. Now, the India Country Study done by the World Commission on Dams puts that figure at as much as 56 million.[16]

Today, India doesn't have a national resettlement policy. The government of Madhya Pradesh, where 80 per cent of Sardar Sarovar-displaced people are from, gave a written affidavit in court saying it did not have enough land to resettle people. The Supreme Court still ordered the construction of the dam to go ahead.

What happens to the people who are driven out from their villages by these development projects and by the general garrotting of India's rural economy? They all migrate to the cities. And there, again, they are non-citizens, living in slums. They are subject to being evicted at a moment's notice, any time a new office complex or a five-star hotel chain covets the land they live on.

You compare the uprooting of these people to a kind of garbage disposal.

That's exactly what it is. The Indian government has managed to turn the concept of non-violence on its head. Non-violent repression. Unlike, say, China or Turkey or Indonesia, the government of India doesn't mow down its people. It doesn't kill people who refuse to move. It just continues to pursue the brutal path of this particular model of 'development' and to ignore the consequences. Because of the caste system, because of the fact that there is no social link between the people who make the decisions and the people who suffer the decisions, it just goes ahead and does what it wants. It's quite an efficient way of doing things. India has a very good reputation in the world as a democracy, as a government that cares. But, that's just not true.

But you say about your own politics that you're 'not an anti-development junkie nor a proselytizer for the eternal upholding of custom and tradition'.[17]

How can I be? As a woman who grew up in a village in India, I've spent my whole life fighting tradition. There's no way that I want to be a traditional Indian woman. So I'm not talking about being against development. I'm talking about the politics of development. I'm talking about more development, not less. More democracy, not less. More modernization, not less. How do you break down this completely centralized, undemocratic process of decision-making? How do you make sure that it's decentralized and that people have power over their lives and their natural resources? I don't even believe in the modern business-like notion of 'efficiency'. It dovetails with totalitarianism, fascism. People say, 'If it's decentralized it will be inefficient.' I think that's fine. Let it be inefficient.

Today the Indian government is trying to present privatization as the alternative to the state, to public enterprise. But privatization is only a further evolution of the centralized state, where the state says that they have the right to give the entire power production in Maharashtra to Enron. They don't have the right. The infrastructure of the public sector in India has been built up over the last fifty years with public money. They don't have the right to sell it to Enron. They cannot do that.

You say private enterprise is going to be more efficient? Look at what Enron is doing. Is that efficient? The same thing is happening in the telecom sector.

Three-quarters of our country lives on the edge of the market economy.[18] You can't tell them that only those who can afford water can have it.

Talk about the material you covered in your essay, 'The End of Imagination':[19] the nuclear testing in India, followed by Pakistan. You say in India the official reasons given for the testing are threats from China and Pakistan and exposing western hypocrisy.

When India carried out the nuclear tests in May 1998, within weeks the Pakistani infiltration of Kargil in Kashmir began. The Indian government didn't do anything about it because they knew how embarrassing it would be to actually admit that the nuclear tests triggered a war. So they allowed it to happen. Hundreds of soldiers got killed.[20] The Indian government and the mainstream media used the Kargil war to whip up more patriotism. It's so frightening, the nationalism in the air in India. I'm terrified by it. It can be used to do anything.

Some of the cheering young Hindu men who were thrilled with the destruction of the Babri mosque in Ayodhya in the northern state of Uttar Pradesh were also celebrating the nuclear tests.

And the same ones were protesting about Coke. The same Bal Thackeray of Shiv Sena who met Rebecca Mark of Enron and signed the 30-billion-dollar deal wants to ban birthday parties and Valentine's Day because they are an attack on Indian culture.[21] Indian intellectuals today feel radical when they condemn communalism, but not many people are talking about the link between privatization, globalization and communalism. Globalization suits the Indian elite. Communalism doesn't. It doesn't create a good 'investment climate'. I think they have to be addressed together, not separately. They are both two sides of the same coin. Growing religious fundamentalism is directly linked to globalization and to privatization. The Indian government is talking about selling its entire power sector to foreign multinationals, but when the consequences of that become hard to manage, the government immediately starts saying, 'Should we build the Ram temple in Ayodhya?' Everyone goes baying off in that direction. Meanwhile, contracts are signed.

It's like a game. That's something we have to understand. It's like a pincer action. With one hand they're selling the country out to multinationals. With the other they're orchestrating this howling cultural nationalism. On the one hand you're saying that the world is a global village. On the other hand governments spend millions and millions patrolling their borders with nuclear weapons.

You use a metaphor of two convoys of trucks, one very large one with many people going off in the darkness and another, much smaller, going into the digital promised land.[22]

Every night outside my house in New Delhi I pass this road gang of emaciated labourers digging a trench to lay fibre optic cables to speed up our digital revolution. They work by the light of a few candles. That is what is happening in India today. The convoy that melts into the darkness and disappears doesn't have a voice. It doesn't exist on TV. It doesn't have a place in the national newspapers. And so it doesn't exist. The people that are in the little convoy on their way to this glittering destination at the top of the world don't care to see or even acknowledge the larger convoy heading into the darkness.

In Delhi, the city I live in, the cars are getting bigger and sleeker, the hotels are getting posher, the gates higher. The guards outside houses are no longer the old chowkidars, watchmen, they are young fellows with uniforms. And yet everywhere the poor are packed like lice into every crevice in the city. People don't see that any more. It's as if you shine a light very brightly in one place, the darkness deepens around it. They don't want to know what's happening. The people who benefit from this situation can't imagine that the world is not a better place.

It's part of that regular diet of contradictions that Indians live with. You made a decision, or the decision was made for you, to identify with, or to be part of, that large convoy.

I can't be a part of the large convoy because it's not a choice that you can make. It's a choice that's made by your circumstances. The fact that I'm an educated person means that I can't be on that convoy. I'm too privileged. Besides, I don't want to be on it. I don't want to be a victim. I don't want to disappear into the darkness.

You talk passionately about taking sides, about not being

a neutral observer, reporting on events in a distant way.

Once you've seen certain things, you can't un-see them, and saying nothing is as political an act as speaking out ... There's no innocence and there isn't any sense in which any of us is perfect or not invested in the system. If I put money in a bank it's going to fund the bombs and the dams. When I pay tax, I'm investing in projects I disagree with. I'm not a completely blameless person campaigning for the good of mankind. But from that un-pristine position, is it better to say nothing or to say something? One is not powerful enough nor powerless enough not to be invested in the process. Most of us are completely enmeshed in the way the world works. All our hands are dirty.

I read somewhere that you once lived in a squatter's colony within the walls of Delhi's Ferozeshah Kotla in a small hut with a tin roof.

That's true. But it's not tragic. It was fun [laughs]. As I said, I left home when I was sixteen. I had to put myself through college. So I used to live there because the mess manager of the canteen in the school of architecture hostel had this little hut. Ferozeshah Kotla was right next to my college. I used to live there with my boyfriend and a whole lot of other people who could not afford to live in the hostel.

What was your experience working in the film industry in India?

I worked on a few films that were a part of the lunatic fringe, films that no one really wanted to see. It wasn't at all part of the film industry. It was very marginal.

Some of these stories that you're telling about resistance and the NBA would seem to be grist for a film or a television series. Is anything like that going on in India?

No. There are a lot of documentary films. Few of them transcend the boundaries between activism and art. I think there are tremendous stories for making films, like the Bhopal tragedy that Union Carbide was responsible for. But I'm a loner. I can't bear the idea of working with a film crew, negotiating with the producer, actors and all the rest of it. I've done it—it's not my thing.

You could write a screenplay.

But then they'll fuck it up [laughs]. One of the things about writing *The God of Small Things* was that I negotiated with nobody. It was just me and my book. A fantastic way to spend four and a half years of my life. No negotiations.

In January 2000, in a village on the banks of the Narmada, there was a protest against the Maheshwar dam. You were among many who were arrested there.

The Maheshwar dam, which is the dam upstream from the Sardar Sarovar, is India's first private hydroelectric project. Its chief promoter is a textile company called S. Kumars. The resistance managed to kick out a whole host of private companies, starting with US companies like Pacgen and Ogden, then German firms like Siemens and HypoVereinsbank. Last year, the villagers decided that they were going to take over the dam site.

I was in the valley in a village called Sulgaon. All night, people were arriving from the surrounding villages, by tractor, by jeep, on foot. By three in the morning there were about 5,000 of us. We started walking in the dark to the dam site. The police knew that the dam site would be captured, but they didn't know from where the people would come.

It was unforgettable. Five thousand people, mostly villagers, but also people from the cities, lawyers, architects, journalists, walking through these byways and crossing streams in absolute silence. There was not a person that lit a bidi or coughed or cleared their throats.

Occasionally a whole group of women would sit down and pee and then keep walking. Finally, at dawn, we arrived and took over the dam site. For hours, the police surrounded us. Then there was a lathi, baton, charge. They arrested thousands of people, including me. They dumped me in a private car that belonged to S. Kumars. It was so humiliating. The jails were full. Because I was there at that time, there was a lot of press and less violence than usual. But people have captured the Maheshwar dam site so many times before, and it doesn't even make it to the news.

What is the status of the Narmada valley project now that the Supreme Court decision of October 2000 has granted permission for the completion of the Sardar Sarovar dam in the state of Gujarat?

The status is totally uncertain. Gujarat is in a shambles from the earthquake last month. What is happening there is ugly. The Gujarat government, and its goon squad the VHP, is commandeering all the relief money. There are reports of how Muslims, Christians and Dalits are being left out of the reconstruction efforts. In Bhuj, one of the worst-hit towns, they have seventeen different categories of tents for the seventeen different castes. It's infuriating to think of how much money these guys must have received from international donors and what they will end up using it for.

Everyone is keeping very quiet about what effect the earthquake will have on the dam. Sardar Sarovar is on a fault line. This is a point that's been brought up again and again. Everybody's ignored it.[23]

The Vishwa Hindu Parishad or VHP is the religious arm of the ruling party, the BJP.

It's a sort of extreme right-wing. There's the RSS and even more right-wing than the RSS is the VHP. Even further to the right is the Bajrang Dal. They are the ones burning churches, destroying mosques and killing priests.[24]

You make the connection between the rise of extreme Hindu-based nationalism and globalization. Are there any local factors at work here?

There are plenty of local factors, but for me this connection explains how disempowerment works. When you have dispossession and disempowerment on this scale as a result of corporate globalization, the anger that it creates can be channelled in bizarre and dangerous ways. India's nuclear tests were conducted to shore up people's flagging self-esteem. India is still flinching from the cultural insult of British colonialism, still looking for its identity. It's about all that.

Are you thinking about writing any more fiction?

I need to write fiction like you need to eat or exercise, but right now it's so difficult. At the moment, I don't know how to manage my life. Just one writer who says quite simply to the people in the Narmada valley, 'I'm on your side,' leads to so much love and so much affection and so many people asking you to join them. Just the fact that you're known as somebody who's willing to speak out opens you to a universe of conflict and pain and incredible suffering. It's impossible to avert your eyes. Sometimes, of course, it becomes ludicrous. A woman rang me up and said, 'Oh, darling, I thought that piece on the Narmada was fantastic. Now could you do one for me on child abuse?' I said, 'Sure. For or against?'

People just assume you're a gun for hire, you can write about anything. I don't know how I'll ever be able to make the space to say, 'I'm writing a book now, and I'm not going to be able to do x or y.' I would love to.

You are a celebrity within India and also outside. How do you handle this?

As a rule I never do things because I'm a celebrity. Also I never avoid doing things because I'm a celebrity. I try to ignore that whole noisy production. Of course I have the whole business of people asking me to inaugurate this or that. I never do that. I stand by what I write. That's what I am—a writer. If I began to believe the publicity about myself, whether for or against, it would give me a very absurd idea of myself. I know that there's a very fine balance between accepting your own power with grace and misusing it.

When I say my own power, I don't mean as a celebrity. Everybody, from the smallest person to the biggest, has some kind of power and even the most powerless person has a responsibility. I don't feel responsible for everybody. Everybody is also responsible for themselves. I don't ever want to portray myself as a representative of the voiceless or anything like that. I'm scared of that.

Gandhi called India's independence 'a wooden loaf'. Many of the issues plaguing the subcontinent are rooted in its partition. What's your perspective on relations between India and Pakistan? India is a multi-cultural, multi-layered country and has one of the largest Muslim populations in the world.

Partition has left a huge and bloody legacy between India and Pakistan. I think both countries are doing their best to keep it alive. The reasons for this range from actual communal hatred and religious suspicion, to governments and bureaucrats making money off arms deals. They use this manufactured conflict and hypernationalism to gain political mileage in their own countries.

I sense some optimism on your part on what you call the 'inherent anarchy' of India to resist the tide of globalizaion.

I don't know whether to be optimistic or not. When I'm outside the cities, I do feel optimistic. In India, unlike perhaps many other countries which are being broken by these new forms of colonialism, there is such grandeur. Ultimately, people prefer to eat rotis and idlis and dosas rather than McDonald's burgers. Whether it's Indian food or textiles, there's so much beauty. I don't know whether they can kill it. I want to think they can't. I don't think that there is anything as beautiful as a sari. Can you kill it? Can you corporatize a sari?

Just before I came here, I went to a market in Delhi. There was a whole plate of different kinds of rajma dal, lentils. Today, that's all it takes to bring tears to your eyes, to look at all the kinds of rajma that there are, all the kinds of rice, and think that they don't want this to exist.

They want to privatize it and control the seeds.

They want to do the same to cultures and people and languages and songs. Globalization means standardization. The very rich and the very poor must want the same things, but only the rich can have them.

'I'm not rural, not urban, not completely "traditional" nor wholeheartedly "modern". I grew up in a village. I saw rural India at work. And yet I had the advantage of having an education. It's like being at the top of the bottom of the heap—without the blinkered single-mindedness of the completely oppressed nor the flabby self-indulgence of the well-to-do.'

'Yet, just as inevitable as the journey that the powerful undertake is the journey undertaken by those who are engaged in the business of resisting power. Just as power has a physics, those of us who are opposed to power also have a physics. Sometimes I think the world is divided into those who have a comfortable relationship with power and those who have a naturally adversarial relationship with power.'

TERROR AND THE MADDENED KING

In conversation with David Barsamian, September 2002.

It's been nineteen months since our last interview. Can you update me on the criminal case filed against you in a district magistrate's court in Kerala for your book, *The God of Small Things*? The charge was 'corrupting public morality'.[1] What has been the outcome of that particular case?

Well, it hasn't had an outcome. It's still pending in court, but every six months or so the lawyer says, 'There's going to be a hearing; can you please come?'

This is one of the ways in which the state controls people. Having to pay a lawyer, or having a criminal case in court, never knowing what's going to happen. It's not about whether you get sentenced eventually or not. It's the harassment. It's about having it on your head, about not knowing what will happen.

More recently you've been charged and found guilty of contempt of court by India's Supreme Court ...

It's McCarthyism—a warning to people that criticizing the Supreme Court could jeopardize your career. You'd have to hire lawyers, make court appearances—and eventually you may or may not be sentenced. Who can afford to risk it?

Based on conversations with David Barsamian in Albuquerque, New Mexico, and Las Vegas, Nevada.

Tell me about Aradhana Seth's film, *DAM/AGE*.[2]

Usually when people ask me to make films with them, I refuse. The request to do *DAM/AGE* came just after the final Supreme Court hearing, when it became pretty obvious to me that I was going to be sentenced, one way or another. I didn't know for how long. I was pretty rattled and thought that if I was going to be in jail for any length of time, at least my point of view ought to be out in the world.

In India, the press is terrified of the court. So there wasn't any real discussion of the issues. It was discussed in a 'Cheeky Bitch Taken to Court' sort of cheap, sensationalist way, but not seriously. After all, what is contempt of court? What does this law mean to ordinary citizens? None of these things had been discussed at all. So I agreed to do the film simply because I was nervous and wanted people to know what this debate was about.

In a very moving segment of the film, you discuss a man named Bhaiji Bhai. Can you talk about him?

Bhaiji Bhai is a farmer in Gujarat, from a little village called Undava. When I first met him, I remember thinking, 'I know this man from somewhere.' I had never met him before. Then I remembered that a friend of mine who had made a film on the Narmada years before had done an interview with Bhaiji Bhai. He had lost something like seventeen of his nineteen acres to the irrigation canal in Gujarat. And because he had lost it to the canal, as opposed to submergence in the reservoir area, he didn't count as a project-affected person and wasn't compensated. So he was pauperized and had spent I don't know how many years telling strangers his story. I was just another stranger that he told his story to, hoping that some day someone would intervene and right this great wrong that had been done to him.

Women seem to be central to the struggle in the Narmada valley. Why do you think women are so actively engaged there?

Women are actually actively engaged in many struggles in India. And especially in the Narmada valley. In the Maheshwar dam submergence villages, the women of the valley are particularly effective. Women are more adversely affected by uprootment than men. Among the adivasi people, it is not the case that men own the land and women don't. But when adivasis are displaced from their ancestral lands, the meagre cash compensation is given by the government to the men. The women are completely disempowered. Many are reduced to offering themselves as daily labourers on construction sites and they are exploited terribly. Women often realize that if they're displaced, they are more vulnerable and therefore they understand the issues in a more visceral and deeper sense than the men do.

You write in your latest essay 'Come September' that the theme of much of what you talk about is the relationship between power and powerlessness. And you write about 'the physics of power'.[3] I'm interested that you use that term, physics. It kind of connects with the mathematical term you used in another of your essays, 'The Algebra of Infinite Justice'. What do you have in mind there?

Unfettered power results in excesses such as the ones we're talking about now. And eventually, that has to lead to structural damage. I am interested in the physics of history. Historically, we know that every empire overreaches itself and eventually implodes. Then another one rises to take its place.

But do you see those excesses as inherent in the structure of power? Are we talking about something inevitable here?

Inevitable would be too fatalistic a term. But I think unfettered power does have its own behavioural patterns, its own DNA. When you listen to George Bush speak, it's as though he has no perspective because he's driven by the crazed impulse of a maddened king. He can't hear the murmuring in the servants' quarters. He can't hear the words of the world's subjects. He's driving himself into a situation and he cannot turn back.

Yet, just as inevitable as the journey that the powerful undertake is the journey undertaken by those who are engaged in the business of resisting power. Just as power has a physics, those of us who are opposed to power also have a physics. Sometimes I think the world is divided into those who have a comfortable relationship with power and those who have a naturally adversarial relationship with power.

You've just spent a couple of weeks in the United States. You spoke in New York and Santa Fe, then took a driving trip through parts of New Mexico. What do you think about the incredible standard of living that Americans enjoy, and the price that is exacted from the developing world to maintain that standard of living?

It's not that I haven't been to America or to a western country before. But I haven't lived here, and I can't seem to get used to it. I haven't got used to doors that open on their own when you stand in front of them, or looking at these supermarkets stuffed with goods. But when I'm here, I have to say that I don't necessarily feel, 'Oh, look how much they have and how little we have.' Because I think Americans themselves pay such a terrible price.

In what way?

In terms of emotional emptiness. Watching Michael Moore's film *Bowling for Columbine* you suddenly get the feeling that here is a country with an economy that thrives on insecurity, on fear, on threats, on protecting what you have—your washing machines, your dishwashers, your vacuum cleaners—from the invasion of killer tomatoes or evil women in saris or whatever other kind of alien.[4] It's a culture under siege. Every person who gets ahead gets ahead by stepping on his brother, or sister, or mother, or friend. It's such a sad, lonely, terrible price to pay for creature comforts. I think people here could be much happier if they could let their shoulders drop and say, 'I don't really need this. I don't really have to get ahead. I don't really have to win the baseball match. I don't really have to come first in class. I don't really have to be the highest earner in my little town.' There are so many happinesses that come from just loving and companionship and even losing.

You write in your essay 'Come September' that the Bush administration is 'cynically manipulating people's grief' after September 11 'to fuel yet another war—this time against Iraq'.[5] You're speaking out about Iraq and also Palestine. Why?

Why not?

But you know that those are stories that are very difficult for most Americans to hear. There's not a lot of sympathy in the United States for the Palestinians, or for the Iraqis, for that matter.

But the thing is, if you're a writer, you're not polling votes. I'm not here to tell stories that people want to hear. I'm not entering some popularity contest. I just say what I have to say, and the consequences are sometimes wonderful and sometimes not. But I'm not here to say what people *want* to hear.

Let's talk a little bit about the mass media in the United States. You write that 'thanks to America's "free press", sadly, most Americans know very little' about the US government's foreign policy.[6]

Yes, it's a strangely insular place, America. When you live outside it, and you come here, it's almost shocking how insular it is. And how puzzled people are—and how curious, now I realize, about what other people think, because it's just been blocked out. Before I came here, I remember thinking that when I write about dams or nuclear bombs in India, I'm quite aware that the elite in India don't want to know about dams. They don't want to know about how many people have been displaced, what cruelties have been perpetrated for their own air conditioners and electricity. Because then the ultimate privilege of the elite is not just their deluxe lifestyles, but deluxe lifestyles with a clear conscience. And I felt that that was the case here too, that maybe people here don't want to know about Iraq, or Latin America, or Palestine, or East Timor, or Vietnam, or anything, so that they can live this happy little suburban life. But then I thought about it. Supposing you're a plumber in Milwaukee or an electrician in Denver. You just go to work, come home, you work really hard, and then you read your paper or watch CNN or Fox News and you go to bed. You don't know what the American government is up to. And ordinary people are maybe too tired to make the effort, to go out and really find out. So they live in this little bubble of lots of advertisements and no information.

***Third World Resurgence*, an excellent magazine out of Penang, Malaysia, had a recent article on the Bhopal disaster of 1984. More than half a million people were seriously injured and some 3,000 people died on December 3, 1984, when a cloud of lethal gas was released into the air from Union Carbide's Bhopal facility in central India. More than 20,000 deaths have since been linked to the gas.**

The article features a leader among Bhopal survivors named Rasheeda Bee—you can tell from the name she's Muslim—who lost five members of her immediate family to cancer after the disaster, and she herself continues to suffer from diminished vision, headache and panic. At the Earth Summit in Johannesburg a few weeks ago, Rasheeda tried to personally hand over a broom to the president of Dow Chemical, which has now taken over Union Carbide, and here's what she said: 'The Indian government has received clear instructions from its masters in Washington, DC. The [Indian] government has made it clear to us [that is, the victims] that if it comes to choosing between

holding Dow [Chemical]/[Union] Carbide liable (or punishing Warren Anderson [who was the CEO of Union Carbide]) and deserting the Bhopal survivors, it will opt for the latter without batting an eyelid.'[7]

Even the absurd compensation that the Indian courts agreed upon for the victims of Bhopal has not been disbursed over the last eighteen years. And now the governments are trying to use that money to pay into constituencies where there were no victims of the Bhopal disaster.[8] The victims were primarily Muslim, but now they're trying to pay that money to Hindu-dominant constituencies, to look after their vote banks.

You were speaking to some students in New Mexico recently and you advised them to travel outside the United States, to put their ears against the wall and listen to the whispering. What did you have in mind in giving them that kind of advice?

That when you live in the United States, with the roar of the free market, the roar of this huge military power, the roar of being at the heart of empire, it's hard to hear the whispering of the rest of the world. And I think many US citizens want to. I don't think that all of them are necessarily co-conspirators in this concept of empire. And those who are not, need to listen to other stories in the world—other voices, other people.

Yes, you do say that it's very difficult to be a citizen of an empire. You also write about September 11. You think that the terrorists should be 'brought to book'. But then you ask the questions, 'Is war the best way to track them down? Will burning the haystack find you the needle?'[9]

Under the shelter of the US government's rhetoric about the war against terror, politicians the world over have decided that this technique is the best way of settling old scores. So whether it's the Russian government hunting down the Chechens, or Ariel Sharon in

Palestine, or the Indian government carrying out its fascist agenda against Muslims, particularly in Kashmir, everybody's borrowing the rhetoric. They are all fitting their mouths around George Bush's bloody words. After the terrorist attack on the Indian Parliament on December 13, 2001, the Indian government blamed Pakistan (with no evidence to back its claim) and moved all its soldiers to the border. War is now considered a legitimate reaction to terrorist strikes. Now through the hottest summers, through the bleakest winters, we have a million armed men on hair-trigger alert facing each other on the border between India and Pakistan. They've been on red alert for months together. India and Pakistan are threatening each other with nuclear annihilation. So, in effect, terrorists now have the power to ignite war. They almost have their finger on the nuclear button. They almost have the status of heads of state. And that has enhanced the effectiveness and romance of terrorism.

The US government's response to September 11 has actually privileged terrorism. It has given it a huge impetus, and made it look like terrorism is the only effective way to be heard. Over the years, every kind of non-violent resistance movement has been crushed, ignored, kicked aside. But if you're a terrorist, you have a great chance of being negotiated with, of being on TV, of getting all the attention you couldn't have dreamt of earlier.

When Madeleine Albright was the US ambassador to the United Nations in 1994, she said of the United States, 'We will behave multilaterally when we can and unilaterally when we must.' I was wondering, in light of the announcement last week [on September 17] of the Bush doctrine about pre-emptive war, if that may not be used as legitimacy for, let's say, India to settle scores with Pakistan.[10] Let's say the Bharatiya Janata Party government in New Delhi says, 'Well, we have evidence that Pakistan may attack us, and we will launch a pre-emptive strike.'

If they can borrow the rhetoric, they can borrow the logic. If George Bush can stamp his foot and insist on being allowed to play

Muslims in Kashmir pray at the Hazratbal shrine in Srinagar.
Photo © Altaf Qadri.

out his insane fantasies, then why shouldn't Prime Minister A.B. Vajpayee or Pakistan's General Musharraf? In any case, India does behave like the United States of the Indian subcontinent.

You know the old expression, 'Beauty is in the eye of the beholder'. Maybe 'terrorist' is the same thing. I'm thinking, for example, Yitzhak Shamir and Menachem Begin were regarded by the British as terrorists when they were controlling Palestine. And today they're national heroes of Israel. Nelson Mandela was considered for years to be a terrorist, too.

In 1987, when the United Nations wanted to pass a resolution on international terrorism, the only two countries to oppose that resolution were Israel and the United States, because at the time they didn't want to recognize the African National Congress and the Palestinian struggle for freedom and self-determination.[11]

Since September 11, particularly in the United States, the pundits who appear with boring regularity on all the talk shows invoke the words of Winston Churchill. He's greatly admired for his courage and he's kind of a model of rectitude to be emulated. In 'Come September' you have a wry, unusual quote from Winston Churchill, that often does not get heard anywhere. Can you paraphrase it?

He was talking about the Palestinian struggle, and he basically said, 'I do not believe that the dog in the manger has the right to the manger, simply because he has lain there for so long. I do not believe that the Red Indian has been wronged in America, or the Black man has been wronged in Australia, simply because they have been displaced by a higher, stronger race.'[12]

And he said this in 1937, I believe.

Yes.

You conclude your essay, 'War Is Peace', by wondering: 'Have we forfeited our right to dream? Will we ever be able to re-imagine beauty?'[13]

That was written in a moment of despair. But we as human beings must never stop that quest. Never. Regardless of Bush or Churchill or Mussolini or Hitler, whoever else. We can't ever abandon our personal quest for joy and beauty and gentleness. Of course we're allowed moments of despair. We would be inhuman if we weren't, but let it never be said that we gave up.

Vandana Shiva, who's a prominent activist and environmentalist in India, told me a story once about going to a village and trying to explain to the people there what globalization was doing to people in India. They didn't get it right away, but then somebody jumped up and said, 'The East India Company has come back.' So there is that memory of being colonized and being recolonized now under this rubric of corporate globalization. It's like the sahibs are back, but this time not with their pith helmets and swagger sticks, but with their laptops and flow charts.

We ought not to speak only about the economics of globalization, but about the *psychology* of globalization. It's like the psychology of a battered woman being faced with her husband again and being asked to trust him again. That's what is happening. We are being asked by the countries that invented nuclear weapons and chemical weapons and apartheid and modern slavery and racism—countries that have perfected the gentle art of genocide, that colonized other people for centuries—to trust them when they say that they believe in a level playing field and the equitable distribution of resources and in a better world. It seems comical that we should even consider that they really mean what they say.

In *DAM/AGE* there's an incredibly moving scene where the Supreme Court in New Delhi is surrounded by people who

have come from the Narmada valley and elsewhere and are chanting your name and giving you support. There was just so much love and affection and tears came to your eyes. As I recount it, I'm getting the chills myself. It was very beautiful.

I was very scared that day. Now that it's over it's okay to say what I'm saying. But while it was happening, while I was surrounded by police and while I was in prison—even though I was in prison for a day—it was enough to know how helpless one can be. They can do anything to you when you are in prison.

I knew that people from the Narmada valley had come. They hadn't come for me personally. They had come because they knew that I was somebody who had said, with no caveats, 'I'm on your side.' I wasn't hedging my bets like most sophisticated intellectuals, and saying, 'On the one hand, this, but on the other hand, that.' I was saying, 'I'm on your side.' So they came to say, 'We are on your side when you need us.'

I was very touched by this, because it's not always the way people's movements work. People don't always come out spontaneously onto the streets. And one of the things about resistance movements is that it takes a great deal of mobilization to keep a movement together and to keep them going and to do things for one another. There are so many different kinds of people putting their shoulders to the wheel. It's not as though all of them have read *The God of Small Things*. And it's not as if I know how to grow soyabeans. But somewhere there is a joining of minds and a vision of the world.

‘The thing is, if you’re a writer, you’re not polling votes. I’m not here to tell stories that people want to hear. I’m not entering some popularity contest. I just say what I have to say, and the consequences are sometimes wonderful and sometimes not. But I’m not here to say what people *want* to hear.’

'When people try to dismiss those who ask the big public questions as being emotional, it is a strategy to avoid debate. Why should we be scared of being angry? Why should we be scared of our feelings, if they're based on facts? The whole framework of reason versus passion is ridiculous, because often passion is based on reason. Passion is not always unreasonable. Anger is based on reason. They're not two different things. I feel it's very important to defend that. To defend the space for feelings, for emotions, for passion.'

DEVELOPMENT NATIONALISM

IN CONVERSATION WITH DAVID BARSAMIAN, NOVEMBER 2002.

You just finished writing an introduction to Noam Chomsky's *For Reasons of State*, which is being reissued after being out of print for several years.[1] What did you learn as you read his essays?

The one fact that shocked me was that Chomsky had searched mainstream US media for twenty-two years for a single reference to American aggression in south Vietnam and had found none. At the same time, the 'free world' is in no doubt about the fact that the Russians invaded Afghanistan, using exactly the same model, the same formula—setting up a client regime and then inviting themselves in. I'm still taken aback at the extent of indoctrination and propaganda in the United States. It is as if people there are being reared in a sort of altered reality, like broiler chickens or pigs in a pen. In India, the anarchy and brutality of daily life means there are more free spaces, simply because it's impossible to regulate. People are beyond the reach of the bar code. This freedom is being quickly snatched away. Reading Chomsky gave me an idea of how unfree the free world is, really. How uninformed. How indoctrinated.

Why did you call your introduction 'The Loneliness of Noam Chomsky'?

There was a poignant moment in an old interview when he talked about being a fifteen- or sixteen-year-old boy in 1945 when the atomic bomb was dropped on Hiroshima. He said that there wasn't a single person with whom he could share his outrage. And that struck me as a most extreme form of loneliness. It was a loneliness which evidently nurtured a mind that was not willing to align itself with any ideology. It's interesting for me, because I grew up in Kerala, where there was a communist government at the time of the war in Vietnam. I grew up on the cusp between American propaganda and Soviet propaganda, which somehow cancelled each other out.

Really the line is between the citizen and the state, regardless of what ideology that state subscribes to. Even now in India, or anywhere else, the minute you allow the state to take away your freedoms, it will. So whatever freedoms a society has exist because those freedoms have been insisted upon by its people, not because the state is inherently good or bad. And in India and all over the world, freedoms are being snatched away at a frightening pace. I think it's not just important but urgent for us to become extremely troublesome citizens, to refuse to allow the state to take away what it is grabbing with both hands just now.

In your essay 'Come September' you write that in country after country freedoms are being curtailed in the name of protecting freedom. In the United States, there's the USA PATRIOT Act, and you have something similar in India, called POTA, the Prevention of Terrorism Act.[2] Do you see any similarities?

Terrorism has become the excuse for states to do just what they please in the name of protecting citizens against terrorism. Hundreds of people are being held in prisons under the anti-terrorism law in India. Many of them are poor people, Dalits and adivasis, who are protesting against 'development projects' that deprive them of their lands and livelihoods. Poverty and protest are being conflated with terrorism. There was a fake 'encounter' in New Delhi's Ansal Plaza just a couple of weeks ago, on November 3. The police claimed that they had foiled a terrorist attack, and that the people they killed were Pakistani terrorists. But from eyewitness reports, it's pretty clear that that police story was concocted.[3]

Similarly, on the thirteenth of December—soon after the

September 11 attack in New York—there was an attack on the Indian Parliament. Five men were killed on the spot. Nobody knows who they really were. The government, as usual, claims they were Pakistanis. They've held four additional suspects in prison for almost a year now: a Kashmiri Muslim professor from Delhi University, two other Kashmiri Muslim men, and a woman who's Sikh but married to Shaukat, one of the accused. During the trial, it seemed as if almost every piece of evidence had been manufactured by the police. As for the professor, Syed Abdul Rehman Geelani, there's no evidence whatsoever to support his arrest. All three men have been sentenced to death. It's outrageous.[4]

In March 2000, just before Bill Clinton came here, there was a massacre of Sikhs in Chittisinghpura in the valley of Kashmir. The army claimed they killed terrorists who were responsible for the massacre. It now turns out that the people they killed were not terrorists, but just ordinary, innocent villagers. The chief minister of Kashmir actually admitted that the DNA samples that were sent to a lab for testing were fake. But nothing happens. You've killed these people, you've admitted to fudging the DNA samples, but nothing happens. Holes are blown into every bit of evidence, but nothing happens.[5]

There's been the *Tehelka* scandal. The secretary of the BJP, Bangaru Laxman, and the secretary of the Samata Party, Jaya Jaitley, were caught on film accepting bribes for fake arms deals. Nothing happens.[6] So there's this kind of marsh into which everything sinks. A citizen's rights are such a fragile thing now.

A few years ago there was a major massacre of Sikhs right here in the capital of India. Thousands of Sikhs were killed after the assassination of Indira Gandhi. And in Bombay after the Babri Masjid was destroyed in Ayodhya, several thousand Muslims were massacred.[7]

Yes, and nothing happened. And in Gujarat now, Narendra Modi is spearheading an election campaign, and the Congress Party and the BJP are both openly talking about playing the Hindu card, or using the caste card vs the Hindu card. So we have to ask ourselves, What is the systemic flaw in this kind of democracy that makes politicians function by creating these vote banks divided along caste lines, or communal lines, or regional lines. As I wrote in my essay 'Democracy: Who Is She When She Is at Home?', democracy is India's greatest strength, but the way in which electoral democracy is practiced is turning it into our greatest weakness.[8]

We both attended a solidarity meeting on behalf of Professor Geelani, who teaches Arabic at Delhi University, and you are on the committee in his support. I'm sure you're besieged with requests to be on such-and-such a committee, to write a letter, to do this and that. How do you make those kinds of choices?

I use my instinct, because that's the only thing I can do. I understand clearly and deeply that no individual matters all that much. It doesn't matter all that much eventually what I do and what I don't do. It matters to me. I can help as much as I can help. But ultimately it isn't the way a battle must be fought—by the support of one individual or another. I don't believe in that kind of celebrity politics.

I just continue to do what I've always done, which is to write, to think about these things. I'm searching for an understanding. Not for my readers, for myself. It's a process of exploration. It has to further my understanding of the way things work. So in a way it's a selfish journey, too. It's a way of pushing myself further and deeper into looking at the society in which I live. If I were to be doing it not as an exploratory thing, but just as a politician might, with some fixed agenda, and then trying to convince people of my point of view, I think I'd become jaded. Curiosity takes me where it takes me. It leads me deep into the heart of the world.

After the publishing of *The God of Small Things*, you could have had your pick of any publisher in New York. I'm sure they were clamouring for you. Yet you chose a small,

independent press based in Cambridge, Massachusetts, South End Press, to publish *Power Politics* and, coming up, *War Talk*. Was that that kind of spontaneous, instinctive choice you made?

It wasn't some big policy decision on my part. I didn't even think at the time, actually, that this is a political step. But I use my political instincts a lot. It's important for me to stay that way. People really imagine that most people are in search of fame or fortune or success. But I don't think that's true. I think there are lots of people who are more imaginative than that. When people describe me as famous and rich and successful, it makes me feel queasy. Each of those words falls on my soul like an insult. They seem tinny and boring and shiny and uninteresting to me. It makes me feel unsuccessful because I never set out to be those things. And they make me uneasy. To be famous, rich and successful in this world is not an admirable thing. I'm suspicious of it all.

Failure attracts my curiosity as a writer. Loss, grief, brokenness, failure, the ability to find happiness in the saddest things—these are the things that interest me. I don't want to play out the role of someone who's just stepped out of *The Bold and the Beautiful.* At the same time, it is interesting to be able to meditate on wealth and fame and success, because I have them and I can play with them, disrespect them, if you know what I mean. I don't suppose that if you haven't been there, you fully understand how empty it all is, in so many ways. And yet, there are wonderful things about being a writer who is widely read.

I can go to Korea, to Japan, to South Africa, to Latin America, and I know that I'll meet kindred souls. And they won't be hard for me to find. I won't have to spend ten years looking for them because my writing has preceded me. I'm a paid-up member of SIN—the Sweethearts International Network. It's a bond between people that arises from literature and politics. I can't think of a more wonderful thing. Writing gives you this gift. It plugs you directly into the world.

There used to be a saying in American journalism—it's not being followed today because of the corporatization of the media—that the function of journalists was to comfort the afflicted and afflict the comfortable. In a way, what you're saying seems to mirror that. That you feel that you want to make those people in power uneasy and uncomfortable.

I don't think that people in power become uneasy and uncomfortable. But you can annoy and provoke them. People who are powerful are not people who have subtle feelings like uneasiness. They got there because of a certain capacity for ruthlessness. I don't even consider their feelings when I write. I don't write for them.

That reminds me of something connected with Chomsky. I've attended many of his lectures. He's often introduced as someone who speaks truth to power. I asked him about that once. He said he doesn't do that. He's not interested in that.

Power knows the truth.

He wants to provide information to people who are powerless, not to those who are oppressing them.

Isn't there a flaw in the logic of that phrase—speak truth to power? It assumes that power doesn't know the truth. But power knows the truth just as well, if not better, than the powerless know the truth. Enron knows what it's doing. We don't have to tell it what it's doing. We have to tell other people what Enron is doing. Similarly, the people who are building the dams know what they're doing. The contractors know how much they're stealing. The bureaucrats know how much they're getting as bribes.

Power knows the truth. There isn't any doubt about that. It is really about telling the story. Good fiction is the truest thing that ever there was. Facts are not necessarily the only truths. Facts can be fiddled with by economists and bankers. There are other kinds of truth. It's about telling the story. As a writer, that's the best thing

I can do. It's not just about digging up facts.

When I wrote *The God of Small Things*, it isn't just that I had a story and then told it. The way you tell a story, the form that narrative takes, is a kind of truth, too. When I wrote 'The Greater Common Good', it isn't that no one knew these facts before. There were volumes and volumes of books on dams—pro-dam, anti-dam, balanced views, and so on. But really, in the end, it's about how you tell that story to somebody who doesn't know it. To me, as a writer, that is something that I take great pleasure in. Telling the story in a way that ordinary people can understand, snatching our futures back from the experts and the academics and the economists and the people who really want to kidnap or capture things and carry them away to their lairs and protect them from the unauthorized gaze or the curiosity or understanding of passers-by. That's how they build their professional stakes, by saying, 'I am an expert on something that you can't possibly understand. My expertise is vital to your life, so let me make the decisions.'

Who tells the stories is absolutely critical. Who is telling the stories in India today?

This is a very important question. When *The God of Small Things* came out, my mother said to me, 'Why did you have to call the village Ayemenem? Why did you have to say the river was the Meenachil?' I said, 'Because I want people to know that we have stories.' It's not that India has no stories. Of course we have stories—beautiful and brilliant ones. But those stories, because of the languages in which they're written, are not privileged. So nobody knows them.

When *The God of Small Things* won the Booker Prize, there was a lot of hostility towards me from regional-language writers, people who write in Hindi, Malayalam, Tamil and Marathi. It was a perfectly understandable hostility. The Indian writers who are well known and financially rewarded are those who write in English—the elite.

All of my political writing is translated into Indian languages, Gujarati, Malayalam, Tamil, Bengali, Hindi and so on. Now I have a relationship with the regional press in Kerala, the Hindi press in the north, the Bengali press in Bengal. Now the English-language media is far more hostile to me than the regional media.

It goes on forever, the question of who tells the story. Even within regional-language writing, the Brahmins and the upper caste have traditionally told the stories. The Dalits have not told their stories. There's an endless pecking order.

Look at, say, the case of Vietnam now. To the world today, thanks to Hollywood and thanks to the US mass media, the war in Indochina was an American war. Indochina was the lush backdrop against which America tested its technology, examined its guilt, worried about its conscience, dealt or did not deal with its guilt. And the 'gooks' were just the other guys who died. They were just stage props. It doesn't matter what the story was. It mattered who was telling it. And America was telling it.

In India, I occupy an interesting space. As a writer who lives in India, writes in English and has grown up in a village in Kerala, I have spent the first half of my life battling traditions, Indian traditions, that wanted me to be a particular kind of Indian woman, which I have refused to be. And now I'm up against the monstrosity of the other side. The monstrosity of the modern world. People like me confront this contradiction. It's a very interesting place to be in, really. Where even politically, you're caught between the fascist regional forces, the BJP and VHP, for instance, versus the monstrous market forces, the Enrons and the Bechtels.

Speaking of Enron, the Houston-based energy giant multinational which was deeply involved in a dam project in Maharashtra, it has collapsed, laying off thousands of workers, most of whom have lost their pensions and retirement benefits. There's been a corporate crime wave in the United States, a huge amount of corruption. You might recall that it wasn't too long ago that the United

States was lecturing a lot of the world about having transparency and clear and open procedures. It's rather ironic.

People often don't understand the engine that drives corruption. Particularly in India, they assume government equals corruption, private companies equal efficiency. But government officials are not genetically programmed to be corrupt. Corruption is linked to power. If it is the corporations that are powerful, then they will be corrupt. I think there have been enough studies that show that corruption has actually increased in the era of privatization. Enron, for instance, openly boasted about how it paid some 20 million dollars to 'educate' Indian politicians.[9] It depends on how you define corruption. Is it just the bribe-taker? Or is the bribe-giver corrupt as well? Today we see a formidable nexus between the powerful elites in the world. Imperialism by email. This time around, the white man doesn't have to go to poor countries and risk diarrhoea and malaria or dying in the tropics. He just has his local government in place, which takes charge of 'creating a good investment climate'. And those who are protesting against privatization and development projects—making investments unsafe—are called terrorists.

You're a critic of corporate globalization. But what kind of arrangements would you like to see, in terms of governance, of relations between different countries?

I am a critic of corporate globalization because it has increased the distance between the people who take decisions and the people who have to suffer those decisions. Earlier, for a person in a village in Kerala, his or her life was being decided maybe in Trivandrum or, eventually, in Delhi. Now it could be in the Hague or in Washington, by people who know little or nothing of the consequences their decisions could have. And that distance between the decision-taker and the person who has to endure or suffer that decision is a very perilous road, full of the most unanticipated pitfalls.

It's not that everything is designed to be malevolent, of course.

Most of it is, but the distance between what happens on paper, in policy documents, and what happens on the ground is increasing enormously. That distance has to be eliminated. Decentralization and the devolving of power to local groups is very important. The current process is fundamentally undemocratic.

You have written that 'a writer's bad dream' is 'the ritualistic slaughter of language'.[10] Can you talk about some examples of how language is constructed?

The language of dissent has been co-opted. WTO documents and World Bank resettlement policies are now written in very noble-sounding, socially just, politically democratic-sounding language. They have co-opted that language. They use language to mask their intent. But what they say they'll do and what they actually do are completely different. The resettlement policy for the Sardar Sarovar dam sounds reasonably enlightened. But it isn't meant to be implemented. There isn't the land. It says communities should be resettled as communities. But just nineteen villages from Gujarat have been scattered in 175 different locations.[11]

The policy's only function is to ease the middle-class's conscience. They all say, 'Oh, how humane the world is now compared to what it used to be.' They can't be bothered that there's no connection between what's happening on the ground and what the policy says. So the issue is not how nice the World Bank president is or how wonderfully drafted their documents are. The issue is, who are they to make these decisions?

There's a sequence in *DAM/AGE* in which World Bank president James Wolfensohn is visiting New Delhi, and he comes out to meet some demonstrators from the NBA. He utters a stream of platitudes about how he cares for the poor, how his focus is on alleviating their suffering and their poverty. In the film you say that you couldn't bear to hang around and wait for him to come out of his meeting, to hear that.

I was there when they blockaded the road. It was evening by the time Wolfensohn was forced to come out. He arrived in his pin-stripe suit like a cartoon white man coming to address the peasants of India. I couldn't bear to hear or see this played out again. At the end of the twentieth century, to see the White Man back again, addressing the peasants of India and saying how concerned he was about them.

Only a few weeks later, I was in London, at the release of the World Commission on Dams report, and Wolfensohn was there.[12] He talked about how he had met with the people of the valley. Missing from his account were the police and those steel separators, and the fact that he had been dragged out of the office and forced to meet them. He made it sound like a genuine grassroots meeting.

There are some exciting things happening culturally in India. In addition to *DAM/AGE*, the documentary by Aradhana Seth, there's another one by Sanjay Kak called *Words on Water*, about resistance in the Narmada valley.[13] Are you encouraged that those kinds of films are being made and seen?

There are many independent film-makers who are doing interesting work. But, more important in India is that there is a vital critique of what is happening. For instance, in Madhya Pradesh there is a huge and growing resistance to the privatization of power. Privatization of the essential infrastructure, water, power, is strangling the agricultural community. Mass protests are building up. The move to corporatize agriculture, the whole business of genetically modified foods, pesticides, cash crops like cotton and soyabean, are crushing the Indian agricultural sector. The myth of the Green Revolution is coming apart. In Punjab, the lands irrigated by the Bhakra dam are becoming salinized and waterlogged. The soil is yielding less and less and the farmers have to use more and more fertilizers. Punjabi farmers, once the most prosperous in India, are committing suicide because they're in debt.

The WTO has now forced India to import rice, wheat, sugar,

milk, all these products which India has in abundance. The government's warehouses are overflowing with excess food grains, while people starve. They're all being dumped. In Kerala, coffee, tea and rubber plantations are closing down, laying off their labour or not paying them.

In India now there is a move toward Hindutva and more and more communal politics. This hasn't happened overnight. People point to December 6, 1992, when the mosque in Ayodhya, the Babri Masjid, was destroyed by Hindu fundamentalists. But it must have its roots deeper than just ten years ago.

It has its roots in the independence movement. The RSS was set up in the 1920s. Today it is the cultural guild to which L.K. Advani and Vajpayee and all of these people owe allegiance. So the RSS has been working toward this for eighty years now. There is a link between religious fascism and corporate globalization. When you impose corporate globalization on to an almost feudal society, it reinforces inequalities. The people who are becoming more and more prosperous are the ones who have had social advantages over many, many years. It's the kind of situation in which fascism breeds.

On the one hand, you have the government privatizing everything, selling off the public sector in chunks—telecommunications, water, power—to multinationals. On the other hand, they orchestrate this baying nationalism, nuclearism, communalism. I've talked about this in my essays 'Power Politics' and 'Come September'.

Every day the *Times of India* has a quote on the front page, and today's is from George Eliot: 'An election is coming. Universal peace is declared, and the foxes have a sincere interest in prolonging the lives of the poultry.'[14] What do you think about elections as a mechanism for democracy? I ask that because people have had enormous influence and impact outside the electoral system, for example,

Gandhi or Martin Luther King, Jr. They never ran for elective office.

I think it is dangerous to confuse the idea of democracy with elections. Just because you have elections doesn't mean you're a democratic country. They're a very vitally important part of a democracy. But there are other things that ought to function as checks and balances. If elections are the only thing that matter, then people are going to resort to anything to win that election.

You can only campaign in a particular constitutional framework. If the courts, the press, the Parliament are not functioning as checks and balances, then this is not a democracy. And today in India, they are not functioning as checks and balances. If they were, Narendra Modi would be in jail today. He would not be allowed to campaign for office. Several candidates would be in jail today. Not to mention several senior people in the Congress Party who ought to have been in jail from 1984 onward for their roles in the massacre of Sikhs in Delhi after the assassination of Indira Gandhi.

The good thing about elections is that however unaccountable politicians are at least every five years they have to stand for election. But the bureaucracy and the judiciary are completely unaccountable. Nobody understands the terrifying role that the judiciary is playing in India today. The Supreme Court is taking the most unbelievable positions. Its decisions affect the lives of millions of people. Yet to criticize them is a criminal offence.

Recently, the Chief Justice of India, B.N. Kirpal, made an outrageous order on the day before he retired.[15] Out of a case that had nothing to do with linking rivers, Kirpal ordered that all the rivers in India should be linked up in ten years' time. It was an arbitrary, uninformed order based on a whim—nothing more. He asked state governments to file affidavits. They never did. The government of India filed an affidavit stating that the project would take forty-one years and cost billions of dollars. This kind of decision is almost as, if not more, dangerous than communal politics. Yet, because of the contempt-of-court law, nobody will question the court. Not the press. Everybody's scared of going to jail.

By sending me to jail, think of what they did: I had a one-year criminal trial, for which you have to have a criminal lawyer which costs an unimaginable amount of money. How is any journalist going to afford a one-year criminal trial and then face the prospect of going to jail, of losing his or her job? What editor, which journalist is going to take that risk? So they've silenced the press. And now the courts have started to rule on vital issues like globalization, privatization, river-linking, the rewriting of history textbooks, whether a temple should be built in Ayodhya—every major decision is taken by the court. No one is allowed to criticize it. And this is called a democracy.

So you're saying that dissent is being criminalized in India.

I'm saying that a democracy has to function with a system of checks and balances. You cannot have an undemocratic institution functioning in a democracy, because then it works as a sort of manhole into which unaccountable power flows. All the decisions are then taken by that institution because that is the one institution that cannot be questioned. So there is a nexus between the judiciary and the executive. All the difficult decisions are being taken by the judiciary, and it looks as if the judiciary is admonishing the executive and saying, 'You're very corrupt. We are forced to become an activist judiciary and to take these decisions.'

If you speak to the middle class, they believe that the Supreme Court is the only institution that functions properly. There's a sort of hierarchical thinking that the buck must stop somewhere. They *like* the fact that the Supreme Court is so supremely unaccountable.

The contempt-of-court law is so draconian that if tomorrow I had documentary evidence to prove that a judge was corrupt, and had taken money from somebody to make a particular decision, I couldn't produce that evidence in court because it would constitute contempt of court. It would be seen to be 'lowering the dignity of the court' and in such a case truth is not a defence.

Are there organizations—NGOs—in the country that are working on this issue? The issue of the autocracy of the court?

It's a very important political issue that we need to fight. But few have understood it yet.

This business of NGOs is a very interesting one in India. I'm no great fan of NGOs. Many of them are funded by various western agencies. They end up functioning like the whistle on a pressure cooker. They divert and sublimate political rage and make sure that it does not build to a head. Eventually it disempowers people.

In the first interview we did, in early 2001, you described India as two separate convoys, going in different directions. One into the digital future of the promised land of glitzy electronic things, and the rest of the country, the poor, the anonymous, going in the other direction. Since then, do you see those convoys coming closer together, or are they getting more and more distant from each other?

The way that the machine of neoliberal capitalism works, that distance has to increase. If what you have to plough back into the system is always your profit, obviously that distance is going to increase. Just mathematically, it's going to increase. Whoever has more makes more, and makes more and makes more.

Tell me about the current situation in the Narmada valley. It seems that despite the heroic efforts and sacrifices that the NBA and its members and supporters have made, it looks like the dams are going through. Is that assessment correct?

Construction on the Maheshwar dam has been stopped for now, but the Sardar Sarovar dam is inching up. That part of the anti-dam movement has really come up against a wall. The question has to be asked: if non-violent dissent is not viable, then what is?

If reasoned, non-violent dissent is not honoured, then by default you honour violence. You honour terrorism. Because you cannot just put this plastic bag over the head of the world and say, 'Don't breathe.' Across India, insurgents and militants have taken over great swathes of territory where they just won't allow the government in. It's not just Kashmir. It's happening all over: Andhra Pradesh, parts of Bihar, Madhya Pradesh and almost the whole of the Northeast, which doesn't consider itself a part of India.

Do you see the possibility of the NBA extending itself beyond its current lifespan into a more national movement of resistance? Could it be a model that people could emulate?

People in cities think that the movement has lost. In one sense, they're right, because the Sardar Sarovar dam is going up. But if you go to the valley, you'll see the great victories of that movement; which are cultural, which are empowering. People know that they have rights. In the Narmada valley, the police cannot treat adivasis, and in particular adivasi women, the way they do elsewhere. These are great and important victories. The section of the NBA that was fighting against the Maheshwar dam are the younger activists in the valley. They have now expanded their operations way beyond the valley and are fighting the privatization of power in the whole state of Madhya Pradesh. They are spearheading the anti-privatization movement.

Do you see any opening for resolving the conflict between India and Pakistan over Kashmir? The Indian prime minister has said, 'Kashmir is ours. They,' presumably the Pakistanis or the Kashmiris, 'will never get it. That decision has been made.'[16] Tens of thousands of Kashmiris have died. It's a militarized state. There's martial law. There's a suspension of the constitution. You know better than I do about the human rights abuses that go on there.

Kashmir is the rabbit that the governments of both India and Pakistan pull out of their hats whenever they're in trouble. They don't want to resolve the conflict. For them, Kashmir is not a problem; it's a solution. Let's never make the mistake of thinking that India and Pakistan are searching for a solution and haven't managed to find one. They're not searching for a solution, because if they were you would not hear intractable statements like this—absurd statements like this—being made.

After the nuclear tests that India and Pakistan conducted, the issue of Kashmir has been internationalized to some extent. That could be a good thing, though not if the US acts as a unilateral superpower and takes it upon itself to impose a 'solution'. Before you would not discuss human rights violations in Kashmir. There were only these militants who were shot in encounters, Pakistani terrorists and so on. That has changed.

Now with the elections, the dislodging of Farooq Abdullah, and Mufti Muhammad Sayeed coming in, I sense a slight break in the refusal to admit what is really happening in Kashmir.[17] I hear people asking questions about the status of Kashmir. I hear more people saying that maybe Kashmiris should be consulted, instead of this being made to seem like an issue between India and Pakistan.

The first step toward a solution would be for India and Pakistan to open up the borders, to allow people to come and go. If you think of the world as a global village, a fight between India and Pakistan is like a fight between the poorest people in the poorest quarters—the adivasis and the Dalits. And in the meantime, the zamindars are laying the oil pipelines and selling both parties weapons.

You're from the southwest of India, Kerala, and now you're living in the north. Language, music, food—there's a completely different vibration between the north and the south. Also it seems that the communal tensions in the south are much less than in the north. Am I misreading that?

Kerala has the highest number of RSS cells now. But so far, you're absolutely right. The BJP just haven't even managed to get a toe-hold in the electoral political scene, but they are very hard at work.

The first time I ever saw an RSS march—with all these men in khaki shorts—was this year in Kerala, when I went to court. I was just shocked to see them marching in the gloom. It put a chill into my heart.

Talk a little bit about the print media.

The difference between Indian newspapers and newspapers that you'd see in America or England or Europe is the number of stories that there are about politics and politicians. Almost too many. Politicians keep us busy with their shenanigans and eventually every single issue, whether it's a caste massacre in Bihar or communal violence in Gujarat or the issue of displacement by dams, is turned into a noisy debate about whether the chief minister should resign or not. The issue itself is never followed up. The murderers are never punished.

If you know anything about a particular issue, if you know the facts and the figures, you see how shockingly wrong newspapers always are. It's quite sad, the lack of discipline in terms of just getting it right, the lack of rigour. The encouraging thing is that there is a tradition of little magazines, community newspapers, pamphlets—an anarchic network of maverick publications, which makes the media hard to control. The big English national dailies don't reach the mass of the people in India. They don't matter as much as they imagine they do. But let's say there's a war against Pakistan or somebody, everybody just becomes jingoistic and nationalistic, just like what happens in the United States. It's no different.

BJP leader L.K. Advani is one of the most powerful members of the government. He took issue with Amartya Sen, the Nobel Prize-winner in economics, on the issue of economics and India.[18]

He said that it was much more important for India to have weapons than to educate people.

Education and health was not the answer for India's development. It was defence.

Advani is the hard core of the centre—though today I was delighted to read on the front page of the papers that Advani has been denounced by the Vishwa Hindu Parishad as a pseudo-secularist. 'Pseudo-secularist' was a term that Advani had coined to dismiss all those who were not communal fascists, and for him to have his own coinage used against him is delightful.[19]

The Sangh Parivar—the Hindu right-wing family of parties, cultural guilds, the Hindutva lot—squabble with each other in public in order to make everybody feel they're at loggerheads. At the end of it all, Vajpayee keeps the moderates happy, Advani keeps the hardliners happy, the VHP and the Bajrang Dal keep the rabid fringe happy. Everybody thinks they actually have differences, but the differences are just short of being serious. It's like a travelling, hydra-headed circus. It's like a Hindi movie. It has everything: sex, violence, pathos, humour, comedy, tragedy. Full value for the money. You go home satiated.

***India Today*, a weekly magazine, has a fairly large circulation. It recently had a cover story entitled 'India Is Now the Electronic Housekeeper of the World'.[20] General Electric, American Express, Citibank, AT&T and other US corporations are shifting what they call their back-office operations to India. It's called the fastest-growing industry in India, and the workers are mostly young women. Many are hired to answer customer service questions for US customers. They might be on the other end of the line when I want someone to look up the balance on my credit card account or when Avis telemarkets a cheap vacation package to San Diego. They take on American names and American personas and tell jokes in American English. The people who are in favour of corporate globalization say this is a great thing. These girls would not ordinarily get jobs, and now they have an opportunity to earn some**

money. Is there anything wrong with that argument?

The call-centre industry is based on lies and racism. The people who call in are being misled into believing that they are talking to some white American sitting in America. The people who work in those call centres are told that they're not good enough for the market, that US customers will complain if they find out that their service is being provided by an Indian. So Indians must take on false identities, pretend to be Americans, learn a 'correct' accent. It leads to psychosis.

One way of looking at this is to say, 'These people at least have jobs.' You could say that about prostitution or child labour or anything—'At least they're being paid for it.' Their premise is that either these workers don't have jobs or they have jobs in which they have to humiliate themselves. But is that the only choice? That's the question.

We hear all this talk about integrating the world economically, but there is an argument to be made for *not* integrating the world economically. Because what is corporate globalization? It isn't as if the entire world is intermeshed with each other. It's not like India and Thailand or India and Korea or India and Turkey are connected. It's more like America is the hub of this huge cultural and economic airline system. It's the nodal point. Everyone has to be connected through America and, to some extent, Europe.

When powers at the hub of the global economy decide that you have to be X or Y, then if you're part of that network you have to do it. You don't have the independence of being non-aligned in some way, politically or culturally or economically. If America goes down, then everybody goes down. If tomorrow the United States decides that it wants these call-centre jobs back, then overnight this billion-dollar industry will collapse in India. It's important for countries to develop a certain degree of economic self-sufficiency. Just in a theoretical sense, it's important for everybody not to have their arms wrapped around each other or their fingers wrapped around each other's throats at all times, in all kinds of ways.

There's a lot of talk about terrorism. In fact, it's become almost an obsession for the media in the United States. But it's a very narrow definition of terrorism.

Yes. It completely ignores the economic terrorism unleashed by neoliberalism, which devastates the lives of millions of people, depriving them of water, food, electricity. Denying them medicine. Denying them education. Terrorism is the logical extension of this business of the free market. Terrorism is the privatization of war. Terrorists are the free marketeers of war—people who believe that it isn't only the state that can wage war, but private parties as well.

If you look at the logic underlying an act of terrorism and the logic underlying a retaliatory war against terrorism, they are the same. Both terrorists and governments make ordinary people pay for the actions of their governments. Osama bin Laden is making people pay for the actions of the US state, whether it's in Saudi Arabia, Palestine, or Afghanistan. The US government is making the people of Iraq pay for the actions of Saddam Hussein. The people of Afghanistan pay for the crimes of the Taliban. The logic is the same.

Osama bin Laden and George Bush are both terrorists. They are both building international networks that perpetrate terror and devastate people's lives. Bush, with the Pentagon, the WTO, the IMF and the World Bank. Bin Laden with Al-Qaeda. The difference is that nobody elected bin Laden. Bush was elected (in a manner of speaking), so US citizens are more responsible for his actions than Iraqis are for the actions of Saddam Hussein or Afghans are for the Taliban. And yet hundreds of thousands of Iraqis and Afghans have been killed, either by economic sanctions or cruise missiles, and we're told that these deaths are the result of 'just wars'. If there is such a thing as a just war, who is to decide what is just and what is not? Whose god is going to decide that?

The United States has only 3 or 4 per cent of the world's population, yet it's consuming about a third of the world's natural resources, and to maintain that kind of disparity and imbalance requires force, the use of violence.

The US solution to the spiralling inequalities in the world is not to search for a more equal world, or a way of making things more egalitarian, but to espouse the doctrine of 'full-spectrum dominance'. The US government is now speaking about putting down unrest from space.[21] It's a terrorist state and it is laying out a legitimate blueprint for state-sponsored terrorism.

Do you find the persistence of romantic images of India in the west—that this is a country of sitar players and yogis and people who meditate, who are in a kind of ethereal zone? Are those clichés still pretty alive and active?

All clichés are structured around a grain of truth, but there are other clichés now, too. I think that the BJP's few years in power have given an ugly edge to India's image internationally. What happened in Gujarat—the pogrom against the Muslim community—has also become a part of the image of what India is: complex, difficult to understand, full of anachronisms and contradictions, and so on. People from India are in the centre of a lot of the intellectual debate about where the world is headed. I think the anarchy of Indian civil society is an important example in the world today, even though India has its back against the wall and is being bullied and bludgeoned by the WTO and the IMF and by our own corrupt politicians. I was in Italy last month at a film festival, and there were documentary films being screened about the Narmada and about other human-rights issues. The whole Italian press had gathered. Journalists were expecting me to talk about how terrible things are in India. I did talk about that. But I said, 'We're not yet in such a bad way that we have a prime minister who owns three television channels and three newspapers and all the publishing houses and the retail outlets and the book shops. And at least when I'm taken to prison, I know that I'm taken to prison. I know that physically my body is being put in prison. It's not like my mind has been indoctrinated to the point that I *think* I'm free when I'm not.'

In India, we are fighting to retain a wilderness that we have. Whereas in the west, it's gone. Every person that's walking down the street is a walking bar code. You can tell where their clothes are from, how much they cost, which designer made which shoe, which shop you bought each item from. Everything is civilized and tagged and valued and numbered and put in its place. Whereas in India, the wilderness still exists—the unindoctrinated wilderness of the mind, full of untold secrets and wild imaginings. It's threatened, but we're fighting to retain it. We don't have to re-conjure it. It's there. It's with us. It's not got signposts all the way. There is that space that hasn't been completely mapped and taken over and tagged and trademarked. I think that's important. And it's important that in India we understand that it's there and we value it.

Just from hearing you speak and the expression on your face, which I wish people could see, it's obvious that you care a lot about this country. You have a deep affection for it.

I'm not a patriot. I'm not somebody who says, 'I love India,' and waves a flag around in my head. It's my place. I'm used to it. When people talk about reclaiming the commons, I keep saying, 'No, reclaim the wilderness.' Not reclaim it, but claim it, hold on to it. It's for that reason that I cannot see myself living away from India. As a writer, it's where I mess around. Every day, I'm taken by surprise by something.

I don't know if I'm making myself clear. There is just a space for the unpredictable here, which is life as it should be. It's not always that the unpredictable is wonderful—most of the time it isn't. Most of the time it's brutal and it's terrible. Even when it comes to my work and myself, I'm ripped apart here. I'm called names. I'm insulted. But it's the stuff of life. The subjects I write about raise these huge passions. It's why I keep saying, 'What's dissent without a few good insults?'[22] You have to be able to take that. If they call you names, you have to just smile and know that you've touched a nerve.

The point is that we have to rescue democracy by being troublesome, by asking questions, by making a noise. That's what you have to do to retain your freedoms. Even if you lose. Even if the NBA loses the battle against the Sardar Sarovar, it has demonstrated the absolute horrors of what it means to displace people, what it means to build a big dam. It's asked these questions. It hasn't gone quietly. That's the important thing. It's important not to just look at it in terms of winning and losing.

If you look at it another way, look at what we're managing to achieve. We're putting so much pressure that the other side is having to strip. It's having to show itself naked in all its brutality. It's having to drop its masks, its disguises, and reveal its raw and crude and brutal nature. And that's a victory. Not just in terms of who's winning and who's losing, because I'm the kind of person who will always be on the losing side by definition. I have to be, because I'm on this side of the line. I'll never be on that side of the line.

Many journalists have come to you, the BBC, Deutsche Welle. What is interesting for you in these interviews? They must have the same questions, like 'When are you going to write another novel?'

I'm the kind of person who sharpens my thinking in public. It could be in an interview or at a lecture. I like talking to strangers. I like talking to people who have read my work. It's a process of thinking aloud. It's not just journalists that ask you the same question. In our lives, whether you're famous or not famous, there's so much repetition, and it's not a terrible thing. If you look at every person you're talking to as a human being, and you're having a conversation with them, then it's never boring. It's only if you're not interested in that person and you're only interested in yourself that it becomes boring. Then you start reciting what amounts to press handouts, which would be terrible.

I'm not necessarily the kind of writer who holes up somewhere and then emerges. I did that with my novel. I don't talk when I'm writing fiction. It's a very private act. But in my political work, I think aloud. I like to pit my mind against another person's, or think together with people. It's not necessarily just with journalists or interviewers with whom I work. It's an interesting process.

There's a great historic figure in American history, the African-American abolitionist Frederick Douglass. He once said that 'power concedes nothing without a demand. It never did and it never will.'[23]

In India, very often, people—not just the government, but people—say, 'Oh look, we're so much better off than, say, people in Afghanistan or people in Nepal or people in Pakistan.' Somehow they seem to suggest that this has to do with the fact that our government is not as violent as the governments in these other countries. But I think it's because the people are more anarchic, in the sense that it is because we are a troublesome people, a troublesome constituency. And that is why it's difficult to imagine India under army rule. It's unthinkable that Indian society would defer to the army like it does in Pakistan. Even if resistance movements like the movement in the Narmada valley don't succeed in their ultimate goal of stopping a particular dam or 'development' project, they do create a spirit among exploited, oppressed people: 'You can't do this to us. And if you do, we're going to be extremely troublesome about it.'

There were a lot of people who were very annoyed with me when I criticized the Supreme Court and I refused to apologize. But you have to ask these public questions. The minute you start giving ground, you're on a slippery slope.

If you put your ear to the ground in this part of the world today, what do you hear?

Communal talk. Talk about religious identity, ethnic identity, tribal identity. Economically, as globalization is pushed down our throats, people are fractured into tribal, communal groups. The world is getting more and more fractured. Nationalism, nuclearism, communalism, fascism, these things are springing up.

There's always been tension between the majority community—the Hindus in India—and the large Muslim minority. But you are clearly seeing an increase in that tension.

There was a terrible episode of bloodshed and massacre and mayhem during the Partition. About a million people were massacred. The wounds of that were never allowed to heal by the Congress Party, which harnessed this hatred and used it to play electoral games. Our kind of electoral democracy seems to demand the breaking up of the electorate into vote banks. But today all the things that the Congress Party did at night, the BJP and its Sangh Parivar does in the daytime. They do it with pride, as policy. Now they're in power, they're in government, they have penetrated every state organ. Whether it's rewriting the history books, or placing their people in the bureaucracy, in the police, in the army. Of course, when the Congress Party was in power, it was their people. But their people were not self-professedly communal people. They did it as a sly, undercover game.

In the past, historians or politicians or bureaucrats would not openly say that India is a Hindu country. But now nobody is shy about saying this. The RSS now has thousands of branches all over the country. They have funds, they have means, they have resources to indoctrinate young minds. Once you inject this poison into the bloodstream, it's very hard to work it out of the system. So now the fact is, whether the BJP wins the next elections or not, their agenda is on the table. The country has been militarized and communalized and nuclearized. The Congress has no means to deal with it. It hasn't been able to counter that in any moral or political way.

Let's say you want to write about a particular topic that interests you. First of all, how do you make that selection, and then how do you go about researching it?

You should never ask me these method questions, because there's never any method! It's not as though I cold-bloodedly go out and select some topic for academic or career reasons. In the case of the nuclear tests, the nuclear tests happened while I was in the United States. My first reaction was one of rage at the hypocrisy there: 'The blacks can't manage the bomb.' Then I came back here and saw the shrill jingoism. So I wrote 'The End of Imagination'. When you start getting into the debate about national security, every country can justify having nuclear weapons. I think it's very important not to enter the debate on their terms, on the terms that the army and the politicians and the bureaucracy would like to set. Because every country can have a pragmatic *realpolitik* justification for why it needs nuclear weapons.

In the case of the Narmada, it was more something that I really had for years wanted to understand. In February 1999, the Supreme Court lifted its stay on the building of the Sardar Sarovar dam. Suddenly it looked as if this battle, which many of us on the outside of this movement had thought was being won, had been dealt a body blow. I started reading. I went to the valley, I met the activists, and felt that the movement needed to tell its story in a way which is accessible to an ordinary reader. It needed a novelist's skill. It's a complex issue and much of the time the establishment depends on the fact that people don't understand. I wanted to build a narrative that could puncture that—to deal with all their arguments, to deal with their facts and figures, to counter them in a way ordinary people could understand.

One thing leads to another. If you read all the political essays, each one dovetails into the next. Going to the Narmada valley, you see that the fight against the Sardar Sarovar, which is a state-built dam, is different from the fight against the Maheshwar dam, which was the first privatized project in India. Then you start asking these questions about the privatization of infrastructure and it leads you to the whole question of privatization and what is going on there. So that led to my essay 'Power Politics'.

It is interesting to see how the establishment deals with dissent. It gives you a fair idea of who the establishment really is. You see who crawls out of the woodwork to take you on. Very often, it's an unexpected person. It's not the people who are completely on the other side of the spectrum, who are completely opposed to your point of view. It will be cowardly people who position themselves as being 'balanced' critics. They really can't deal with the real questions, because they're instinctively undemocratic. There is nothing they condemn more passionately than passion. But I insist on the right to be emotional, to be sentimental, to be passionate. If displacement, dispossession, killing and injustice on the scale that takes place in India does not enrage us, what will?

When people try to dismiss those who ask the big public questions as being emotional, it is a strategy to avoid debate. Why should we be scared of being angry? Why should we be scared of our feelings, if they're based on facts? The whole framework of reason versus passion is ridiculous, because often passion is based on reason. Passion is not always unreasonable. Anger is based on reason. They're not two different things. I feel it's very important to defend that. To defend the space for feelings, for emotions, for passion. I'm often accused of the crime of having feelings. But I'm not pretending to be a 'neutral' academic. I'm a writer. I have a point of view. I have feelings about the things I write about—and I'm going to express them.

That reminds me of a famous Urdu couplet by Muhammad Iqbal: 'Love leaped into Nimrod's fire without hesitation./ Meanwhile, reason is on the rooftop, just contemplating the scene.'[24] There is that kind of juxtaposition of the intellect versus feeling.

I think the opposite. I think that my passion comes from my intellect. So much of the way I love comes from the way I think. Thinking makes great loving. I don't acknowledge this artificial boundary between the intellect and the heart. They're not as separate as literature and poetry makes them out to be. Their fusion is what makes artists and writers. I believe in succumbing to the beauty of feelings and I believe in the rigour of the intellect, too. I don't believe in over-ripe passion. But I believe that there isn't anything as wonderful as a fierce intellectual passion.

Do you ever experience writer's block, where you have real difficulty in writing? Do you have any techniques to get out of it? Do you exercise or walk around the block or eat oranges?

No. I haven't gone through that. Not yet. I don't look at writing as a profession, a career. If I can't write, I won't write. I'll do something else. It's important to understand that one is not that significant. It doesn't matter. If you can do something, great; if you can't do it, it's okay.

Often I tell myself, 'Don't do it. Don't write.' Because I don't want to enter an arena that I know will consume my soul. I don't want to take on Narendra Modi or write about the riots in Gujarat. But, it's very hard to keep quiet. This hammering sets up in my head. My non-fiction is wrenched out of me. It's written when I don't want to write. So when people say, 'You're very brave' or 'You're very courageous,' I feel a bit embarrassed. Because it isn't bravery or courage. I have to do it. Often I don't want to see or understand. But I can't not, because the story clamours to be told and then I'm just the go-between that sits down and tells it, in some way.

What advice would you give to people, in terms of thinking outside the box, outside of what's called conventional wisdom, for example?

I'm very bad at giving advice!

For yourself, then, how do you do it? And how did you develop it, because it's something that's acquired. It's not necessarily innate, like a sense of smell.

I wonder. I didn't grow up within a conventional kind of family and I wasn't in a city. I was this child who was wandering all over the place, spending hours on the river alone, fishing. My childhood's greatest gift was a lack of indoctrination. So it's not that I'm somebody who's remarkable because I've learned to think outside the box. The fact is that the box was never imposed on me. I never went to a formal school until I was about ten. There was a delightful absence of a box.

We were in a way very cosmopolitan and in a way completely local and rural. It's an odd combination. I always had trouble if anyone asked me the most normal questions, like, 'Where are you from, what's your name, what's your mother tongue, what does your father do?' I had no answers for any of these questions, because I just didn't know my father and it was difficult to explain the complexities of my childhood. But if you asked me completely unconventional questions, then I could answer them, because I would think about them. These normal things were not easy for me to reply to.

As you've grown older, have you got an opportunity to know your father?

I've met him. Yes. At least I know what he looks like.

I was at Delhi University a few days ago, and a student asked me, 'What would you do in a public sector that is inefficient and has an overbloated bureaucracy and is losing money?' What's wrong with privatizing that?

People in India especially, but in the third world generally, are being made to believe that this is the only choice. You have a choice between a corrupt public sector and an efficient private sector. If those are the only two options, anyone would say, 'I'll have the efficient private sector.' In fact, many of the public sector units that are being privatized were actually profit-making. For instance, Bharat Heavy Electricals Limited, which manufactures turbines and heavy electrical machinery, was one of the foremost manufacturers in the world. As soon as the government decided to privatize it about ten years ago, they deliberately allowed everything to go to seed and then they said, 'Look, isn't it terrible?' It's propaganda, this opposition of the sleek, efficient private sector and the corrupt, terrible government. Of course, the public power sector has been incredibly corrupt and inefficient. The transmission and distribution losses have been tremendous. But what does the government do? It signs up with Enron. What is happening with Enron today? The government is paying Enron not to produce electricity, because it's so expensive.

So Enron, even though it's bankrupt in the United States and disgraced, is still sucking money out of the Indian economy?

There's a big litigation process on, but, yes, that's the situation.

Bill Gates of Microsoft, one of the sahibs of the new world economic order, was shopping in Delhi last week. He met with top government officials and CEOs. You saw something very interesting on TV about how Indians view Gates.

I was watching some music channel—not MTV, but some other music channel—this morning. On the screen it said, 'What does Bill Gates really want?' Then they had interviews with maybe twenty young students. Every single one of them said he's here to blow open the market for Windows and he's just trying to get publicity by giving money for AIDS. Nobody was under any illusions about what his visit was about.

Does that encourage you, that people have that understanding?

Three or four months ago, I went to a seminar on the power sector, and I thought to myself, 'What are you doing here? How can you be sitting in this seminar on the privatization of power?' If someone had told me four years ago that I would be attending meetings about electricity, I would have laughed. But it was uplifting to listen to the kind of minds that are at work here. People can just take the whole thing apart and critique it. The first critique of the Power Purchase Agreement with Enron came from a small NGO in Pune called Prayas.[25] Everything they said has come true. That is a great thing about India. There is a very strong intellectual ability to take something apart, in a way that I really appreciate and admire.

To what extent do you think that the British used 'divide and rule' as a strategy to maintain control of India—a vast country? The British had very few soldiers and administrators here.

The British certainly used divide-and-rule tactics, but the British empire survived because it co-opted the Indian elite. It's the same technique that empire uses now to propagate its neoliberal reign.

Have you read the work of Martin Luther King, Jr? He was influenced by Gandhi. People in the United States generally know about his 'I Have a Dream' speech from the 1963 March on Washington, but not a lot of Americans know about the speech he gave in New York in 1967 at Riverside Church. He became increasingly radical later in his life, and in New York he said, 'True compassion is more than flinging a coin to a beggar. It comes to see that an edifice which produces beggars needs restructuring.'[26]

That is the terrible dilemma of living in India, isn't it? Every moment of every day, you're faced with the brutal inequalities of the society you live in. So it is impossible to forget, even for a moment. Just to enjoy the ordinary daily things—the clothes you wear, the fun you have, the music you listen to, the roof over your head, the meal in the evening—involves knowing that other people don't have these privileges.

We have been taught that peace is the opposite of war. But is it? In India, peace is a daily battle for food and shelter and dignity.

Martin Luther King, Jr wrote in his 'Letter from Birmingham Jail' that true peace is not merely 'the absence of tension' but 'the presence of justice'.[27]

Or at least the journey toward justice, toward some vision of egalitarianism. Which is what I think is fundamentally the problem with the whole ethic of neoliberal neocapitalism. You make it all right to grab. You say that it's all right to get ahead by hitting the next person on the head. It's all right to accumulate capital and profits at someone else's expense. It destroys the fabric of concern and fellow-feeling. There is a finite amount of capital in the world, and if you accumulate, you're grabbing from somebody. That's not right.

Another of the sahibs who recently has been in Delhi is Paul O'Neill, the US treasury secretary. He was talking on November 22 to an audience of corporate leaders, and he was very critical of India, a country, he said, where 'corruption and bribery are widespread, frightening away honest businessmen and investors'.[28]

If it's frightening away investors like Enron and Bechtel, it can only be a good thing.

It's interesting that he should be lecturing Indians about corruption and bribery, because the United States has just gone through what *Business Week* calls the most unprecedented 'corporate crime wave' in its history.[29] Not just Enron, but WorldCom, Xerox, Tyco, Arthur Andersen—a huge number of corporations have been guilty of insider trading and all kinds of shenanigans.

When have America's own shortcomings prevented it from lecturing to other people? That's par for the course.

Howard Zinn, the great American historian, said there was the Bronze Age, the Iron Age, and today we live in the Age of Irony.[30]

Irony is a kind word for the crimes of the American empire.

In your essay entitled 'Come September' you are very

critical of US policy in support of Israel and its repression of the Palestinians. You must know that this is a hot-button issue in the United States. It's difficult to talk about Israel critically without immediately being labelled in the most unflattering terms. Why did you choose to talk about this?

I was talking about the eleventh of September, and I thought I should remind people that the eleventh of September 1922 was when imperial Britain marked out a mandate on Palestine, after the Balfour Declaration. Eighty years on, the Palestinians are still under siege. How can one come to the United States and not mention Israel's illegal occupation of Palestinian territory? The US government is funding it and supporting it politically and morally. It's a crime.

Diaspora communities are notorious for having very inflammatory views. If you look at the most right-wing, unreasonable, vituperative Hindus, many live in the United States. Every time you get a letter to the editor saying, 'I think there should be nuclear war and Pakistan should be destroyed,' it will be somebody who lives in Urbana-Champaign or some other US town. I've never been to Israel, but I've been told that in Israel the media reflects a broader spectrum of opinion than you see in the United States.

What do you think of the report that just came out looking at the Indian diaspora community in the United States? Apparently, some segments of it are sending a lot of money to support Hindu fundamentalist organizations.[31]

The report seems quite credible. It's quite important that this kind of dogged work is being done. These groups hide behind the fact that they do charity work, though their charity is all about the Hinduization of tribal people. But in India, these things will not be investigated.

What was your take on the US presidential election in the year 2000, especially in light of the US tendency to be

very critical of how elections are conducted in other countries?

I have to say that I didn't follow it very closely, because if you don't live in America, whether it's Bush or Clinton or Gore, it doesn't seem to make that much difference. I personally feel that if the September 11 attacks had happened when Clinton was in power, it could have been worse for the world in a way, because he at least doesn't sound as stupid as Bush. Bush is vicious but he's comical. He's easy meat. Whereas Clinton is far cleverer and more calculating. He's more of a showman. I don't think there's much to choose between them.

You have used the word 'bully' to describe the United States and its policies. I think maybe some Americans might have difficulty identifying their state as a bully because of a lack of information about what's going on outside.

People from poorer places and poorer countries have to call upon their compassion not to be angry with ordinary people in America. I certainly do. Every time I write something, that anger does come out, and then I pull it back, because I tell myself, 'They don't know. These are people who don't know what is being done in their name.' Yet, I keep wondering if that's because it suits them not to know. I have to remind myself about the extent of the brainwashing that goes on there. But I think that if most people knew what was being done in their names, they would be mortified. The question is: how do we let them know?

Ben Bagdikian and others have written extensively about how the corporate media operates in the United States, and by extension in the rest of the world because of its enormous reach.[32] Do you think that the people who work for these corporations know the reality, know the facts about what's going on and are repressing it? Or are they truly ignorant?

I'm sure the senior people know. The junior people are sent on a beat and told to cover something and they cover it. So I don't think everybody knows the key secret and is suppressing it. Journalists have the illusion of independence. But certainly the people who make the decisions know.

Where are the spaces for dissidents in the Indian context? What about television?

There's no space on TV whatsoever. Not even to show a documentary film, like, say, Sanjay Kak's film on the Narmada. We don't even begin to think that it will be shown on TV.

Why not? Why isn't there a station or a network?

Why not? You can't even have a private screening of a documentary film without a censor certificate. When Anand Patwardhan made his documentary about the nuclear issue, the censor board told him, 'You can't show politicians in your film.' *You can't show politicians in your film!* What does that mean? You can't have politicians making political speeches in your film![33] It's really Kafkaesque. Yet they can't police everything. It's too difficult.

In a country like the United States where books like Chomsky's *9-11* are starting to reach wider audiences, aren't people going to feel a bit pissed off that they had no idea about what was going on, and what was being done in their name?[34] If the corporate media continues to be as outrageous in its suppression of facts as it is, it might just lift off like a scab. It might become something that's totally irrelevant, that people just don't believe. Because, ultimately, people are interested in their own safety.

The policies the US government is following are dangerous for its citizens. It's true that you can bomb or buy out anybody that you want to, but you can't control the rage that's building in the world. You just can't. And that rage will express itself in some way or the other. Condemning violence is not going to be enough. How can you condemn violence when a section of your economy is based on selling weapons and making bombs and piling up chemical and biological weapons? When the soul of your culture worships violence? On what grounds are you going to condemn terrorism, unless you change your attitude toward violence?

With very few exceptions, the September 11 attacks are presented as actions by people who simply hate America. It's separated from any political background. That has confused a lot of people.

It was a successful strategy, this isolation of the events of September 11 from history, insisting that terrorism is an evil impulse with no context. The minute you try and put it into a context, you are accused of excusing it or justifying it. It's like telling a scientist who is researching drugs for malaria that he or she is in cahoots with the female anopheles mosquito. If you're trying to understand something, it doesn't mean you're justifying it. The fact is, if you can justify all the wars that you have fought, all the murders that you've committed, all the countries that you've bombed, all the ecologies that you've destroyed, if you can justify that, then Osama bin Laden can certainly use the same logic to justify September 11. You can't have a political context for one kind of terrorism and no political context for another.

So if you were to talk to an average American, what would be something that you would say, in terms of trying to understand why there is animosity toward the United States, why there is rage and anger?

I was in America in September 2002, as you know. I was very reluctant to come. I thought there just wasn't any point in saying these things, because I don't believe in 'speaking truth to power'. I don't believe that there is any way in which you can persuade that kind of power to act differently unless it's in its own self-interest. There isn't any point. But my editor, Anthony Arnove, persuaded me to come, and I'm so glad that I did, because it was very, very nice for me to see how human and open the people I met were. People were clearly trying to understand what was going on in the world. It was an important trip for me.

I had exactly the opposite experience from what I expected. I had people coming up to me on the street saying, 'Thank you for saying what you said' and 'We can't say it because we're so scared, but thank you.' It was wonderful for me that it happened. It made me believe that the reason that so much energy and money is poured into manipulating the media is because the establishment fears public opinion. They know that ordinary people are not as ruthless, as cold, as calculating, as powerful people. Ordinary people do have a conscience. Ordinary people don't necessarily always act in their own selfish interests. If the bubble were to burst, and people were to know all of the horrendous things that have been carried out in their name; I think it would go badly for the American establishment. And I think it has begun. I think all of America's family secrets are spilling out backstage on the Green Room floor. I really think so. Yes, it's true that the corporate media just blanks out everything, but on the Internet, some of the most outraged, incandescently angry pieces are written by Americans. A film like *Bowling for Columbine* has been shown everywhere and it connects the dots in ways which ordinary people can understand. This is important. I think it's beginning to unravel, actually. I think the propaganda machine is going to come apart.

What about the role of intellectuals in the propaganda machine? In the United States, intellectuals are supposed to be neutral. They're supposed to accumulate facts and present them without presuming to be on one side or the other. They're encouraged to use obscure jargon. For example, there are no ideas—everything is a 'notion'. No one talks, it's all 'discourse'. It's what we call pomo, postmodernism. Do you have something like that in India?

We have pomo in India, too. Definitely. A lot of it has to do with the sad business of creating a little expertise, so that you come off sounding special, as if the world couldn't do without you. A little hunk of expertise that you can carry off to your lair and guard against the unauthorized curiosity of passers-by. My enterprise is the opposite: to never complicate what is simple, to never simplify what is complicated. But I think it's very important to be able to communicate to ordinary people what is happening in the world. There's a whole industry working hard at trying to prevent people from understanding what is being done to them.

Chomsky calls them a mandarin class of specialists.

Experts take away from people the ability to make decisions. In courts, language has evolved in such a way that ordinary people simply can't understand. You have this phalanx of lawyers and judges who are deciding vitally important issues, but people can't understand what is being said, what the procedure really is, what's going on.

I noticed that in the film *DAM/AGE*, it was difficult to follow some of the pronouncements from the Supreme Court.

'Vicious stultification and vulgar debunking cannot be allowed to pollute the stream of justice' [laughs]. What is the other one? 'Contumacious violation ...' I've forgotten. I used to know it by heart.

Do you see any role for specialized knowledge?

I see a role for specialized knowledge, but I think that it's important for there to be an arena where it is shared, where it is communicated. It's not that somebody shouldn't have specialized knowledge. The ability to dig a trench and lay a cable is a kind of specialized knowledge. Farmers have specialized knowledge too. The question is: what sort of knowledge is privileged in our societies? I don't think that a CEO is more valuable to society and ought to be paid ten million dollars a year, while farmers and labourers starve.

The range of what is valued has become so extreme that one lot of people have captured it and left three-quarters of the world to live in unthinkable poverty, because their work is not valued. What would happen if the sweepers of the city went on strike or the sewage system didn't work? A CEO wouldn't be able to deal with his own shit.

Macaulay, a Raj official in the nineteenth century, imperiously declared that 'a single shelf of a good European library [is] worth the whole native literature of India and Arabia'. In recent years there's been an enormous surge of writing produced not only by Indian writers such as yourself but also writers of Indian origin who live outside of India, like V.S. Naipaul. Why is that happening now?

It's not that enormous a surge, actually. I remember when my novel was first published, the *New Yorker* organized to shoot one big photograph of Indo-Anglian writers.[36] There were maybe ten or fifteen of us. They'd organized this huge bus to take us to lunch, but the bus was still pretty empty. Everyone's talking about this surge but you can count the people who are known on your fingertips. It's being made out to be something more than it is, I think.

Like a fad?

There are people writing, but it's not some renaissance or anything that's happening. If it is a fad for the western world, then that's their business. I don't care.

Some people might say that writing in English automatically means you're writing for a yuppie audience, because English in India particularly is a language of privilege.

That's true. But at the same time, any language in India is very limited. If you write in Malayalam, only someone from Kerala can read it. If you write in Hindi, only those from a few states in the north can read it. So language is a very complicated issue in India. It's interesting that *The God of Small Things* has been published in forty languages, so in a way it's about language, but not as in English or German or French or Hindi. It's something more than that. It's language as communication, more or less.

My political writing is published in many, many Indian languages. The Hindi translation of *The God of Small Things* is almost ready. So it's no longer just for yuppies. And anyway it's not just yuppies who speak English in India. There are more people who speak English in India than in England. It's a huge number.

One of the pleasures for me about having written *The God of Small Things* is that many of the people who are reading it would not normally read an English novel. So a sub-inspector from Muzaffarnagar or some person from some village somewhere will come to me and say, 'I read it with a dictionary. I understood it.' So I love the range of readers—from John Updike to a policeman in Muzaffarnagar.

Your articles and essays appear in the *Nation* magazine, and you're publishing now with South End Press. *Power Politics* is your first book with them and *War Talk* is the next one. Are you getting a lot of response from outside India? Are people writing to you?

I do receive a lot of letters, but it's difficult for me to deal with the volume of responses and requests that I get. I'm under pressure to turn myself into an institution, to have an office and secretaries and people dealing with my mail and my accounts. I'm just not like that. I can't be like that. So I choose the inefficient model, which is not to deal with it. I do what I can. Obviously I have a literary agent in America and in England. They help me. But in my own space, I just don't have that. It's hard, but it's a choice that I make, that I just continue to be an individual who gets a lot of mail and can't handle it.

Himanshu Thakkar is someone whom you admire. You mention him in the introduction to *The Cost of Living*.[37] I happened to meet him and he told me, 'You know, it's remarkable. The women are the leaders in the country. The women are advancing the movements for social justice.' Why is that?

I don't know but it's absolutely correct. In India, the legacy of the freedom struggle has been a great respect for non-violent resistance. The pros and cons of violent and non-violent resistance can be debated, but I don't think there can be any doubt that violent resistance harms women physically and psychologically in deep and complex ways. Having said that, Indian society is still deeply disrespectful of women. The daily violence, injustice and indignity heaped on women is hard to believe sometimes.

But this takes place against a backdrop of an institutionalized misogyny that is deeply culturally imbedded. One example was a report in the *Times of India* a couple of days ago that there's a crisis in Haryana because there are not enough marriageable girls?[38] Why aren't there enough marriageable girls? Because of female foeticide? The families have to buy brides for their sons from outside the state and their community. It's interesting that the *Times* said that 'Desperate boys are willing to marry girls from any caste.' That's another one of these incredible contradictions.

That is India. We don't even blink when someone brings up a contradiction. What is interesting is that a lot of the women who are involved in resistance movements and who are activists are also redefining what 'modern' means. They are really at war against their community's traditions on the one hand, and against the kind of modernity that is being imposed by the global economy on the other. They decide what they want from their own tradition and what they will take from modernity. It's a high-wire act. Very tiring but exhilarating.

Another thing everyone probably has to deal with here is the persistence of colour, the emphasis on being fair-skinned. I was reading about Kareena Kapoor, a rising young hollywood starlet (who is opening, incidentally, a Pizza Hut in Gurgaon), and she was described as 'cream coloured'. It's a very favourable designation.

I'm so glad that you brought this up, because most people, foreigners, don't even notice that there's a colour difference between white Indians and black Indians. But it's something that really drives me crazy here. India is one of the most racist modern societies. The kind of things people will say about being black-skinned are stunning.

There was a television programme a few years ago about this. In the audience there was a Sudanese man, an albino man, and a Punjabi woman who runs a marriage bureau. I've never seen anything more ridiculous. The Sudanese man talked about how terrible it was for him to live here and how girls would cross to the other side of the road. How people would pull his hair on the bus and call him *hubshi*, which is roughly equivalent to 'nigger'. Then the albino said, 'I don't know whether I would be considered fair or dark.' So he asked the woman who runs the marriage bureau whether she could get him a bride. She looked at him and said, 'I can get you a polio victim.'

This was all being done without irony. At the end of it, the man who was presenting the show said, 'It looks like all of us are very colour conscious. In actual fact, why do we spend so much time thinking about the packaging? Black people are also nice from underneath.'

If you look at the newspapers, you see advertisements for some cream called Afghan Snow or Fair and Lovely. And all these white women in Bollywood films! Ninety per cent of the women in India are black. But, according to Bollywood, if you're not white, you're not beautiful. The rising international popularity of Bollywood films worries me. Most of them reinforce some terrible, some very disempowering values.

Poor people, the Dalits and the adivasis, are mostly black. There's an apartheid system at work here, for anyone who cares to notice.

Let's go to another Bombay Bollywood star, from an older generation, Nargis. She complained bitterly about Satyajit Ray, the great Indian film-maker, saying that his films only

show poverty. Then she was asked, 'Well, what would you rather see in Indian cinema?' And she said 'dams'.[39]

'You're not showing India in a proper light.' That's the great middle-class complaint: 'Why can't you show McDonald's and Pizza King?' Because here, you see, people have learned not to see the poverty. They have these filters, these contact lenses, that filter it out. They don't understand why 'outsiders' get so exercised about it. They take it as a kind of affront.

I'm interested in how that operates. I've seen it myself, and see it in myself when I'm here. How do you look away from someone who's terribly poor and indigent?

It's a survival technique. Meaning, how else are you to survive? You have to find a way of continuing with your life. So you just filter it out.

'When people describe me as famous and rich and successful, it makes me feel queasy. Each of those words falls on my soul like an insult. They seem tinny and boring and shiny and uninteresting to me. It makes me feel unsuccessful because I never set out to be those things. And they make me uneasy. To be famous, rich and successful in this world is not an admirable thing. I'm suspicious of it all.'

'It's one thing to have a dictator who commits genocide. It's another thing to have an elected government with officials who have been accused of actively abetting mass murder being re-elected. Because then, all of us must bear the shame of that. All of us must bear some responsibility for that. I don't see that it's all that different from the American public electing president after president who has killed and massacred and bombed people all over the world.'

GLOBALIZATION OF DISSENT

IN CONVERSATION WITH DAVID BARSAMIAN, MAY 2003.

In March 2002, a pogrom was carried out against the Muslim population of Gujarat. You've written an essay on this entitled 'Democracy: Who Is She When She Is at Home'. What happened in Gujarat?

In February 2002, the BJP was gearing up for elections in Uttar Pradesh. They had trundled out their favourite campaign issue, the building of the Ram temple in Ayodhya. Communal tension was at a fever pitch. People were travelling to Ayodhya by train to participate in the building of the temple. At the time, Gujarat was the only major state in India to have a BJP government. It had for some time been the laboratory in which Hindu fascism had been conducting an elaborate experiment. In late February, a train carrying belligerent VHP and Bajrang Dal activists was stopped by a mob outside the Godhra station. A whole compartment of the train was set on fire and fifty-eight people were burnt alive.[1]

Nobody really knew who was responsbile for the carnage. Within hours, a meticulously planned pogrom was unleashed against the Muslim community. About 2,000 Muslims were killed. One hundred and fifty thousand were driven from their homes. Women were publicly gang-raped. Parents were bludgeoned to death in front of their children. The leaders of the mob had computer-generated lists marking out Muslim-owned shops, homes and businesses, which were burned to the ground. Muslim places of worship were desecrated. The mob was equipped with trucks loaded with thousands of gas cylinders that had been hoarded weeks in advance. The police did not merely protect the mob, but provided covering fire. Within months, Gujarat's chief minister, Narendra Modi, announced proudly that he wanted to have early elections. He believed that the pogrom would win him Hindu hearts.

Modi was right, wasn't he?

Modi's re-election is something that has shaken many of us to the core of our beings. It's one thing to have a dictator who commits genocide. It's another thing to have an elected government with officials who have been accused of actively abetting mass murder being re-elected. Because then, all of us must bear the shame of that. All of us must bear some responsibility for that.

But thinking deeply about it, I don't see that it's all that different from the American public electing president after president who has killed and massacred and bombed people all over the world. A child asked me quite recently, 'Is Bush better or is Modi better?' I said, 'Why are you asking?' He said, 'Because Modi killed his own people, and Bush is killing other people.' That's how clear children can be. Eventually, after thinking about it, I said, 'Well, the people they killed are all people.' We have to think like that.

What happened in Gujarat has raised very serious questions. When you speak to somebody and tell them that 2,000 Muslims were massacred on the streets of Gujarat, and women were raped, and pregnant women had their stomachs slit open, normal people, or people who are outside that situation, recoil in horror. But people inside that situation say things like, 'They deserved it.' And how do you deal with that?

It isn't a coincidence that the massacre of Muslims in Gujarat happened after September 11. Gujarat is also one place where the toxic waste of the World Trade Centre is being dumped right now.[2] This waste is being dumped in Gujarat and then taken off to Ludhiana and places like that to be recycled. I think it's quite a metaphor. The demonization of Muslims has also been given legitimacy by the world's superpower, by the emperor himself. We are at a stage where democracy—this corrupted, scandalous version of democracy—is the problem. So much of what politicians do is with an eye on elections. Wars are fought as election campaigns. In India, Muslims are killed as part of election campaigns. In 1984, after the massacre of Sikhs in Delhi, the Congress Party won, hands down. We must ask ourselves very serious questions about this particular brand of democracy.

What was the response of the political class in India and the media to Modi being re-elected?

The media in India can roughly be divided into the national English media and the local regional-language newspapers. Typically, their understandings of similar events are completely different. The local Gujarati press was vehemently anti-Muslim. It manipulated events and supported what was happening. But the English press was very outspoken and condemnatory of what Modi was doing in Gujarat.

It's important to understand that the killing in Gujarat had a long run-up. The climate was created soon after the BJP came to power and India conducted nuclear tests. This whole business of unfettered Hindu nationalism, where else was it going to lead?

The national press supported that idea from the beginning. It supported the Kargil war uncritically. The English-language press in India supports the project of corporate globalization fully. It has no time for dispossession and drought and farmers' debts, the ravages that the corporate globalization project is wreaking on the poor of India. So to suddenly turn around and condemn the riots is a typical middle-class response. Let's support everything that leads to the conditions in which the massacre takes place, but when the killing starts, you recoil in middle-class horror and say, 'Oh, that's not very nice. Can't we be more civilized?'

Once Modi won the elections, the English-language press began to whip itself and say, 'We got it wrong. Maybe the secularists are taking too much of an anti-Hindu position,' and rubbish like that. They began to negotiate with the fascists, basically. The Chamber of Indian Industry apologized to Modi for having said things about the fact that genocide was bad for business. They promised to re-invest in Gujarat. So as soon as he won this election, everybody was busy

Armed police personnel patrol the streets of Ahmedabad, Gujarat during the organized violence against Muslims in 2002. Photo courtesy Anandabazar Picture Archives.

negotiating and retracting. I've lost track of the number of references I've seen in the media to 'Modi magic'.

What was the response of the so-called intellectual class, academics and writers, to Gujarat and Modi's re-election?

I think everybody felt whipped and beaten, because Modi was gloating. Everybody felt as if they had taken a pounding, which they had, to an extent. I think it threw the opposition—I don't mean the Congress Party when I say the opposition, but the critics of this kind of politics—into disarray, because they felt that, and they were made to feel that, they had no place in modern India. These voices of sanity and reason felt that they had no place.

Academics have this problem. If you are an economist, you are only an economist. If you are a sociologist, you are only a sociologist. If you are a historian, you're only a historian. And now, to understand what's going on, you must cross disciplines and you must see the connections between the dispossession and the despair created by corporate globalization, flowing into the bitterness of Partition, flowing into the rhetoric of cultural nationalism. All these things come together to create this situation.

Gujarat is also, ironically, the home state of Mahatma Gandhi. In 1930, there was a very interesting event there. He led a Salt March to the coastal town of Dandi. Why don't you recount that, so that people have another kind of historical perspective?

Whatever critique one may or may not have of him, Gandhi's understanding of politics and public imagination is unsurpassed, I would say, by any politician in world history. He knew how to strike at the heart of empire. The Salt March—the Dandi march—when Indians marched to the sea to make salt, was a strike against the salt tax. It wasn't just a symbolic weekend march, but struck at the heart of the economic policies of the colonial regime. What has happened in the evolution of non-violent resistance is that it's become more and more symbolic, and less and less real. When a symbol unmoors itself from what it symbolizes, it loses meaning. It becomes ineffective.

Fifteen million people marched against the war in Iraq on 15 February 2003, in perhaps the biggest display of public morality ever seen. It was fantastic. But it was symbolic. Governments of today have learned to deal with that. They know to wait out a demonstration or a march. They know the day after tomorrow, opinions can change, or be manipulated into changing. Unless civil disobedience becomes real, not symbolic, there is very little hope for change.

That's a very important lesson that we need to learn from the civil disobedience and the non-violent resistance of the Indian independence struggle. It was fine political theatre, but it was never, ever merely symbolic. It was always a real strike against the economics of imperialism. What was swadeshi about? It was saying, 'Don't buy British products.' It was saying, 'Make your own yarn. Make your own salt. We have to take apart the economic machinery of empire now and strike at it.' These marches and songs and meetings of today—they are beautiful, but they are often mostly for us. If all our energies go into organizing these things, then we don't do any real damage to the establishment, to the empire.

There's a lot of talk in the United States now about empire. A new book by British historian Niall Ferguson, *Empire*, celebrates the many positive aspects of imperialism, particularly of British rule. The jewel in the crown of Britain, of course, was colonial India.[3]

It's rather staggering that people like Ferguson are touting the benefits of imperialism. By the middle of the eighteenth century, just about the time that the British took it over, India accounted for nearly 25 per cent of the world's global trade. When the British left in 1947, this figure had dwindled to around 4 to 5 per cent. Much scholarly research has demonstrated that during British rule, India's economy underwent a process of peasantization, where urban areas were ruralized, essentially.

Recently, travelling to the west, it's the first time it's even occurred to me that people can actually justify imperialism. Let me say categorically that—politically, socially, economically—there is no justification for colonialism. Next, these people will be justifying genocide or slavery. Weren't they the foundations of the American empire?

Do you think that the people of South Africa, or anywhere on the continent of Africa, or India, or Pakistan are longing to be kicked around all over again? Is Ferguson aware of how many million people died in India in the late nineteenth century because of the drought and the famine while food and raw materials were being exported to England? How dare they even talk like this? It's grotesque that anybody can sit down and write a reasoned book on something like this. It is nothing short of grotesque.

Thomas Friedman, the Pulitzer Prize-winning columnist for the *New York Times*, has written that 'America is in an imperial role here, now. Our security and standing in the world ride on our getting Iraq right.'[4]

Well, it isn't doing it right, is it? But the point is that the justification for going to war against Iraq has been forgotten. The weapons of mass destruction have not been found. You were told in the United States that Iraq was going to annihilate you, just as Cuba was, and Nicaragua was, and El Salvador was, and all the tiny little countries of the world were. After the war, you were told, America was going to be secure. But today, after the war, the terrorist alerts keep being set to purple, or whatever the highest register is. And now you're saying, 'Al-Qaeda is in Iran, or maybe it's in Syria, or maybe it's in North Korea.'

The point is that any kind of justification, any kind of nonsense works because there isn't any real media left in the United States. It's just a kind of propaganda machine that spews out whatever suits the occasion and banks on people's short memory span.

When you spoke at the World Social Forum in Porto

Alegre, Brazil, in late January 2003, you were certain that the United States was going to attack Iraq. In fact, you said, 'It's more than clear that Bush is determined to go to war against Iraq, regardless of the facts—and regardless of international public opinion.'[5]

I don't think you needed to be a genius to be certain. There is a strategy at work which has nothing to do with the propaganda that's being put out. And when you start to see the pattern, then you have a sense of what is going to happen. After the attack on Afghanistan, you started to see the preparations for the next war against Iraq. And now they are laying the basis for even more wars.

I find it shocking that people should think that world public opinion should have changed because the United States 'won' the war. Did anybody think it wasn't going to? Here is a country that is so ruthless in what it is prepared to do that it's going to win every war that it fights, except if its own people do something about it. There isn't any country that can fight a conventional war against US forces and win.

Talk about how war is viewed as a product to be marketed and sold to the consumers, in this case the American public.

Referring to the timing of the Iraq war, a Bush administration spokesperson said, 'From a marketing point of view, you don't introduce new products in August.'[6] They were asking themselves, what's the best season to introduce this new product? When should you start the ad campaign? When should you actually launch it? Today, the crossover between Hollywood and the US military is getting more and more promiscuous.

War is also an economic necessity now. A significant section of the American economy depends on the sale of weapons. There has to be a turnover. You can't have cruise missiles lying around on the factory floor. The economies of Europe and the United States depend on the sale and manufacture of weapons. This is a huge imperative to go to war. Apart from this, the United States needs millions of barrels of oil a day to keep its bloated economy chugging along. It needs Iraq. It needs Venezuela.

What accounts for the brazenness of the Bush administration? For example, Paul Wolfowitz, the deputy secretary of defence, was talking about Syria, saying it was 'behaving badly', like the headmaster wagging his finger at the bad student.[7] How is this attitude seen outside the United States?

I think, in two ways. On the one hand, it's seen as a kind of uncouth stupidity. On the other hand, it's seen as just the insulting language of power. You speak like that because you can.

In an interview you did in the *Socialist Worker*, you said, 'The greatest threat to the world today is not Saddam Hussein, it's George Bush (joined at the hip to his new foreign secretary, Tony Blair).'[8] Talk about Tony Blair. Why has he attached himself to American power with such fervour and vigour?

That's a much more intriguing question than why the Bush regime is so brazen. The combination of stupidity, brutality and power is an answer to the first question. But why is Blair behaving the way he is? I've been thinking about it, and my understanding is that what has happened is that the American empire has metamorphosed from the British empire. The British empire has morphed into the American empire. Tony Blair wants to be part of empire because that's where he thinks he belongs. That's where his past, his country's past, has been, and it's a way of staying in the imperial game.

I was reading an article in the *New York Times* the other day that was appropriately called something like 'Feeding Frenzy in Iraq'.[9] It said that countries 'representing their corporate interests' are bidding for subcontracts from Bechtel and Halliburton. Among the countries that are petitioning Bechtel and Halliburton, Bush administration officials said that Britain has the best case, because it 'shed blood in Iraq'. I wondered what they meant by that, because the little British blood that was shed was basically shed by Americans. And since they hadn't specified whose blood was shed, I presume they mean that the British shed Iraqi blood in Iraq. So their status as co-murderers means that they ought to be given privileged access to these subcontracts.

The article went on to say that Lady Symons, who is the deputy leader of the House of Lords, was travelling in the United States with four British captains of industry. They were making the case that they should be given preference not only because they were co-murderers but because Britain's had a long and continuous relationship with Iraq since imperial days, right up to the time of the sanctions, which means that they were trading with Iraq, were doing business in Iraq, through Saddam Hussein's worst periods.

The idea that you're actually trying to petition for privilege because you were once the imperial master of Iraq is unthinkable for those of us who come from former colonies, because we think of imperialism as rape. So the way the logic seems to work is, first you rape, then you kill, and then you petition to rape the corpse. It's like necrophilia. On what grounds are these arguments even being made? And made without irony?

What factor does racism play in this construction of imperial power?

Racism plays the same part today as it did in colonial times. There isn't any difference. I mean, the only people who are going to argue for the good side to imperialism are white people, people who were once masters, or Uncle Toms. I don't think you're going to find that argument being made by people in India, or people in South Africa, people in former colonies. The only ones who want colonialism back in its new avatar of neoliberalism are the former white masters and their old cohorts—the 'native elites'—their point men then and now.

The whole rhetoric of 'We need to bring democracy to Iraq' is absurd when you think of the fact that the United States supported Saddam Hussein and made sure that he ruled with an iron fist for all those years. Then they used the sanctions to break the back of civil society. Then they made Iraq disarm. Then they attacked Iraq. And now they've taken over all its assets.

The people who supported the military attack on Iraq may concede today, 'Well, those reasons that we gave perhaps are not valid. We can't find the plutonium and uranium and biological and chemical weapons. Let's say we concede those points. But, after all, Miss Roy, we've got rid of a terrible dictator. Aren't the Iraqi people better off now?'

If that were the case, then why are they busy supporting dictators now all over central Asia? Why are they supporting the Saudi regime?

We're told that 'Saddam Hussein is a monster who must be stopped now. And only the United States can stop him.' It's an effective technique, this use of the urgent morality of the present to obscure the diabolical sins of the past and the malevolent plans for the future. This present 'urgency' can always be used to justify your past sins and your future sins. It's a non-argument.

Islam is being targeted and demonized in much of the media, and also among what I can only describe as mullahs and ayatollahs here in the United States, people like Franklin Graham, son of Billy Graham, who called Islam 'a very evil and wicked religion.' Jerry Falwell said Mohammed was a 'terrorist'. Jerry Vines, who is a very prominent preacher, described Mohammed as a 'demon-obsessed paedophile'.[10]

This seems to integrate with a lot of rhetoric coming from the Hindu nationalists in India, about Islam. Vajpayee said recently, 'Wherever Muslims are, they do not want to live peacefully.'[11]

The mullahs of the Islamic world and the mullahs of the Hindu world and the mullahs of the Christian world are all on the same side. And we are against them all. I can tell you that, insult for insult, you will find the mullahs in Pakistan or in Afghanistan or in Iran saying the same things about Christianity. And you will find the mullahs in India and the RSS people in the Hindu right-wing saying the same things about each other. I see Praveen Togadia of the VHP and Paul Wolfowitz and John Ashcroft and Osama bin Laden and George Bush as being on the same side. These are artificial differences that we waste our time on, trying to figure out who is insulting who. They are all on the same side. And we are against them all.

You've travelled to the United States on several occasions. You give talks and you meet and talk with lots of people. Why do you think Americans have been so susceptible to the Bush propaganda, specifically about Iraq being such an imminent threat to the national security of the United States, and that Iraq was responsible for September 11, and that Iraq is connected to Al-Qaeda, when there is simply no empirical evidence to support any of those assumptions?

I think, on one level, the fact is that the American media is just like a corporate boardroom bulletin. But on a deeper level, why are Americans such a frightened people? After all, many of us routinely live with terrorism. If Iraq or El Salvador or Cuba is going to destroy America, then what is the point of all these weapons, these 400 billion dollars spent every year on weapons, if you are that vulnerable in the end? It doesn't add up.

It's 400 billion dollars a year, not including the Iraq war, which is a supplemental expenditure.

So what is it that makes a country with all these bombs and missiles and weapons the most frightened country and the most frightened people on earth? Why is it that people in a country like India, which has nothing in comparison, are so much less scared? Why do we live easier lives, more relaxed lives?

People are so isolated, and so alone, and so suspicious, and so competitive with each other, and so sure that they are about to be conned by their neighbour, or by their mother, or by their sister, or their grandmother. What's the use of having 50 per cent of the world's wealth, or whatever it is that you have, if you're going to live this pathetic, terrified life?

Michael Moore's documentary *Bowling for Columbine* explores this to some degree.

What is wonderful about *Bowling for Columbine* is that it's accessible to ordinary people. It broke through the skin of mainstream media.

The language of the Left must become more accessible, must reach more people. We must acknowledge that if we don't reach people, it's our failure. Every success of Fox News is a failure for us. Every success of major corporate propaganda is our failure. It's not enough to moan about it. We have to do something about it. Reach ordinary people, break the stranglehold of mainstream propaganda. It's not enough to be intellectually pristine and self-righteous.

There is a growing independent media movement in the United States, and it's connected with movements and organizations, such as Sarai.net in New Delhi, and Independent Media Centres all over the world. There are a lot of young people getting involved in the media who are frustrated with the corporate pablum that they receive, and they're doing something about it. You're in touch with some of these activists in India.

The fact that hundreds of thousands of people in the United States were out on the streets, marching against the war, was partly because of that independent media. Unfortunately, it's not enough to walk out on the street on a weekend. One of the things that needs to be done is for the alternative media to reach a stage where the corporate media becomes irrelevant. That has to be the goal. Not that you attack it, but that you make it irrelevant, that you contextualize it.

How do you develop the ability to discern fact from fiction in approaching news from mainstream outlets?

I think the only way to do it is to follow the money. Who owns which newspaper? Who owns the television network? What are their interests? Assume that corporate media has an agenda. And so the least you can do is to cross-check a particular story with other sources of information that are independent. If you can do that, you can see the discrepancies. Compare, for example, the way the US media and the British media covers the same war, the same event. How does this differ from how Al Jazeera covers it? It's not as if these other media don't have an agenda. But if you look at the two, at least your head is not being messed with completely.

In the United States, there are a number of very well funded right-wing think tanks. And these think tanks provide many of the voices that are heard and seen in the media. For example, one of the most prominent is the American Enterprise Institute. Someone there—the holder of the Freedom Chair, incidentally—Michael Ledeen, said this, reported on the *National Review* online: 'Every ten years or so, the United States needs to pick up some small, crappy little country and throw it against the wall, just to show the world we mean business.'[12]

What can one say to that?

How are voices like this given such prominence in the media, while voices like Noam Chomsky or Howard Zinn or Edward Said or Angela Davis and others are completely marginalized?

But that's the project, isn't it? That's the Project for the New American Century. Why are we asking these questions or feeling surprised? We know that. And the brazenness of it is perhaps not such a bad thing. I'm for the brazenness, because at least it clarifies what is going on. And you know, you have to believe that eventually all empires founder, and this one will.

Beyond the immediate excitement of being with people from many, many countries, what value is there in gatherings like the World Social Forum? Earlier you suggested that maybe we need to move beyond the marches and the typical demonstrations.

There's a tremendous value in the World Social Forum, and it has been central to making us feel that there is another world. It's not just possible. It is there. But I think it's important that we don't sap all our energies in organizing this event. It's an act of celebration of solidarity, but it's for us. It's not a strike against them. If you want to send out one million emails and enjoy the World Social Forum, you can, but let's reserve our energies for the real fight.

And that real fight is waiting to happen now. We need to clearly demarcate the battle lines. We cannot take on empire in its entirety. We have to dismantle its working parts and take them on one by one. We can't use the undirected spray of machine-gun fire. We need the cold precision of an assassin's bullet. I don't mean this literally. I am talking about non-violent resistance. We need to pick our targets and hit them, one by one. It's not possible to take on empire in some huge, epic sense. Because we simply don't have the kind of power or reach or equipment to do that. We need to have an agenda, and we need to direct it.

At a press conference in New York, the day before your Riverside Church speech, you said, 'We have to harm them.'[13] In what way can we harm them? Do we stop buying their cars? Do we stop travelling on their planes?

First of all, we have to understand that we cannot be pure. You can't say, 'Arundhati, if you are against empire, then why are you flying to America?' Because we can't do it in any virginal, pristine way. All of us are muddy. All of us are soiled by empire and included in it in some way. We can only do our best. But certainly I believe that, for instance, a great starting point would be to target a few companies that have been given these reconstruction contracts in Iraq and shut them down, just to show ourselves that we can do it, if nothing else.

If Bechtel or Halliburton was trying to establish some business in India, you would think that Indians should boycott them.

Absolutely—but also target their offices around the world, their other privatization projects around the world, target the CEOs, the members of the board, the shareholders, the partners, and let them know we will not allow them to profit off the occupation of Iraq. We need to disrupt business as usual.

The US civil rights movement was ignited in 1955 by a bus boycott in the city of Montgomery, Alabama.

That's the thing. We need to be very specific now about what we have to do. Because we know the score. Enough of being right. We need to win.

You felt that the massive demonstrations on February 15 made a very powerful moral statement.

I think so. I think there was a huge difference between the display of public morality on the streets of the world and the vacuous, cynical arguments in the UN Security Council. We know all that talk about morality by old imperialists was rubbish. The minute war was announced, these supposed opponents of the war rushed to say, 'I hope you win it.' But I also think that the demonstrations and the peace movement really stripped down empire, which was very important. It stripped off the mask. It made it very clear what was going on. And if you look at general public perception of what the US government is about, it's very different today. Not enough people knew what the US government was up to all these years. People who studied it knew. Foreign policy scholars knew. Ex-CIA people knew. But now it's street talk.

The *National Security Strategy of the United States of America*, which formally lays out the doctrine of pre-emption, actually has the statement in it that the events of September 11 presented the United States with 'vast, new opportunities'.[14]

It did. Which is why I keep saying Bush and bin Laden are comrades in arms. But contained within those 'opportunities' are the seeds of destruction. The fact is that here is an empire that, unlike other empires, has weapons that could destroy the world several times over and has people at the helm of power who will not hesitate to use them.

What was the position of the Indian government on the attack on Iraq?

It was pretty inexcusable. There was a very subdued response to it in India. Because you see, the right-wing Indian government is trying very hard to align itself with the Israel–US axis.

What do you mean by that?

Ariel Sharon is coming to India to visit quite soon. And the rhetoric against Muslims in the United States locks in with the fascist rhetoric against Muslims in India. Meanwhile India and Pakistan are behaving like the begums of Sheikh Bush, competing for his attention.

Explain what 'begum' means.

A begum is part of the sheikh's harem.

How much of the traditional Orientalism that Edward Said has written about plays a factor in shaping and forming public opinion about the East, or 'them', or 'those people over there'?

I think outright racism would be a more accurate explanation. We are all expendable, easily expendable. Orientalism is a more gentle art. Crude racism powers all this.

You spoke in New York at the Riverside Church on May 13, 2003. How did you prepare for that, knowing that that church was where Martin Luther King gave his April 4, 1967 speech opposing the Vietnam war?

It was important to me to come to the United States and speak in that church. Apart from what I said in the talk, which is available as a text, there was a lot unsaid which was very political. A black woman from India speaking about America to an American audience in an American church. It's always historically been the other way around. It's always been white people coming to black countries to tell us about ourselves. And if anybody from there comes here, it's only to tell you about us and what a bad time we're having. But here something else is happening. Here citizens of an empire want to know what other people think of what that empire is doing. Globalization of dissent begins like that. That process is very, very important.

You've used the phrase 'the chequebook and the cruise missile'. What do you mean by this?

Once you understand the process of corporate globalization, you have to see that what happened in Argentina, the devastation of Argentina by the IMF, is part of the same machine that is destroying Iraq. Both are efforts to break open and to control markets. And so Argentina is destroyed by the chequebook and Iraq is destroyed by the cruise missile. If the chequebook won't work, the cruise missile will. Hell hath no fury like a market scorned.

W.B. Yeats lamented in one of his most famous poems that 'the best lack all conviction, while the worst are full of passionate intensity'. I think when it comes to you, it's the exact opposite. You have that passionate intensity, and the total conviction. Thank you very much.

You're welcome, David. I am always happy to be flattered [laughs].

‘If the chequebook won’t work, the cruise missile will. Hell hath no fury like a market scorned.’

'The system of electoral democracy as it stands today is premised on a religious acceptance of the nation state, but the system of corporate globalization is not. The system of corporate globalization is premised on the fact that liquid capital can move through poor countries at an enormous scale, dictating the agendas, dictating economic policy in those countries by insinuating itself into those economies. Capital requires the coercive powers of the nation state to contain the revolt in the servants' quarters. But it ensures that individual countries cannot stand up to the project of corporate globalization alone.'

SEIZE THE TIME!

IN CONVERSATION WITH DAVID BARSAMIAN, NOVEMBER 2004.

I'd like to start with a quote from a recent interview I did with you, published in the July–August issue of the *International Socialist Review*. You said, 'It's that we're up against an economic system that is suffocating the majority of the people in this world. What are we going to do about it? How are we going to address it?'[1] So I thought that would be a really easy way to begin. What are we going to do about it, and how are we going to address it?

I've only been in the United States for three days now, and I obviously have felt the electricity in the air about the coming election.[2] Just in May, we had a very important election in India. I think one of the dangers that we face is that politics becomes a discussion only about personalities, and we forget that the system is in place, and it doesn't matter all that much who is piloting the machine. So as I said in my talk at the American Sociological Association in San Francisco, this whole fierce debate about the Democrats and the Republicans and whether Bush or Kerry is better is like being asked to choose a detergent. Whether you choose Tide or Ivory Snow, they're both owned by Procter & Gamble.[3]

And so, first of all, we have to understand that elections are just an apparent choice now. In India, we were faced with outright fascism with the Bharatiya Janata Party (BJP) and the covert communalism that the Congress Party had indulged in for fifty years, preparing the ground in many ways for the right-wing. It was the

---

'Seize the Time!' first appeared in International Socialist Review.

Congress Party that actually opened India's markets to corporate globalization. But the one difference was that in their election campaign at least they had to lie; at least they had to say that they were against their old policies.

But here, in the United States, they don't even do you the dignity of that. The Democrats are not even pretending that they're against the war or against the occupation of Iraq. And that, I think, is very important, because the anti-war movement in America has been so phenomenal a service, not just to people here, but also to all of us in the world. And you can't allow them to hijack your beliefs and put your weight behind somebody who is openly saying that he believes in the occupation, that he would have attacked Iraq even if he had known there were no weapons of mass destruction,[4] that he will actually get UN cover for the occupation, that he will try and get Indian and Pakistani soldiers to go and die in Iraq instead and that the Germans and the French and the Russians might be able to share in the spoils of the occupation. Is that better or worse for somebody who lives in the subject nations of empire?

The fact is that we all know that what is happening is that there is a system of economic disparity that is being entrenched in the world today. It isn't an accident that 580 billionaires in the world have greater income than the GDP of the 135 poorest countries. The disparities in the world are huge. And the disparities are not between rich countries and poor countries, but between rich people and poor people. So what do we do about it?

We understand a few things. One is that the system of electoral democracy as it stands today is premised on a religious acceptance of the nation state, but the system of corporate globalization is not. The system of corporate globalization is premised on the fact that liquid capital can move through poor countries at an enormous scale, dictating the agendas, dictating economic policy in those countries by insinuating itself into those economies.

Capital requires the coercive powers of the nation state to contain the revolt in the servants' quarters. But it ensures that individual countries cannot stand up to the project of corporate globalization alone, which is why you have even people like Lula

Inácio da Silva[5] of Brazil or Nelson Mandela of South Africa, who were giants in the opposition but reduced to dwarfs on the global stage, blackmailed by the threat of capital flight.

So theoretically the only way to confront this is with what all of us are involved with, which is the globalization of dissent, which is the joining of hands of people who do not believe in empire. We have to join hands across countries and across continents in very specific ways and stop this. Because globalization isn't inevitable. It is signed by specific contracts with specific signatures and specific governments and specific companies. And we have to bring that to its knees.

Imperialism, years ago, was only the province of certain Marxist scholars. It was a dirty word that couldn't be spoken in polite company. But today you have people like Michael Ignatieff, who seems to have unlimited access to the *New York Times* magazine, writing cover stories extolling the virtues of what he calls 'imperialism lite'.[6] And you have someone like Salman Rushdie writing that America in Afghanistan 'did what it had to do, and did it well'.[7] I wonder now, given three years since the attack on Afghanistan, with the return of the warlords, the huge surge in opium trafficking, what your views are on the situation there?

Afghanistan has just been thrown back to the warlords the way it was abandoned after the American government funded the mujahideen in order to get the Russians out. And today Hamid Karzai, the CIA man who worked for Unocal, can't even entrust Afghans with his own security. He has to bring in private mercenaries. Just as everything else has been privatized, now security and torture and prison administration and all of this is being privatized. So what can you say to Michael Ignatieff?

I've grown up in India, and I've lived all my life there. I've never spent any large amounts of time in the West. So you come here and you listen to people like Ignatieff, and you think, even our fascists are not saying that. I've often been asked to come and debate imperialism, and I think it's like asking me about the pros and cons of child abuse. Is it a subject that I should debate? Do they imagine that in every little bylane that we walk down in India there are people saying 'Bring the British back, we miss colonialism so badly'? So it's a kind of new racism. And it isn't even all that new. We can't even give them points for originality on this. These debates have taken place in the colonial time in almost exactly the same words: 'civilizing the savages', and so on. So that isn't even something I think is worth the dignity of a debate. It is just an aspect of power. It is what power always will say. And we can't even allow it to deflect our attention for six seconds.

In an earlier interview, you recalled growing up as a kid in Kerala during the 1960s and wondering whether you would be considered a 'dink' or a 'gook'. And today the language is 'raghead', 'towelhead' and 'Haji'.

Yes, Kerala was very much like Vietnam. We too had rice fields and rivers and communists. We were just a few thousand miles west of Vietnam. So I do remember wondering whether we would be blown out of the bushes while you had some Hollywood background score playing.

Nothing has changed all that much except that it's gone back to the workshop and come out with its edges rounded. This year at the World Social Forum in Mumbai, the talk I gave was called 'Do Turkeys Enjoy Thanksgiving?'[8] And there is a small passage in it which I'll read to you, which sort of talks about the new imperialism.

> Like Old Imperialism, New Imperialism relies for its success on a network of agents—corrupt local elites who service Empire. We all know the sordid story of Enron in India. The then Maharashtra government signed a power purchase agreement that gave Enron profits that amounted to 60 per cent of India's entire rural development budget. A single American company was guaranteed a profit equivalent to

funds for infrastructural development for about 500 million people!

Unlike in the old days, the New Imperialist doesn't need to trudge around the tropics risking malaria or diarrhoea or early death. New Imperialism can be conducted on email. The vulgar, hands-on racism of Old Imperialism is outdated. The cornerstone of New Imperialism is New Racism.

The best allegory for New Racism is the tradition of 'turkey pardoning' in the United States. Every year since 1947, the National Turkey Federation has presented the US President with a turkey for Thanksgiving. Every year, in a show of ceremonial magnanimity, the President spares that particular bird (and eats another one). After receiving the presidential pardon, the Chosen One is sent to Frying Pan Park in Virginia to live out its natural life. The rest of the 50 million turkeys raised for Thanksgiving are slaughtered and eaten on Thanksgiving Day. ConAgra Foods, the company that has won the Presidential Turkey contract, says it trains the lucky birds to be sociable, to interact with dignitaries, school children and the press. (Soon they'll even speak English!)

That's how New Racism in the corporate era works. A few carefully bred turkeys—the local elites of various countries, a community of wealthy immigrants, investment bankers, the occasional Colin Powell or Condoleezza Rice, some singers, some writers (like myself)—are given absolution and a pass to Frying Pan Park. The remaining millions lose their jobs, are evicted from their homes, have their water and electricity connections cut, and die of AIDS. Basically they're for the pot. But the Fortunate Fowls in Frying Pan Park are doing fine. Some of them even work for the IMF and the WTO—so who can accuse those organizations of being anti-turkey? Some serve as board members on the Turkey Choosing Committee—so who can say that turkeys are against Thanksgiving? They participate in it! Who can say the poor are anti corporate globalization? There's a stampede to get into Frying Pan Park. So what if most perish on the way?

As part of the project of New Racism we also have New Genocide. New Genocide in this new era of economic interdependence can be facilitated by economic sanctions. New Genocide means creating conditions that lead to mass death without actually going out and killing people. Denis Halliday, who was the UN humanitarian coordinator in Iraq between 1997 and 1998 (after which he resigned in disgust), used the term genocide to describe the sanctions in Iraq. In Iraq the sanctions outdid Saddam Hussein's best efforts by claiming more than half a million children's lives.

In the new era, apartheid as formal policy is antiquated and unnecessary. International instruments of trade and finance oversee a complex system of multilateral trade laws and financial agreements that keep the poor in their bantustans anyway. Its whole purpose is to institutionalize inequity. Why else would it be that the US taxes a garment made by a Bangladeshi manufacturer twenty times more than a garment made in Britain? Why else would it be that countries that grow cocoa beans, like the Ivory Coast and Ghana, are taxed out of the market if they try to turn it into chocolate? Why else would it be that countries that grow 90 per cent of the world's cocoa beans produce only 5 per cent of the world's chocolate? Why else would it be that rich countries that spend over a billion dollars a day on subsidies to farmers demand that poor countries like India withdraw all agricultural subsidies, including subsidized electricity? Why else would it be that after having been plundered by colonizing regimes for more than half a century, former colonies are steeped in debt to those same regimes and repay them some $382 billion a year?

Colonies went out of fashion several decades ago, but with

the US occupation and colonization of Iraq, you're calling for something rather dramatic in terms of what the US should do.

Not dramatic, just reasonable. They should pull out and pay reparations.

But 'the maddened king', as you call George W. Bush, says, 'the world is a safer place.'[9] Do you feel safer in India now that Saddam Hussein is no longer in power in Iraq?

I really miss the amazing Technicolour terror alerts in India—the polka-dotted and salmon-pink and orange and lavender or whatever it is that day. In India—I'm not talking about the elite, but among normal people—there is a distinction between the government and the people, between the sarkar, as we call it, and the public. But here, this whole regime of synthetically manufactured fear has bonded people to the government. And that bond is not because of public health care, or looking after the old, or education, or social services, but fear. I think it would be a disaster for the American government if all of you started feeling safe. If you look at, say, India, from 1989 to today, would you possibly believe that in the last fourteen years 80,000 people have been killed in Kashmir? Every day there are terrorist attacks. In states like Andhra Pradesh, 200 extremists are killed every year. Every day there are militant strikes. But none of us goes around feeling terrified. We all know that everybody has to just continue living as they do. People would laugh at the government if they started this Technicolour terror alert thing, because everyone has so many other problems. So, I think not to be frightened here is a political act.

Of course, the Indian corporate press is no different from the American corporate press. In a twisted sense, the only lucky thing is that most people can't read it, so the lies and the indoctrination don't penetrate very deep.

Talking about the media, in *The Checkbook and the Cruise Missile*, you say that Americans live in a 'bubble of lots of advertisements and no information'.[10] How do you

break through the bubble?

I think we need to think about what is it that the mass media are doing to us. People who live outside the United States sometimes find it hard to actually believe the levels of indoctrination that take place here. Somehow, in a more anarchic society, like India, you can't indoctrinate people so easily. One day you have the Kumbh mela with millions of people, and a Naga sadhu trying to pull the district collector's car with his penis. And you can't tell him that corporate globalization is the answer to all his problems. Just drink more Coke. So sometimes it's hard for us to understand the reach and penetration of television and newspapers here.

But I think one of the mistakes a lot of us make is in railing against the corporate media to a point where we don't know what to do. And I think that there are two things to keep in mind. One is that you do have very strong alternative media here. You have *Alternative Radio*. You have *Democracy Now!* You have the Internet. There is so much going on, so many places to look for information. But also I think there is a kind of ad busting to be done, which is you read the mainstream media, but what you gather from it is not what they want to tell you. You have to learn to decode it, to understand it for the boardroom bulletin that it is. And therefore, you use its power against itself. And I think that's very important to do, because many of us make the mistake of thinking that the corporate media supports the neoliberal project. It doesn't. It *is* the neoliberal project.

It's become so blatant. In the United States, just think of what was going on in this country in 2001, and think of what is going on now. What a huge victory so many of you have won in terms of having been in this flag-waving, frightening place. I remember in 2003, when I spoke in Porto Alegre, at the World Social Forum, I didn't even believe what I was saying at that time. It was just wishful thinking. There in Brazil, I said activists and musicians and writers, so many people have worked together to strip empire of its sheen. And we've exposed it, and now it stands too ugly to behold itself in the mirror. That much I believed. And the next sentence was, 'Soon it will not be able to rally its own people.' And look what's happened. It's happening here. And it's because of you. So between that time and now, what used to be America's secret history is now street talk. And that's because of you. And you mustn't lose focus. You can't think that now, if Kerry comes to power, we can all go back home and be happy.

The global demonstrations against the Iraq war on February 15, 2003, turned out at least 10 million people and by some accounts up to 15 million people. You've called that one of the greatest affirmations of the human spirit and morality. But then the war started and many people went home.

This is something we have to ask ourselves about, because the first part of this question is that you did have this incredible display of public morality. In no European country was the support for a unilateral war more than 11 per cent. Hundreds of thousands marched on the streets here. And still these supposedly democratic countries went to war. So the questions are, A: Is democracy still democratic? B: Are governments accountable to the people who elected them? And, C: Are people responsible in democratic countries for the actions of their governments? It's a very serious crisis that is facing democracies today. And if you get caught in this Ivory Snow vs Tide debate, if you get caught in having to choose between a detergent with Oxy-Boosters or Gentle Cleansers, we're finished. The point is, how do you keep power on a short leash? How do you make it accountable?

And the fact is that we can't also only feel good about what we do. What we have done has been fantastic, but we must realize that it's not enough. And one of the problems is that symbolic resistance has unmoored itself from real civil disobedience. And that is very dangerous, because governments have learned how to wait these things out. They think we're like children with rattles in a crib. Just let them get on with their weekend demonstration and we'll just carry on with what we have to do. Public opinion is so fickle and so on. The symbolic aspect of resistance is very important. The theatre is very important. But not at the cost of real civil disobedience. So we have to find ways of implementing what we're saying seriously.

And you look at what's happening today. I feel that the Iraqi resistance is fighting on the frontlines of empire. We know that it's a motley group of former Baathists and fed-up collaborationists and all kinds of people. But no resistance movement is pristine. And if we are going to only invest our purity in pristine movements, we may as well forget it. The point is, this is our resistance, and we have to support it.

And you have to understand that the American soldiers who are dying in Iraq are conscripts of a poverty draft from the poorest parts of the United States being sent to war. In fact, they as well as the Iraqis are victims of the same horrendous system that asks for their lives in return for a victory that will never be theirs.

The book that we did together is called *The Checkbook and the Cruise Missile*. And the fact is that sometimes the cruise missile is highlighted, and you're thinking about the torture and the invasion and the army and the people dying and so on. But, meanwhile, the contracts are being signed, the pipelines are being laid, everything is being put in place for the time when they can withdraw the cruise missile. But the system of appropriation is already in place. And you have these companies like Bechtel and Halliburton, who did business with Saddam Hussein and who are now profiting in the billions from the destruction and the reconstruction of Iraq. And those same companies were in Cochabamba, Bolivia, engaged in water privatization.[11] Those same companies are in India, along with Enron. Enron and Bechtel, for instance, were involved in the first private power project in India, where the profits were equal to 60 per cent of India's entire rural development budget.

The point I'm trying to make is that Iraq is on the frontlines of this war on empire, but each of these companies that are involved there have economic outposts across the world. So it gives us a foothold. It gives us a way of bearing down on single individual corporations and companies. And if we can't shut them down, if we can't prevent them from doing what they're doing, then how can we call ourselves a resistance? We have to do it. We have to find a way of doing it.

And the thing is, it's not going to happen without us paying a price. It's not going to happen on weekends or anything like that. People in poor countries are being battered by the system. It's not only that empire arrives in their lives in the form of military intervention, as it has in Iraq. It also arrives in the form of exorbitant electricity bills that they can't pay, of their water being cut off, of their being dismissed from their jobs and uprooted from their lands.

If you look at a country like India, we are old hands at the game. You have the Armed Forces Special Powers Act, which allows a non-commissioned army officer to kill anybody on suspicion of creating public disturbance.[12] All over the Northeast, all over Kashmir, you have the Gangster Act, you have the Special Areas Security Act, you have the Terrorist and Disruptive Activities Act (TADA), which has now lapsed but under which people are still being tried.[13] And then you have the equivalent of the USA PATRIOT Act,[14] which is Prevention of Terrorism Act (POTA), under which thousands of people are just being picked up and held without trial.[15] And their crime is poverty. It isn't that they're terrorists. They're being called terrorists, but their crime is poverty. So terrorism and poverty are being conflated. And states are becoming very sophisticated in their repression. And how do we counter that?

This battle is not going to be won without us paying a price. That's one thing we have to understand. It's not going to be a cute war.

The Prevention of Terrorism Act—or, as you and others have called it, the Production of Terrorism Act—has its counterpart in the United States in the PATRIOT Act, which has greatly enhanced the ability of the state to surveil and imprison its citizens.

Fundamentally the thing about these acts that we have to understand is that they are not meant for the terrorists, because the terrorists, or suspected terrorists, are just shot or taken, in the case of America, to Guantánamo Bay. Those acts are meant to terrorize you. So basically all of us stand accused. It prepares the ground for the government to make all of us culprits and then pick off whichever one of us it wants to.

And once we give up these freedoms, will we ever get them back? In India, at least when the Congress Party was campaigning, it said it was going to withdraw POTA. It probably will, but not before it enacts other kinds of legislation that approximate it. So it won't be POTA, it will be MOTA or whatever. But here, are they even saying that they will repeal the PATRIOT Act? It's an insult to you that they don't even think they have to say it. Is it populist to say that we are going to deal in sterner ways with terror and we are going to make America stronger and safer and have more oxy-boosters? It's a crazy situation that they don't even lie. I know a lot of people say that, 'Oh, you know, Kerry is saying this, but when he comes to power, he will be different.' But nobody moves to the Left after they come to power; they move only to the Right.

One of your essays in your new collection, *An Ordinary Person's Guide to Empire*, is called 'When the Saints Go Marching Out: The Strange Tale of Martin, Mohandas and Mandela'.[16] Talk about Gandhi. He was able to devise strategies which exploited cracks in the empire.

Gandhi was one of the brightest, most cunning and imaginative politicians of the modern age. What he did was what great writers do. Great writers expand the human imagination. Gandhi expanded the political imagination. But, of course, we mustn't ever think that the Indian freedom struggle was a revolutionary struggle. It wasn't. Because the Indian elite stepped very easily into the shoes of the British imperialists. Nor was it only a non-violent struggle, because that's the other myth, that it was an entirely non-violent struggle. It wasn't. But what Gandhi did was democratic because of the ways in which he devised strategy. It included a lot of people. He found ways of including masses of people. For instance, in 1931, when they did the Dandi march, where they decided to march to the coast—it took twenty-one days, I think—to make salt in order to break the British salt tax laws which prevented Indians from making salt, it was symbolic. But also, then, millions of Indians began to make salt, and it struck at the economic underpinning of empire. So that was his brilliance.

But I think we really need to re-imagine non-violent resistance, because there isn't any debate taking place that is more important in the world today than the one about strategies of resistance. There can never be one strategy. People are never going to agree about one strategy. It can't be that while we watch the American war machine occupy Iraq, torture its prisoners, appropriate its resources, we are waiting for this pristine, secular, democratic, non-violent, feminist resistance to come along. We can't prescribe to the Iraqis how to conduct their resistance, but we have to shore up our end of it by forcing America and its allies to leave Iraq now.

I think a lot of people here have on their minds the November 2 election and what to do, who to vote for. Tariq Ali, who is very critical of Kerry, recently said, 'If the American population were to vote Bush out of office, it would have a tremendous impact on world opinion. Our option at the moment is limited. Do we defeat a warmonger government or not?' What do you think of Ali's perspective?

Look, it's a very complicated and difficult debate, in which I think there are two things you can do: you can act expediently, if you like, but you must speak on principle. I cannot sit here with any kind of honesty and say to you that I support Kerry. I cannot do that. I'll tell you a small example. In India, you may or may not be aware of the levels of violence and jingoism and fascism that we've faced over the last five years. In Gujarat, rampaging mobs murdered, raped, gang-raped, burnt alive 2,000 Muslims on the streets, drove 150,000 out of their homes. You have this kind of plague of Hindu fascism spreading. And you had a central government that was supported by the BJP. A lot of the people who I know and work with work in the state of Madhya Pradesh, in central India, where there was a Congress state government for ten years. This government had overseen the building of many dams in the Narmada valley. It had overseen the privatization of electricity, of water, the driving out from their homes and lands of hundreds of thousands of people, the disconnection of single-point electricity connections because they signed these huge contracts for privatization with the Asian Development Bank. The activists in these areas knew that a lot of the reasons that Congress was so boldly doing these things was [as the Congress was] saying, 'What option do you have? Do you want to get the BJP? Are you going to campaign for the BJP? Are you going to open yourself up not just to being physically beaten but maybe even killed?' But I want to tell you that they didn't campaign for the Congress. They didn't. They just said, 'We do not believe in this, and we are going to continue to do our work outside.' It was just a horrendous situation, because the BJP was pretending to be anti-'reform', saying, 'We'll stop this, we'll change that.' They did come to power, the BJP, and within ten days they were on the dam site saying, 'We are going to build the dam.' So people are waiting for their houses to get submerged. This was the dilemma.

The point is, then, you have to say, 'Look, can you actually campaign for a man who is saying, "I'm going to send more troops to Iraq"?' How? So I think it's very important for us to remain principled. Let me tell you that during the Indian elections, people used to keep asking me, 'Aren't you campaigning for the Congress?' Because, of course, I had spent the last five years denouncing the BJP. I said, 'How can I campaign for the Congress that also oversaw the carnage of Sikhs in Delhi in 1984, that opened the markets to neoliberalism in the early 1990s?' And every time, you're put under this pressure. I said, 'I feel sometimes when I'm asked this question like I imagine what a gay person must feel when he's watching straight sex: I'm sort of interested but not involved.' I think it's very important for us to understand that we are people of principle and we are soldiers who are fighting a different battle, and we cannot be co-opted into this.

So you've got to refuse the terms of this debate; otherwise you're co-opted. I'm not going to sit here and tell you to vote for this one or vote for that one, because all of us here are people of influence and power, and we can't allow our power to be co-opted by those people. We cannot.

[Going] back to the subject of the American election. You have to force the Democrats to say that they are against the war, otherwise you're not going to support them. They can't tell you what to do. They're the public servants. You have to tell them what to do.

Do you have any ideas about reaching beyond the choir? One of the frequent charges that's levelled against the Left or progressives is that we talk among ourselves, we have a good time and everyone nods their head and then has a beer and goes home, and nothing happens. There is some truth to that. How do we get to a larger audience?

First of all, I don't get that feeling where I come from, because what we are saying is what a majority of India's poor are saying. So there is no question of preaching to the choir there. It's just that the choir, millions of people, aren't heard. That's a different matter. But it isn't ghettoized thinking at all. If it were, then we would be politically wrong, don't you think? Because we are saying that this is a view that is on the side of the world's poor. So I don't think I accept that charge, that we just have a good time and have a beer and go to bed.

I think, on another level, it is true that there is a sort of suspicion of success, of popularity, among Left intellectuals. You like to have this language that is sort of impenetrable. Not quite as bad as the postmodernists, but getting there. So I think it's very important to know that Fox News's success is our failure.

One of the things that I really think we have to try to do is to snatch our future back from the world of experts, to say, 'I'm sorry, but it's not that hard to understand and it's not that hard to explain.' And if you think of it, just a few years ago—when the confrontation happened in Seattle at the WTO convention, for many of us in the subject nations of empire, it was a delightful thing to know that even people in imperialist countries shared our battles. It was really the beginnings of the globalization of dissent.

Corporate globalization wasn't something that was as palpable earlier. Nobody really knew what it meant. The enemy wasn't corporeal. But it is now, and that is because of the efforts of so many people. Now you go into any bookshop in the United States and look at the books there and ask yourself; seven, eight, nine years ago would they have been there? No. And that's what we've done. And must continue to do. I think even, say, in documentary film-making—and I'm not only talking about the high end of it; I'm not only talking about *Fahrenheit 9/11*—technology has enabled documentary film to become such a powerful tool both to the Right and to the Left. But the fact is that in countries like India, it's become such an important political tool that governments are really frightened—and are exploring how to censor it, how to stop it, now that these film-makers who used to need grants from the Ford Foundation and some state film corporation can just go and do it on their own with a little camera. And those films are so subversive and so gripping. You go to a little village in India with a projector and a player and show films, and thousands of people will come. So these are new tools that are being honed.

Michael Moore has been very successful in terms of reaching a much larger audience.[17] In fact, he has two books on the best-seller list right now. His *Fahrenheit 9/11* has been seen by millions of people and will soon be out on DVD. What can we learn from those kinds of interventions?

The obvious, I think, that those kinds of interventions have a space now and have to be exploited, because it blows open spaces. It changes what people expect from cinema, makes it all so much more exciting. I think there are other films, like *Control Room*.[18]

By Jehane Noujaim.

Yes. Everything has to become out of control now. We just sort of become really bad.

A couple of years ago, you were at the United World College in Las Vegas, a small town in northern New Mexico. You were talking to the students there, and I took these notes. 'It's difficult to be citizens of an empire, because it's hard to listen. Put your ear to the wall. Listen to the whisper.' If you put your ear to the wall now, what would you hear?

I don't feel qualified to answer that properly, because I've just been here for a few days, and speaking in places like this, where it's not exactly like I'm on the street listening to things. But I must say that soon after September 11, I wrote an essay called 'The Algebra of Infinite Justice'.[19] And when I wrote it, I did think to myself, here is me writing this essay that's probably going to annoy this huge and powerful country, and that's the end of me here. But then, as a writer, if I can't write what I think, that would be the end of me anyway. So let me just do it.

And instead I find that it's just so wonderful to arrive here and to know that you all are heroes. It gives so much strength to people. And I'm always called, of course, for strategic reasons, anti-American. And I'm so far from being anti-American, because I have such a deep respect for what you do. I can assure you that if India and Pakistan were at war, it would be hard for me to find people to come out in the numbers in which you have come out and protested against what your government is doing. So power to you. That's just fantastic, what you do. And it is something which encourages people everywhere. It blurs these national borders: you're this, I'm that. You don't even talk like this: you're an American, and I'm an Indian, and so-and-so is a Moroccan. We are finding a different kind of language in which to talk to each other, which is important.

I've said this just now, but I'll say it again. This idea that America's secret history is street talk is what I hear. That is all out in the open now. And the fact is that empires always overreach themselves and then crumble. Power has a short shelf life.

Kathy Kelly is an extraordinary woman.[20] She's one of the founders of Voices in the Wilderness.[21] She just served a four-month sentence in jail for civil disobedience at the School of the Americas training camp in Fort Benning, Georgia. Again, talking about courage, she says it's the ability to control fear, and we catch courage from one another. I know you've spent a lot of time with some very extraordinary women in the Narmada valley. What kind of courage were you able to catch?

One of the facts is that one of the great things about the non-violent political resistance in India, its legacy, is that it really has women at the heart of it, it really allows women into the heart of it. When movements become violent, then not only does the state react with huge coercive power, but that violence by people on your own side is very soon turned on women. So because we have this legacy, I think, in places like the Narmada valley, women also realize that they are far bigger victims than the men are. Say, a hundred thousand people are being displaced by a dam and they're not being given land for land, because there is no land. The men are given some cash as compensation. The men buy motorcycles or get drunk, and then it's finished. And the women are left in a terrible situation. So they are fighting this battle much more fiercely. And everywhere you go you see that they're really at the forefront of it.

I think, of all the women's resistances, the most remarkable today is RAWA, the Revolutionary Association of the Women of Afghanistan.[22] What a tremendous battle they have waged and continue to wage. And what a principled battle. They were faced with the Taliban and the Northern Alliance and the Americans in between. And we were made to feel that America was fighting a feminist war in Afghanistan. But look at their situation now. They didn't say, 'Yes, yes, we'll support you and come in.' At no point did they take an expedient position. I think we have to learn this from that.

In one of your essays in your book *War Talk*, you conclude with a paraphrase of Shelley's poem 'Mask of Anarchy': 'You be many, they be few'.[23] Talk about that.

That is what is happening. It is in the nature of capitalism, isn't it? The more profit you make, the more you plough back into the machine, the more profit you make. And so now you have a situation in which, like I said, 500 billionaires have more money than the GDP of 135 countries. And that rift is widening. I think today's paper said that the rift between the rich and the poor of the United States is widening even more. Everywhere that's happening. And the fact is that I believe that wars must be waged from positions of strength. So the poor must fight from their position of strength, which is on the streets and the mountains and the valleys of the world, not in boardrooms and parliaments and courts. I think we are on the side of the millions and that is our strength. And we must recognize it and work with it.

There is an alternative to terrorism. What is it?

Justice.

How do we get there?

The point is that terrorism has been isolated and made to look like some kind of thing that has no past and has no future and is just some aberration of maniacs. It isn't. Of course, sometimes it is. But if you look at it, the logic that underlies terrorism and the logic that underlies the war on terror is the same: both hold ordinary people responsible for the actions of governments. And the fact is that Osama bin Laden or Al-Qaeda, in their attacks on September 11, took the lives of many ordinary people. And in the attacks in Afghanistan and on Iraq, hundreds of thousands of Iraqis and Afghans paid for the actions of the Taliban or for the actions of Saddam Hussein. The difference is that the Afghans didn't elect the Taliban, the Iraqis didn't elect Saddam Hussein. So how do we justify these kinds of wars?

I really think that terrorism is the privatization of war. Terrorists are the free marketeers of war. They are the ones who say that they don't believe that legitimate violence is only the monopoly of the state. So we can't condemn terrorism unless we condemn the war on terror. And no government that does not show itself to be open to change by non-violent dissent can actually condemn terrorism. Because if every avenue of non-violent dissent is closed or mocked or bought off or broken, then by default you privilege violence. When all your respect and admiration and research and media coverage and the whole economy is based on war and violence, when violence is deified, on what grounds are you going to condemn terrorism?

Whatever people lack in wealth and power they make up with stealth and strategy. So we can't just, every time we're asked to say something, say, 'Oh, terrorism is a terrible thing,' without talking about repression, without talking about justice, without talking about occupation, without talking about privatization, without talking about the fact that this country has its army strung across the globe.

And then, of course, even language has been co-opted. If you say 'democracy', actually it means neoliberalism. If you say 'reforms', it actually means repression. Everything has been turned into something else. So we also have to reclaim language now.

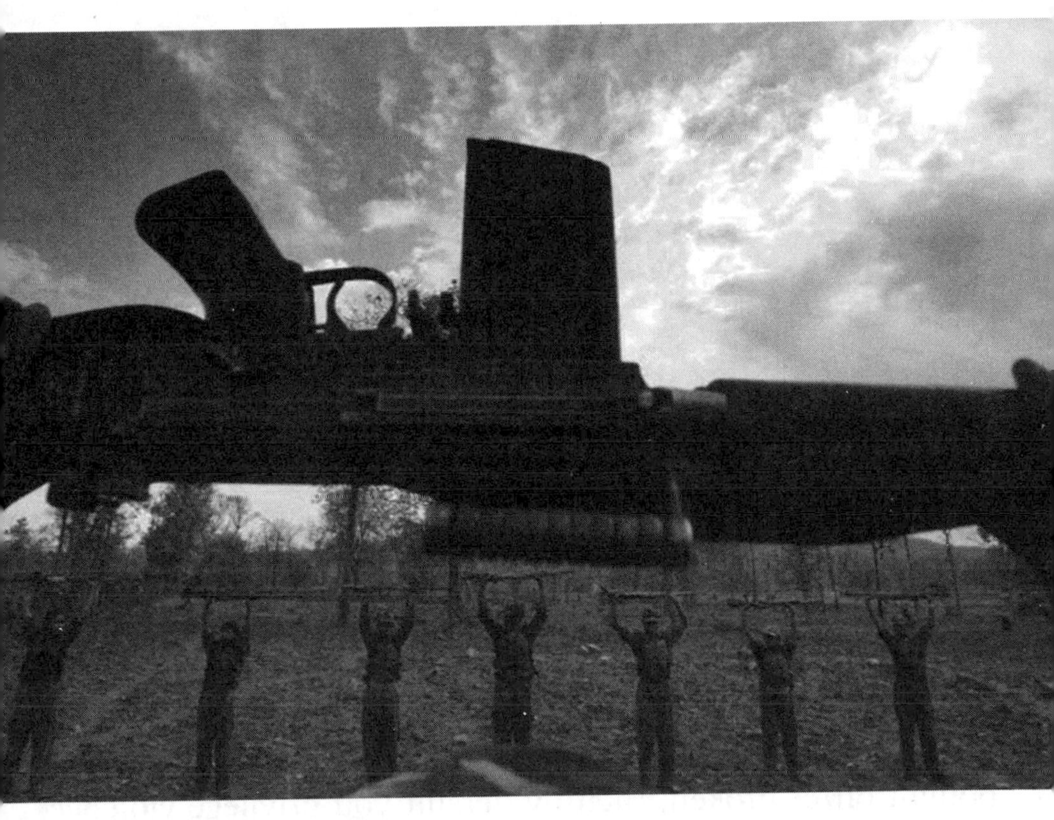

Maoists at a temporary base in the forests of Chhattisgarh.
AP Photo/Mustafa Quraishi.

'If every avenue of non-violent dissent is closed or mocked or bought off or broken, then by default you privilege violence. When all your respect and admiration and research and media coverage and the whole economy is based on war and violence, when violence is deified, on what grounds are you going to condemn terrorism?'

The Shape of the Beast

‘Freedom means mass murder now. In the US, it means fried potatoes (freedom fries). Liberation means invasion and occupation. When you hear the words “humanitarian aid”, it’s advisable to look around for induced starvation. We all know what collateral damage means. When the US invaded South Vietnam and bombed the countryside, killing thousands of people and forcing thousands to flee to cities where they were held in refugee camps, Samuel Huntington called this a process of “urbanization”.’

THE OUTLINE OF THE BEAST

In conversation with Anthony Arnove, April 2003.

The corporate media ask the question over and over again: What can be done about Saddam Hussein? What's your response?

The question is disingenuous. Let's turn it around and ask instead: What do we do with George Bush and Tony Blair? Should we just stand by and watch while they bomb and kill and annihilate people? Saddam Hussein is a killer, and in the past, the US and the UK governments have supported many of his worst excesses.

The US and UK have bombed Iraq's infrastructure, fired depleted uranium into Iraq's farmlands, blocked vaccines and hospital equipment, contributing to hundreds of thousands of deaths of children under five. Denis Halliday, the former UN humanitarian coordinator in Iraq, has called the sanctions a form of genocide.[1]

If you lifted the sanctions, Iraqi society might have gained the strength to overthrow their dictator (just like the people of Indonesia, Serbia, Romania overthrew theirs).

And if it's repression, sectarianism and human rights abuses we're concerned about, let's also turn our attention to Colombia, Turkey, Saudi Arabia, Egypt, the Central Asian Republics, Israel, Russia, China, India, Pakistan, Burma and, of course, America. Shall we pre-empt Saddam and bomb them all? Then he won't have anyone left to kill.

The greatest threat to the world today is not Saddam Hussein, it's George Bush (joined at the hip to his new foreign secretary, Tony Blair).

'The Outline of the Beast' first appeared on the website www.socialistworker.org

Bush says that he's leading an 'international coalition' against Iraq. What's your reaction to that?

The international Coalition of the Bullied and the Bought is what that coalition is more commonly called.

The important thing to keep in mind is that it is governments that have been coerced, one way or another. Even the major 'shareholders' in the coalition—governments of countries like Spain and Australia—don't have the support of the majority of their people.

There have been some interesting studies showing the nature of the regimes of some of the countries in this 'coalition'. Many of them are high up on the list of human rights violators—and have no business to criticize Saddam Hussein given their own reputations.

Bush also says that this war is 'defensive' and that it would be 'suicidal' not to attack Iraq.

That's like an elephant taking a long run-up to smash an ant to death—and then saying that it was 'defensive' and that to let the ant remain alive would have been suicidal. It would be fair to call the elephant paranoid and unstable.

Oh, and that doesn't include the business of using the UN to disarm the ant before the elephant attacks. Apart from calling it paranoid and unstable, you could also call it a coward and a cheat.

In an interview on the Pacifica Radio programme *Democracy Now!*, you spoke about the 'murder of language'. Can you elaborate on that?

Freedom means mass murder now. In the US, it means fried potatoes (freedom fries). Liberation means invasion and occupation. When you hear the words 'humanitarian aid', it's advisable to look around for induced starvation. We all know what collateral damage means.

Of course, none of this is new. When the US invaded South Vietnam and bombed the countryside, killing thousands of people and forcing thousands to flee to cities where they were held in refugee camps, Samuel Huntington called this a process of 'urbanization'.[2]

The *New York Times* magazine recently ran a cover that read 'The New American Empire (Get Used to It.)'.[3] How is that message playing in India and elsewhere outside the United States?

In India, there is a dissonance between what people think of the war and the American Empire, and the deliberately ambiguous position of the Indian government. This war against Iraq has fuelled a lot of anger among a majority of people, but there are the opportunists, among the elite in particular, who are rather stupidly hoping to be thrown some crumbs in the 'reconstruction' era. They're like hyenas. Vultures.

No one's going to 'get used' to the American Empire—no one can. This is because that empire can only survive and hold its position if it continues with its agenda of mass murder and mass dispossession.

These are not things people get used to, however hard they try. You can expect to be killed, but you can't get used to the idea.

It will be a bloody battle, this battle for the establishment and perpetuation of hegemony. The world is not a static place. It's wild and unpredictable. The American Empire isn't going to have all that easy a ride. The people of the world will not be lining the streets raining roses on the emperor.

More than 10 million people demonstrated around the world on 15 February, including millions in the countries leading the war on Iraq. Why do you think we are seeing such large protests?[4]

I think that there's only one reason. America has been stripped of its mask. Its secret history of brutal interventions and unforgivable manipulations is street talk. The dots have been joined and the shape of the beast has emerged.

'It will be a bloody battle, this battle for the establishment and perpetuation of hegemony. The world is not a static place. It's wild and unpredictable. The American Empire isn't going to have all that easy a ride. The people of the world will not be lining the streets raining roses on the emperor.'

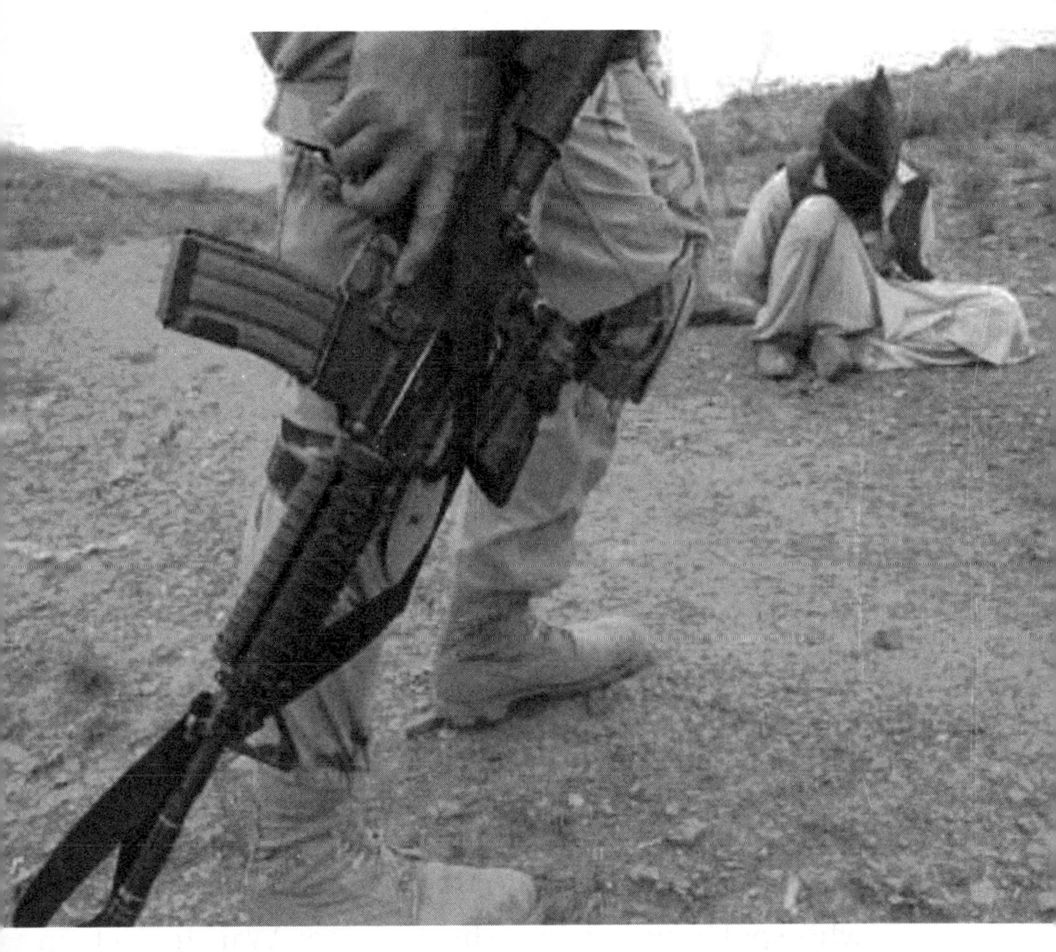

An American soldier stands over a Person Under Control (PUC) in eastern Afghanistan, one of a number of people taken prisoner during Operation Dragon Fury in 2003. Photo © David Orr

'I think speaking out against the occupation is the bravest thing that a soldier can do. I have always admired the US soldiers who spoke out against the Vietnam War. In fact, in places like India, when people get randomly racist and anti-American, I always ask them: When do you last remember Indian soldiers speaking out against a war, any war, in India?'

THE WAR THAT NEVER ENDS

IN CONVERSATION WITH ANTHONY ARNOVE, SEPTEMBER 2003.

The war on Iraq has become an occupation. Is Iraq a new colony?

Yes, but it's proving to be a pretty recalcitrant one. Maybe we should rethink the notion that Iraq has been 'conquered'. American soldiers are dying every day, more now than during the war.

The US government has been threatening Iran, Syria and North Korea.[1] Do you think Iran was just a prelude?

In this particular chapter of War and Empire, the war on Afghanistan was the real prelude. Basically 'The War on Terror' is Bush's perfect war, the war that never ends. The weapons deals that never stop. The oil fields that never dry up.

But maybe those who supported the wars in Afghanistan and Iraq were too quick to declare victory. In both countries now, US troops are bogged down in a kind of quicksand. That's why the US government is trying to coerce other countries like India and Pakistan to clean up the mess it has left behind.

If the United States now attacks Iran, Syria or North Korea, its troops will be further strung out across the globe. But then the physics of Empire seems to be encrypted in some way—overreach and implode. Maybe that's what will happen. But the downside is that the US arsenal of nuclear weapons might ensure that the American Empire is the last empire the human race will ever know.

'The War That Never Ends' first appeared on the website www.war-times.org

Halliburton just announced increased profits largely because of its Iraq operations.'[2] Who's profiting from this war and who isn't?

Halliburton is an old player in Iraq. It's not every corporation that can boast of having the army and the entire military might of the most powerful country on earth at its disposal, risking life and limb in order to increase its margins of profit.

If I were a US soldier, risking my life and sanity in the 100-plus-degree deserts of Iraq, I'd be asking some pretty serious questions of the CEOs of companies like Halliburton. How much do you earn? How much do I earn? What do you risk? What do I risk?

Equally, if I were a student, or a schoolteacher, or a health worker, or a single mother in the United States, reading about the huge cuts in public spending, I'd be asking a very simple question about this war: Who pays, who profits?

I think what I find most insulting of all is the complete confidence with which George Bush the Lesser and his henchmen do what they do, assuming that American people are just plain stupid and that public memory is fickle.

America's poor are being exploited and put on the frontlines to ensure further profits for America's rich. It's for this reason that it's ridiculous and self-defeating to be 'anti-American'. America is not one homogeneous mass of brutality.

One-fifth of the armed forces are African-American.[3] I don't imagine anywhere close to one-fifth of the profits of this war go to African-American people. Asians and Latinos are in the army, hoping to get citizenship. What a great system. Get the blacks, Asians, Latinos and poor whites to fight your boardroom battles for you …

Iraq is being opened up for privatization in the name of democracy.[4] What is privatization about?

It's quite unbelievable. The kinds of things that are being done these days in the name of 'democracy' would be laughable if it weren't so savage. Privatization is the antithesis of democracy. It is the process of transferring public assets, held in trust for the public good, to private companies to amass private profit. It is simply unacceptable.

Soldiers and their families are speaking out against the occupation. Will this help rally international opposition?[5]

I think speaking out against the occupation is the bravest thing that a soldier can do. I have always admired the US soldiers who spoke out against the Vietnam War. In fact, in places like India, when people get randomly racist and anti-American, I always ask them: When do you last remember Indian soldiers speaking out against a war, any war, in India?

When soldiers speak out, people really sit up and listen. I cannot think of a better way of rallying international opposition to the occupation. To those American soldiers who have had the courage to speak out, I send my heartfelt salaams.

President Bush has asked India to send troops to help 'control' Iraq. What is your reaction?

Bush probably knows that right-wing religious fundamentalists, regardless of what religion they subscribe to, are brothers in arms. George Bush, Osama bin Laden, Ariel Sharon, the mullahs of Pakistan and the L.K. Advanis and Narendra Modis of India have no trouble understanding each other.

In India, the present government is not just right-wing, it is skating very close to fascism. For the first time in the history of independent India, the Indian government (the coalition led by the Bharatiya Janata Party) is trying hard to align itself with the US–Israel axis. It is not a coincidence that the massacre of Muslims in Gujarat, conducted with the brazen collusion of the government and the police, took place so soon after September 11. Neither is it a coincidence that the case is closed internationally, because killing Muslims now, after September 11, is somehow seen as acceptable.

If Indian troops aren't sent to Iraq, the reason won't be a lack of will on the part of the Indian government. It will be because the proposal has caused serious outrage among Indian people, a majority of whom were also incensed by the war in Iraq.

'If I were a US soldier, risking my life and sanity in the 100-plus-degree deserts of Iraq, I'd be asking some pretty serious questions of the CEOs of companies like Halliburton. How much do you earn? How much do I earn? What do you risk? What do I risk?'

‘Why is it that every time a government goes to war, the only reasons offered are moral reasons? “To spread democracy, freedom, feminism, to rid the world of evil-doers.” Why is it that states expect morality of us, but we as individuals can’t debate an issue in moral terms?’

INDEPENDENCE DAY SPECIAL

IN CONVERSATION WITH S. ANAND, AUGUST 2005.

I was about to buy batteries for my recorder for this interview and was avoiding, as usual, a certain unrepentant brand associated with the Bhopal gas tragedy. Sometimes, such independent choices are not even possible in this world which some say is becoming flat. What are your thoughts?

We live in an Age of Spurious Choice. Eveready or Nippo? Coke or Pepsi? Nike or Reebok?—that's the more superficial, consumer end of the problem. Then we have the spurious choice between the so-called 'corrupt' public sector and the 'efficient' private sector. The real question is, does democracy offer real choice? Not really, not any more. In the recent US elections, was the choice between Bush and Kerry a real choice? Was the choice between Blair and his counterpart in the Conservative Party a real choice? For the Indian poor, has the choice between the Congress and the BJP been a real choice? They are all apparent choices accompanied by a kind of noisy theatre which conceals the fact that all these apparently warring parties share an almost complete consensus. They just exchange slogans depending on whether they're in the opposition or in the government.

So there's a lack of choice despite political democracy?

The last Lok Sabha election was fundamentally about two issues: the economy and right-wing Hindu nationalism. I would say that in

---

'Independence Day Special' first appeared in Outlook.

most rural areas, issues of economy were at the forefront of the voter's mind. During the countdown, the campaign rhetoric of the Congress was about marginalizing disinvestment, taking a new look at privatization, taking a new look at 'corporate globalization'? But as soon as it won, even before they took office, senior Congress leaders had begun reassuring the market that it would not make any radical change. Look at what's happening now. Privatization and corporatization are proceeding apace. Meanwhile, by arbitrarily adjusting the poverty line, by redefining what constitutes poverty, the Planning Commission drastically reduces the official number of poor people to 27 per cent of the population.[1] Half of India's rural population has a food energy intake below the average of sub-Saharan Africa. Yet one of the first things Finance Minister P. Chidambaram does is to slash the rural development budget to the lowest it has ever been! The one ray of hope was the Rural Employment Guarantee Act.[2] But I'm not at all sure it will go through. Is it just smoke and mirrors, a game of Good Cop/Bad Cop that trades on the almost saintly status of Sonia Gandhi and the credibility of some extraordinary people in the National Advisory Council in order to garner the Congress some brownie points?

Prime Minister Manmohan Singh, who lost a Lok Sabha poll from the posh south Delhi constituency in 1999, is called a decent, incorruptible statesman. Is he able to carry off a neoliberal agenda because of this non-politician halo?

I don't know why technocrats like President Kalam and this new breed of bureaucrat-politician seem to have the middle class and the mass media in their thrall. Maybe because they have power without being frayed at the edges by real political engagement. Maybe because they are the architects of the process separating the Economy from Politics—and thereby keeping power where they think it really belongs, with the elite. Manmohan Singh, Montek Singh Ahluwalia and P. Chidambaram have fused into the Holy Trinity of neoliberalism. Their vision of the New India has been fashioned at the altar of the world's cathedrals: Oxford, Harvard Business School, the World Bank and the IMF. They are the regional head office of the Washington Consensus. They are part of a powerful network of politicians, bureaucrats, diplomats, consultants, bankers, businessmen and retired judges who trade jobs, contracts, consultancies and vitally—contacts. Right now, for example, there's a lot in the news about the scandalous Enron contract being 're-negotiated' for the third time—the contract that resulted in Maharashtra State Electricity Board (MSEB) having to pay Enron millions of dollars not to produce electricity. The renegotiation is all very secret (like the initial Enron negotiation). The nodal ministry involved in the re-re-negotiation is the finance ministry headed by P. Chidambaram who, until the day he became finance minister, was Enron's lawyer. The other members on the committee are Montek Ahluwalia and Sharad Pawar—the two who were instrumental in signing the disastrous contract in the first place. It's like asking an accused in a criminal case to investigate the crimes he's been accused of.

Do people in rural India view these technocrats and bureaucrat-politicians differently?

A few years ago (when Manmohan Singh was between jobs), I was in Raipur at a meeting of iron ore workers from the neighbouring districts. I'll never forget a young Hindi poet who read a poem, called 'Manmohan Singh Kya Kar Raha Hai Aaj Kal?' (What's Manmohan Singh Doing These Days?). The anger in the poem was so acute, so shocking, even to me. All the more so because it was aimed at such a gentle, soft-spoken man. The first two lines were: Manmohan Singh kya kar raha hai aaj kal/Vish kya karta hai khoon mein utarne ke baad? (What does poison do once it has entered the bloodstream?) At the time, I came away disturbed and shaken. But today? The thing is, rural India is in real distress—and many do link their distress to Manmohan Singh's reforms when he was finance minister in the early '90s.

What did you make of the prime minister's Oxford address?[3]

Timing is everything; it was an unambiguous political statement. Right now, western powers and several right-wing academics, like the historian Niall Ferguson, have embarked on a project of valorizing imperialism. This is the argument they use to justify the invasion and occupation of Iraq and Afghanistan and all the ones still to come. At this point in history, for the Indian PM to publicly and officially declare himself an apologist for the British Empire is pretty devastating. After a few cautious caveats in his speech, Manmohan Singh thanked British imperialism for everything India is today. Ironically, at the top of his list was all the machinery of repression put in place by a colonial regime—the bureaucracy, the judiciary, the police, Rule of Law. He then went on to express gratitude for the gift of the English language—the language that separates India's elite from its fellow countrymen and binds its imagination to the western world. Macaulay couldn't have asked for a more dedicated disciple.

The only people who might have a valid reason to view the British Empire with less anger than the rest of us are Dalits. Since to the white man all of us were just natives, Dalits were not especially singled out for the bestial treatment meted out to them by caste Hindus. But somehow, I can't imagine Manmohan Singh bringing a Dalit perspective to colonialism while receiving an honorary PhD in Oxford.

You once said that on several issues—Babri, N-bombs, big dams, privatization—the Congress sowed and the BJP swept in to reap a hideous harvest. With the Congress at the helm, what has fundamentally changed?

I'll be honest. When the BJP lost the elections, in spite of my intellectual analysis of the situation that nothing was going to change economically, I certainly feel less hunted. This is a totally selfish point. I think this incredible communal churning has ceased. The BJP has a far more vicious way of implementing the same policies. I don't think we can deny that.

Kar Sevaks demolishing the Babri Masjid in Ayodhya on 6 December 1992. Photo courtesy Anandabazar Picture Archives.

What is the future of the BJP?

It's different in the centre and the states (like Rajasthan, Gujarat and Madhya Pradesh). If you look at the number of seats it won and its vote-share, it does not indicate that it should have fallen apart like it has. It seems to have been held together by the glue of power. And when that went, it fell apart. I am not mourning this. They seem to have exhausted this Ramjanmabhoomi agenda totally. But we also need to have a strong opposition in this country ...

The BJP doesn't seem to have the time for that. But the Left thinks it is playing opposition.

I think the Communist parties run the risk of making themselves ridiculous by contesting everything initially and then caving in eventually. They are playing the role of a 'virtual opposition'. This Left–Congress combine could well become the secular version of the Parivar. All the arguments are reduced to being family squabbles.

What does it mean to be independent today? Has Independence Day become a mere annual ritual?

As corporatization and privatization proceed apace and more and more people are rendered jobless, homeless, and have no access to natural resources, anger and unrest will build. The central function of the state will increasingly be to oversee the repression of an unemployed, dispossessed population on behalf of the corporates. The state will have to evolve into an elaborate tyranny which retains all the rhetoric of democracy. Look at what's happening in Orissa—the new crucible of corporate globalization. Multinational mining companies—Sterlite, Vedanta, Alcan—are devastating Orissa's hills and forests for bauxite. They say Kashmir is like Palestine. True. But Orissa is getting there too. Orissa is a police state now. For some years now, there has been a resilient, feisty, anti-mining movement in Kashipur. You ask what independence means to most Indians—visit Kuchaipadar, the extraordinary little adivasi village at the heart of the Kashipur struggle, and you will have your answer. Kuchaipadar is surrounded by police. People cannot move from one village to the next. Cannot hold meetings, rallies or protests. Over the last two years, they have been shot, beaten, lathi-charged, jailed and several have been killed. Last year, on Independence Day, Kuchaipadar's villagers hoisted a black flag. That's what independence means to them. Oh, and who's on the board of directors of Vedanta, one of the biggest mining companies prospecting in Orissa? P. Chidambaram, who resigned on the day he was appointed finance minister; David Gore-Booth, former UK high commissioner in India; Naresh Chandra, former cabinet secretary and ex-Indian ambassador to the US and former chairman of the Foreign Investment Promotion Bureau. It's a bedroom farce with blood on the tracks.

There's been an outsourcing boom. The Indian Information Technology (IT) and IT-enabled services business touched $17.2 billion in 2004–05. Fifty per cent of Fortune 500 companies are clients of Indian IT firms. Surely, some people are benefiting?

Of course, some people benefit. Otherwise there wouldn't be the kind of vocal support that it does have among sections of the people and the national media. The outsourcing industry has created thousands of jobs, mostly in urban areas, and in India that small percentage amounts to a huge number of people. But in return, there is a larger section that gets disempowered, dispossessed. The point, as always, is, who pays, who profits? This section that benefits is full of the joy of having cars, mobile phones, lifestyles that they could not even have dreamt of a few years ago. They control the media, television, they make the movies, they fund them, act in them, distribute them. They form a little universe of their own, sending each other signals of light. For the rest, the darkness deepens. However, be assured, if at any point outsourcing begins to cost America, if it begins to affect their population seriously, outsourcing operations will be shut down in a flash. We live on sufferance. And that's not a safe place to build a home.

While the United Progressive Alliance (UPA) government initially promised to ensure some kind of affirmative action in the private sector, twenty-one leading industrialists led by Ratan Tata have pronounced the entire generation of Dalit/tribal people with degrees from Indian institutions 'unemployable'. They have decided to create a new generation of Dalits/adivasis through 'skill upgradation'.

When it appears that Dalits and other backward classes are getting represented suddenly in our democracy, people in power will find ways of undermining this process. That's what privatization and corporatization are about. Dalits, adivasis and other dispossessed people should realize that they can't bank on the politics of compassion. Because there is none left, and they have no leverage on Ratan Tata.

Dalit spokespersons such as Chandrabhan Prasad have been arguing that if US corporates can employ blacks under the policy of diversity, can't Ford and GE do similar social engineering here?[4]

It was not an act of compassion on the part of Ford and GE. At the time in the US, the black civil rights movement was an international force to be reckoned with. So some negotiation had to happen. Power concedes nothing unless it is forced to. No one knew that better than Ambedkar. It was at the centre of his brilliant demolition of Gandhi's argument in 'The Annihilation of Caste'. Right now, the Dalits have no leverage.

Today, the Dalit movement is fractured and scattered. We need a strong Dalit movement. Unfortunately, it is not a movement that anyone has to negotiate with, least of all India Inc.

The UN this April appointed two special rapporteurs to investigate and find solutions for caste-based discrimination

in India. Can something come out of this internationalization of the Dalit issue?[5]

The UN is such a shaky organization. It has not been able to bring any kind of authority to international issues of late, as we have seen from what happened in Iraq. The UN was used to disarm Iraq before the attack and then was just kicked aside. Maybe their (the UN rapporteurs') coming is a good thing. But I'll believe it when I see something really happening. Because today India is a market. All the major corporations are looking at India with greedy, greedy little eyes. Whether it is the genocide that took place in Gujarat, or whether it is everyday discrimination against Dalits, I don't see any of this being allowed to come in the way of Thomas Friedman's dreamland project. The treatment of Dalits in India is by no means any less grotesque than the treatment of women by the Taliban. But is any of the violence against Dalits in the Indian or international mainstream press? But if you are a willing and open market, will they bomb the caste system out of India, like they wanted to bomb feminism into Afghanistan? I am not a believer in these UN-driven institutional therapies. You have to wage your struggles; you have to put your foot in the door.

That brings us to Friedman's dreamland, New Gurgaon, an outsourcing hub. The Congress harped on the 'aam aadmi' before the election. But the aam aadmi got pulped in Gurgaon. What lessons do we learn?

Unfortunately, underpaid as they are, and humiliated as they have been, the Honda workers are not aam aadmi.[6] They're supposed to be the real beneficiaries of globalization. At least they have work. Far from the glare of TV cameras, the aam aadmi has been facing not just the lathi, but also goli—in Orissa, Bihar, Andhra Pradesh, Jharkhand, Chhattisgarh, Madhya Pradesh, Kerala. The atrocity on the Honda workers happened at the heart of corporate paradise. In Thomas Friedman land. Trouble broke out in the bubble. Gurgaon is one of three New Economic Zones where existing labour laws have never really applied. In the race to the bottom—cheaper labour, longer hours, more 'efficiency'—the company's labour contractors, like all labour contractors, hired 'trainees' and paid them stipends, not salaries. When their 'training' was through, they fired them in order to hire more 'trainees'.

The TV coverage cuts both ways—it can either frighten people or enrage them. I think the police was given instructions to be so brutal and repressive in order to make an example of workers so that others would not dare to do this again anywhere. But the uproar that has ensued and the fact that Honda has been forced to reinstate those who it sacked could mean that workers realize that when they act together they do become a force to reckon with.

Doesn't the Indian elite and the middle class conveniently vent its anger on the political class and yet align with the state on most issues?

This is again about the hollowing out of democracy. Even as we sell our credentials on the international stage as a democracy, even if there's democracy at the level of panchayati raj or Laloo and Mayawati, there's a certain amount of fear in the Indian elite that the underclasses are being elected. How do you undermine that? You undermine it by corporatization, by creating a situation in which the politicians may hold the theatre and the audience, but the real economic power has shifted from their hands. The elite in Pakistan have seen so little democracy. So, strangely enough, they know the difference between themselves and the state. Najam Sethi can be rounded up, beaten up and put in jail.[7] People tell me: If you had been in Pakistan, you would have been shot by now. But whoever comes to power (in India), the chances of that happening to N. Ram or Vinod Mehta are still quite remote. The Indian elite is fused with the state in many ways. We think like the state. We're all wannabe policy-makers. No one's just a citizen.

What do you think of India's new role as a US ally?

The Indian government should seriously study the history and fate of former and present US allies—the world is littered with the carcasses of their people. Only a few years ago, they were shaking hands with Saddam Hussein and a little before that they were doing it with the mujahideen. Pakistan, Iran, Indonesia, Egypt, Saudi Arabia, Chile, other countries in Latin America and Africa. Look what happened to Argentina. And the former USSR. We are tying ourselves into an intricate economic and strategic web. Once we're in, there's no out. We're in the belly of the beast. Once you're there, you eat predigested pap. You behave. You do what you're told, buy what you're sold. If you disobey, you're in trouble. Already, you can see the signs. Condoleezza Rice says the oil pipeline deal with Iran will be a bad idea. Manmohan, on cue, promptly declares to the *Washington Post* that he thinks it will be very hard to raise money for the project. What's that supposed to mean?

But experts say the nuclear deal with the US puts India in a 'win–win' situation.

If a swordfish signs a deal with a crocodile, can it be a win–win deal? Right now, it's strategically important for the US to allow us to believe our own publicity about being a superpower. India is not a superpower. It's just super poor. It's not enough to discuss the nuclear 'deal' as an issue about nuclear energy and nuclear bombs—though that's important too. Where are the studies that show that the right kind of energy for India is nuclear energy? Have we seriously explored alternative forms of energy? Why has the debate been posited as one solely between nuclear energy and fossil fuels? What are the pros and cons of nuclear energy versus energy from fossil fuels? Why has there been no public debate about these things? But the real issue is not about whether India has escaped nuclear isolation. It's not about whether the government has capped its nuclear programme. It's about whether it has capped its imagination. It's about whether it has restricted its room to manoeuvre politically, economically and morally. Has it imbricated itself intimately into an embrace it can never escape?

But both General Musharraf and Manmohan Singh want to be Bushies.

We have two begums competing for the attention of Sheikh Bush. Both of them are fighting for attention and are jealous of each other.

Edward Said would have perhaps approved of this interesting Orientalist metaphor. But seriously, what should be the terms of the nuclear debate?

Actually, it is Orientalist and sexist. I shouldn't have said it ... anyway. For all these experts appearing to debate and disagree on the nuclear issue, these are matters of state and foreign policy which are not to be debated in terms of morality and principles, because that's not how foreign policy works. It's about 'strategy'. I know that. But I don't want to think like the state. As a human being, I ask: Is it all right for our prime minister, on behalf of all of us, to dine at the high table and wave from the balcony arm-in-arm with a liar and a butcher called President George Bush? A man who has lied about WMDs in Iraq, whose lies have been exposed, whose military cowardly killed 100,000 Iraqis after getting the UN to disarm Iraq and killed 25,000 more subsequently? It's worth keeping in mind that collaboration in wars against sovereign nations is a war crime. And also, if Bush is so acceptable to them [the Congress], why lose sleep over Modi, our own overseer of mass murder? We are told it's a strategic alliance with the US, and morality doesn't apply. But why is it that every time a government goes to war, the only reasons offered are moral reasons? 'To spread democracy, freedom, feminism, to rid the world of evil-doers.' Why is it that states expect morality of us, but we as individuals can't debate an issue in moral terms? I don't understand.

You've travelled in Kashmir ...

It's impossible to pronounce knowledgeably on Kashmir after just a few short trips. But some things are not a mystery. Sixty-nine thousand have lost their lives in this conflict. Both Pakistan and India have played a horrible, venal role in Kashmir. But among ordinary Kashmiri people, Pakistan still remains an unknown entity—and for that reason it's become an attractive idea, an ideal even, conflated by many with the yearning for 'azaadi'. It's ironic that a country that is a military dictatorship should be associated with the notion of liberation. The ugly reality of Pakistan is not something that most Kashmiris have experienced. The reality of India, however, to every ordinary Kashmiri, is an ugly, vicious reality they encounter every day, every ten steps at every checkpost, during every humiliating search. And so India stands morally isolated—it has completely lost the confidence of ordinary people. According to the Indian army, there are never at any time more than 3,000–4,000 militants operating in the Valley. But there are between 500,000–800,000 Indian soldiers there. An armed soldier for every ten to fifteen people. By way of comparison, there are 160,000 US soldiers in Iraq. Clearly, the Indian army is not in Kashmir to control militants, it is there only to control the Kashmiri people. It is an army of occupation the Indian media—and here I include the film industry—has played a pretty unforgivable part in. In totally misrepresenting the truth of what's really going on. How can we even talk of 'solutions' when we simply deny the reality?

State repression, religious fundamentalism and corporate globalization seem interconnected. But hasn't resistance to this nexus become symbolic, tokenistic, NGO-ized and even a career for some professionals, including, some would say, for you?

Sometimes NGOs wreck real political resistance more effectively than outright repression does. And yes, it could be argued that I'm yet another commodity on the shelves of the Empire's supermarket, along with Chinese cabbages and freeze-dried prawns. Buy Roy, get two human rights free! But between the NGOs and Al-Qaeda—frankly, I'm with the many millions who are looking for the Third Way.

And the prognosis for the War on Terror?

Clearly, it's spreading. Empire is overstretched. The Iraqis have actually managed to mire the US army in what looks like endless, bloody combat. More and more US soldiers are refusing to fight. More and more young people are refusing to join the army. Manpower in the armed forces is becoming a real problem. In a recent article, the remarkable un-embedded journalist Dahr Jamail interviews several American marines who served in Iraq. Asked what he would do if he met Bush, one of them says: 'It would be two hits—me hitting him and him hitting the floor.'[8] It's for this reason that the US is looking for allies—preferably low-cost allies with low-cost lives. Because the media is completely controlled, no real news makes it out of Iraq. But last month, I was on the jury of the World Tribunal on Iraq in Istanbul. We heard fifty-four horrifying testimonies about what is going on there, including from Iraqis who had risked their lives to make it to the tribunal. The world knows only a fraction of what's going on. The anger emanating out of Iraq and Afghanistan is spreading wider and wider. It's a deep, uncontrollable rage that you cannot put a PR spin on. America isn't going to win this war.

It has been eight years since *The God of Small Things*.[9] Is there a second novel in you or has too much politics meant the end of Arundhati Roy's imagination? You have also been talking of disengaging from political writing?

All writing is political. Fiction is especially subversive. But it's time for me to change gear. I am sort of up for anything right now, which is exciting. Let's see what happens.

Any positive thoughts to end this dark conversation?

Let me share a sweet little thing. I saw a news report about two adivasi girls getting married to each other. And the whole village was saying: If that's what they want, it's fine. They had this ceremony, with all the rituals and customs, and they let them get married. That's a moment of magic. It reveals their level of modernity, of their sophistication. Of their beauty.

‘I saw a news report about two adivasi girls getting married to each other. And the whole village was saying: If that’s what they want, it’s fine. They had this ceremony, with all the rituals and customs, and they let them get married. That’s a moment of magic. It reveals their level of modernity, of their sophistication. Of their beauty.’

'In India we are at the moment witnessing a sort of fusion between corporate capitalism and feudalism—it's a deadly cocktail. We see it unfolding before our eyes. Sometimes it looks as though the result of all this will be a twisted implementation of the rural employment guarantee act. Half the population will become Naxalites and the other half will join the security forces. And what Bush said will come true. Everyone will have to choose whether they're with "us" or with the "terrorists". We will live in an elaborately administered tyranny.'

THE QUESTION OF VIOLENCE

In conversation with Amit Sengupta, November 2005.

I start with an old question: When *Tehelka* was being cornered, you had said there should be a Noam Chomsky in India. What is this idea of Noam Chomsky in a context like India?

I think essentially that whether it is an issue like *Tehelka* being hounded or all the other issues that plague us, much of the critical response is an analysis of symptoms; it's not radical. Most of the time it does not really question how democracy dovetails into majoritarianism which edges towards fascism, or what the connections are between this kind of 'new democracy' and corporate globalization, repression, militancy and war. What is the connection between corruption and power?

At one point when the *Tehelka* exposé happened, I thought, thank god the BJP is corrupt, thank god someone's taken money, imagine if they had been incorruptible, only ideological, it would have been so much more frightening.[1] To me, pristine ideological battles are really more frightening.

In India we are at the moment witnessing a sort of fusion between corporate capitalism and feudalism—it's a deadly cocktail. We see it unfolding before our eyes. Sometimes it looks as though the result of all this will be a twisted implementation of the rural employment guarantee act. Half the population will become Naxalites and the other half will join the security forces and what Bush said will come true. Everyone will have to choose whether they're with 'us' or with the 'terrorists'. We will live in an elaborately administered tyranny.

But look at the reaction to the growing influence of the

'The Question of Violence' first appeared in Tehelka.

Maoists—even by political analysts it's being treated as a law and order problem, not a political problem—and like militancy in Kashmir and the Northeast, it will be dealt with by employing brutal repression by security forces or arming local people with weapons that will eventually lead to a sort of civil war. That seems to be perfectly acceptable to Indian 'civil society'.

Those who understand and disagree with the repressive machinery of the state are more or less divided between the Gandhians and the Maoists. Sometimes, quite often the same people who are capable of a radical questioning of, say, economic neoliberalism or the role of the state, are deeply conservative socially—about women, marriage, sexuality, our so-called 'family values'; sometimes they're so doctrinaire that you don't know where the establishment stops and the resistance begins. For example, how many Gandhian/Maoist/Marxist Brahmins or upper-caste Hindus would be happy if their children married Dalits or Muslims, or declared themselves to be gay? Quite often, the people whose side you're on, politically, have absolutely no place for a person like you in their social, cultural or religious imagination.

That's a knotty problem; politically radical people can come at you with the most breathtakingly conservative social views and make nonsense of the way in which you have ordered your world and your way of thinking about it and you have to find a way of accommodating these contradictions within your world view.

In the Hindi heartland, the same terrain that had Munshi Premchand, Muktibodh, Nirala, Kaifi Azmi is still one of the most stagnating, backward, poverty-stricken terrains of India. But in terms of the lilt of the languages here, humour, bawdy jokes, hard politics, there is a vibrant churning going on; there is Dalit churning. This is engagement with reality in a very different manner. There are new theatre, literary, cinema journals, a vibrant culture.

There is a lot of excitement in the air and it is actually happening here in India, an excitement that is in a way absent in the west. If you live in America or Europe it is almost impossible to really believe that another world is possible. Over there, anybody who talks about life beyond capitalism is part of a freak show; they're just considered nuts and weirdos going through teenage angst.

But here, it actually still exists, though they are being rapidly destroyed. It is very important, the anarchy of what you were saying, there are magazines and little pamphlets, all over India, which cannot be controlled by the corporate establishment, and that's very important, the way communication links are kept alive. We are in a very striking phase. But how powerful are these alternative ways of communication? You can see these mighty structures of capitalism. Can you fight them with these alternatives? The only way you can be optimistic is to insist on being irrational, unreasonable, magical, stubborn, because what you see happening is an inevitable crunching through of these structures.

Is it possible for anyone to stand up against these structures, as Chomsky has done again and again, or you, and not be hounded out by the entire apparatus?

Until recently, we all hoped that it was a question of getting the facts out, getting the information out, and that once people understood what was going on, things would change. Their conscience would kick in and everything would be all right. We saw it, rather stupidly, as a question of getting the information out. But getting the story out is only one small part of the battle. For example, before the American elections, Michael Moore's film was in every small-town cinema hall everywhere; the film was an evidence-based documentary, it was by no means a piece of radical political thought, it was just a fact-based political scandal about the House of Bush, but still, Bush came back with a bigger majority than the earlier elections.

The facts are there in the world today. People like Chomsky have made a huge contribution to that. But what does information mean? What are facts? There is so much information that almost all becomes meaningless and disempowering. Where has it all gone? What does the World Social Forum mean today? They are big questions now. Ultimately, millions of people marched against the war in Iraq. But the war was prosecuted; the occupation is in full stride. I do not, for a moment, want to undermine the fact that unveiling the facts has meant a huge swing of public opinion against the occupation of Iraq, it has meant that America's secret history is now street talk, but what next? To expose things is quite different from being able to effectively resist things.

I am more interested now in whether there are new strategies of resistance. The debate between strategies of violence and non-violence ...

One option is to keep digging, keep digging and there is always the danger of stagnation, becoming self-righteous, dogmatic, moralistic, losing your sense of humour, songs, masti. You stop laughing. As if the poor or the working class don't laugh ...

You are absolutely right on that one. In India, particularly, self-righteousness is the bane of activists or public thinkers. It's also the function of a kind of power that you begin to accumulate. Some activists have unreasonable power over people in their 'constituencies', they have adulation, gratitude, it can turn their heads. They begin to behave like mainstream politicians. Somebody like me runs a serious risk of thinking that I'm more important than I actually am—because people petition me all the time, with serious issues that they want me to intervene in. And, of course, an intervention does have some momentary effect, you begin to think that it is in your power to do something. Whereas actually is it or is it not? It's a difficult call.

At the end of the day, fame is also a gruesome kind of capitalism, you can accumulate it, bank it, live off it. But it can suffocate you, block off the blood vessels to the brain, isolate you, make you lose touch. It pushes you up to the surface and you forget how to keep your ear to the ground.

I think it is important to retreat sometimes. Because you can really get caught up in fact and detail, fact and detail, and forget how to think conceptually, and that's a kind of prison. Speaking for myself, I'm ready for a jailbreak.

You mean even anti-conformism can become a conformist trap?

There is the danger, especially for a writer of fiction, that you can become somebody who does what is expected of you. I could end up boring myself to death. In India, the political anti-establishment can be socially very conservative (Bring on the gay Gandhians!) and can put a lot of pressure on you to become something which may not necessarily be what you want to be: they want you to dress in a particular way, be virtuous, be sacrificing, it's a sort of imaginary and quite often faulty extrapolation of what the middle class assumes the 'people', the 'masses' want and expect. It can be maddening, and I want to say like Bunty in *Bunty aur Babli*,[2] 'Mujhe aisi izzat aur sharafat ki zindagi se bachao …'

There are all kinds of things that work to dull, leaden your soul … to weigh you down …

I like Jean Paul Sartre. He used to say money must keep circulating. He used to blow his money on taxis, without any purpose. Blow it up on booze. Money should etherize. That does not take away his strange involvement with histories or literature: the Spanish civil war, Stalin. I don't agree with the term 'intellectual'. Anybody with skills and intelligence can be intellectual. A cobbler is an intellectual.

I don't really want to work out the definitions. It's just the opposite of what novelists do. They really try to free their thinking from such definitions.

As for money, I have tried to take it lightly. Really, I have tried to give it away, but even that is a very difficult thing to do. Money is like nuclear waste. What you do with it, where you dump it, what problems it creates, what it changes, these are incredibly complicated things. And eventually, it can all blow up in your face. I'd have been happier with less. Yeh Dil Maange Less. Less money, less fame, less pressure, more badmashi. I hate the fucking responsibility that is sometimes forced on me. I spent my early years making decisions that would allow me to evade responsibility, and now ...

People are constantly in search of idols, heroes, villains, sirens—in search of individuals, in search of noise. Anybody in whom they can invest their mediocre aspirations and muddled thinking will do. Anyone who is conventionally and moderately 'successful' becomes a celebrity. It's almost a kind of profession now—we have professional celebrities—maybe colleges should start offering a course.

It's indiscriminate—it can be Miss Universe, or a writer, or the maker of a ridiculous TV soap, the minimum requirement is success. There's a particular kind of person who comes up to me with this star-struck smile—it doesn't matter who I am—they just know I'm famous; whether I'm the 'BookerPrizeWinner' or the star of the *Zee Horror Show* or whatever is immaterial.

In this freak show, this celebrity parade, there's no place for loss, or failure. Whereas to me as a writer, failure interests me. Success is so tinny and boring. Everyone is promoting themselves so hard.

You gave your Booker money to the NBA.[3] Your Sydney Prize money to aborigine groups. The Lannan Prize money you gave to fifty organizations who are doing exemplary work.[4] You trusted them. You gave away your money, okay, it's not your money, the money came from somewhere; but you gave it away. Very few people do that in this world. No one does that. So you can't stop society [looking] at you in a certain way.

Well, I haven't given it all away. I still have more than I need. If I gave it all away I might turn into the kind of person that I really dread—'the one who has sacrificed everything' and will no doubt, somewhere along the way, extract a dreadful price from everybody around. I've learned that giving money away can help, but it can also be utterly destructive, however good your intentions may have been. It is impossible to always know what the right thing to do is.

It can create conflict in strange and surprising places. I am not always comfortable with what I do with my money. I do everything. I give it away extravagantly. I blow it up extravagantly. I have no fix on it—it comforts me, it bothers me, I'm constantly glad that I can afford to pay my bills. I'm paranoid about its incredible capacity for destruction. But the one thing I'm glad about is that it is not inherited. I think inherited money is a curse.

Giving money away is dangerous and complicated and in some ways against my political beliefs—I do not subscribe to the politics of good intentions—but what do I do? Sit on it and accumulate more? I'm uncomfortable with lots of things that I do, but can't see a better way—I just muddle along. It's a peculiar problem, this problem of excess, and it's embarrassing to even talk about it in a land of so much pain and poverty. But there it is …

Last question. There is a conflict within oneself. There is a consistency also, of positions, commitments, knowledge. And there are twilight zones you are grappling with. So why can't you jump from this realm to another: there is no contradiction in saying, what is that, 'Mujhe izzat …'

I think we all are just messing our way through this life. People, ideologues who believe in a kind of redemption, a perfect and ultimate society, are terrifying. Hitler and Stalin believed that with a little social engineering, with the mass murder of a few million people, they could create a new and perfect world. The idea of perfection has often been a precursor to genocide. John Gray writes about it at some length. But then, on the other hand, we have the placid acceptance of karma which certainly suits the privileged classes and castes very well. Some of us oscillate in the space between these two ugly juggernauts trying to at least occasionally locate some pinpoints of light.

'To expose things is quite different from being able to effectively resist things. I am more interested now in whether there are new strategies of resistance. The debate between strategies of violence and non-violence …'

Zahoor Ahmad's mother hugs his grave in the Martyrs' Graveyard in Srinagar. Ahmad was killed by security forces in March 1996.
Photo © Altaf Qadri

'When there is such massive army presence I do not understand how anybody, any agency, can say that there are free and fair elections in Kashmir, regardless of how many people turn out or do not turn out to vote. Because when you have a permanent army presence you do not need to send people on the end of a bayonet to voting booths.'

I HOPE KASHMIR WILL BE IN ALL THE BOOKS I WRITE ...

IN CONVERSATION WITH P.G. RASOOL, MARCH 2006.

You recently visited earthquake-hit areas of Uri (Kashmir)—your impressions.[1]

I really spent a very short time in Uri. I saw the Athrot [helping hand] camp office, really dedicated people. When all the other NGOs were gone, they were distributing thermocol sheets, tin sheets, etc. It is incredible, the isolation and supervision under which people live. The people instead of giving their names answer with card numbers as if living in prison. In this situation, whether it is the politicians, the Hurriyat or the government, no one can claim to know what the people want. I could see people paralysed by the nexus of soldiers and informers. There was one village on the other side [of the river Jhelum]. It was snowing and we were told that people were slowly freezing. With all the army and helicopters, nobody seemed to know how to get them food, etc. particularly now that the publicity blitz was over.

And, of course, the Line of Control was not a line, but a whole expanse of area, sixty kilometres wide, beyond the reach of even Kashmiri civil society and administered only by the army.

A lot of development is being talked about and particularly the corporate world is being requested and provided facilities to 'uplift' Kashmir now. How do you see that?

One of the striking differences between Kashmir and north India is that you do not see abject poverty like in other parts of India.

'I Hope Kashmir Will Be in All the Books I Write ...' first appeared in Greater Kashmir.

Obviously one of the reasons for this was the radical land reform in the 1950s by the Sheikh Muhammad Abdullah government which gave Kashmiris a level of self-sufficiency that has helped them survive the terrible events of the last seventeen years. Also the governments, both at the state and at the centre were so occupied with the occupation that they did not seem to have the time or the inclination to pursue what they call 'development' of the kind that they practice in the rest of India which has resulted in the rich cornering all the natural resources and the poor being robbed of everything they ever had. This neoliberal corporate model only accelerates the speed of manufacturing extreme wealth for the minority and extreme poverty for the majority.

When corporate-style development comes to Kashmir, it will basically destroy the template of egalitarianism that land reforms had created. I think the government's strategic hope is that it will create a situation where the struggle for self-determination is converted into a class war where the very rich will have increasing 'stakes' in peace and the poor will be so disempowered that what they want will not matter. It is an attempt to break what the Indian state knows to be a more or less stubborn consensus about self-determination. The schism between the Kashmiri elite and the rest of the population has already begun to show.

One of the unintentional, inadvertent advantages of the fact that there is an armed struggle in Kashmir is that Kashmiris have been saved from the savage impoverishment that the Indian government's chosen 'development model' has inflicted on the rest of India.

You refused the Sahitya Akademi award for your book *The Algebra of Infinite Justice*, a collection of political essays.[2]

Well, I gave what I thought were clear reasons for why I could not accept the award in a letter to the Akademi.[3] Here I can only repeat the contents of the letter. I wrote that even as we call ourselves a democracy, Indian security forces control and administer Kashmir, Manipur and Nagaland and the numbers of the dead and the disappeared continue to mount. I thanked the jury of the Sahitya

Akademi for giving me the Award. I said I am proud that the jury felt that a collection of political essays deserved to be given India's most prestigious literary prize. The essays, written between 1998 and 2001, are deeply critical of the Indian state on big dams, nuclear weapons, increasing militarization and on economic neoliberalism. However, even today, the incumbent government shows a continuing commitment to these policies and is clearly prepared to implement them, ruthlessly and violently, whatever the cost. The government has seen it fit to declare itself an ally of the US government and, thereby, the American invasion of Afghanistan and its illegal occupation of Iraq which under the Nuremberg principles constitutes the supreme crime of a war of aggression.[4] I have great respect for the Sahitya Akademi, for the members of this year's jury and for many of the writers who have received these awards in the past. But to register my protest and reaffirm my disagreement—indeed, my absolute disgust—with these policies of the Indian government, I refused to accept the Sahitya Akademi Award.

During the BJP regime I was convicted for contempt of court and sent to jail. During the Congress regime, I am being given an award. Though these seem different ways of dealing with the writer, to my mind they are both ways to neutralize a troublesome writer.

Last year your speech on 'International Day of the Disappeared' became a topic of discussion in the media.

I wish the fact that there are approximately 8,000–10,000 disappeared people in Kashmir would become a topic of hot discussion. Even notorious regimes like Pinochet's Chile cannot boast such numbers. But because India has the reputation of being a democracy, it quite literally gets away with mass murder. But of course, it is so much more convenient for such media to discuss and try and discredit me instead of paying attention to the real issue which [because of the] organic relationship between the media and the state and the corporations [they] would like to avoid even mentioning.

You often talk about the disproportionate number of

Indian armed forces in Kashmir. Would you like to elaborate upon it?

We know that there are approximately 700,000 soldiers present in Kashmir [and] by the army's own admission, at any given time, a maximum of 3,000 militants operating there. So clearly the army is there to control the people and not the militants. Let's keep in mind that the US has less than 150,000 troops in Iraq and that should tell us seriously what's going on in Kashmir. These Indian security forces are present twenty-four hours a day, seven days a week, year in and year out. When there is such massive army presence I do not understand how anybody, any agency, can say that there are free and fair elections in Kashmir, regardless of how many people turn out or do not turn out to vote. Because when you have a permanent army presence you do not need to send people on the end of a bayonet to voting booths. The presence of such a heavy number of troops is in itself proof of coercion. So when an army gets into the business of administering and governing a civilian population, it becomes just that—a business. It begins to develop economic stakes in continuing to run the business. And it becomes productive for them to continue to remain 'needed'. This is a very dangerous situation for everybody, for the Kashmiris, for the army and for Indian society as well.

Why have Indian intellectuals and the civil society remained silent over the huge injustices and oppression in Kashmir?

The easy answer is that the media has managed to almost completely twist and distort and disappear the Kashmiri story. To understand, one has to actually go there and spend a long time. Many go there but fall into the army/NGO/government network and do the approved guided tour. And because of the massive army presence, intelligence gathering network and the presence of informers, it becomes very difficult for ordinary people to trust strangers and tell them what's happening to their lives and society. However I do not want to make any excuses for the silence from the Indian intellectuals and India's wealth of social activists. I am sure it will return to haunt them.

You have mentioned Kashmir in your books *An Ordinary Person's Guide to Empire*[5] and *The Checkbook and the Cruise Missile*[6] and you have been visiting Kashmir also. Do you plan any book on the subject?

I do not think of Kashmir as a subject. It's much more than that. For a writer, it's really a place which gives you an understanding of power, powerlessness, brutality, bravery and the dilemmas of the human condition. I would not want to write a book 'about' Kashmir, I hope Kashmir will be in all the books I write.

'I refused to accept the Sahitya Akademi Award. During the BJP regime I was convicted for contempt of court and sent to jail. During the Congress regime, I am being given an award. Though these seem different ways of dealing with the writer, to my mind they are both ways to neutralize a troublesome writer.'

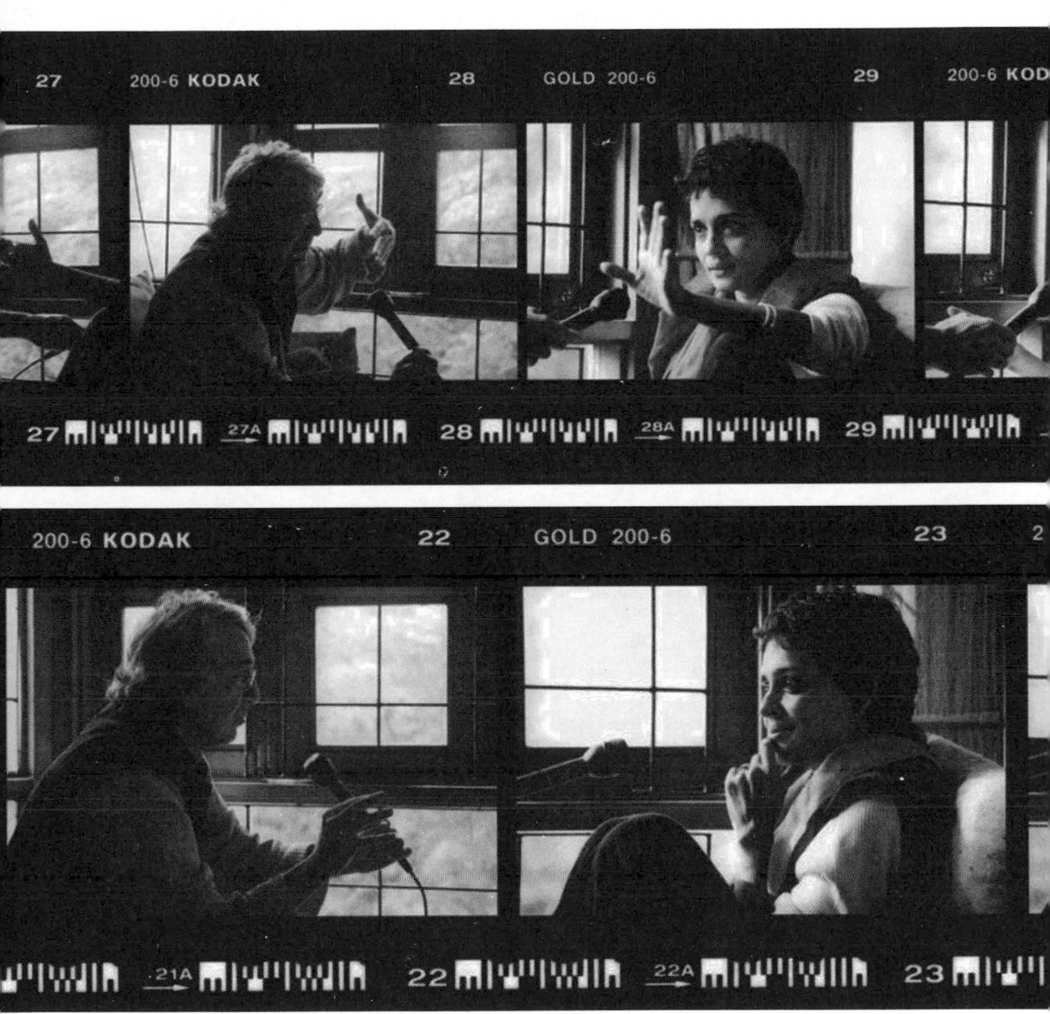

David Barsamian and Arundhati Roy in New Delhi, November 2002.
Photo © Sanjay Kak.

'I'd say our views paint us out of the small corner—the small, rich, glittering, influential corner. The corner with "the voice". The corner that owns the guns and bombs and money and the media. I'd say our views cast us onto a vast, choppy, dark, dangerous ocean where most of the world's people float precariously. And from having drifted there a while, I'd say the mood is turning ugly.'

THERE'S A FURY BUILDING UP ...[1]

In conversation with Shoma Chaudhury, April 2006.

The media has been playing up the recent Supreme Court verdict on the Narmada case as a victory for all sides.[2] How do you read it? What does this verdict really mean?

It may well be a victory for the Gujarat government but it's by no means a victory for the Narmada Bachao Andolan. The prime minister has washed his hands off an unequivocal report by members of his own cabinet. The minister for water resources, Saifuddin Soz, had the rare courage to put down on paper what he actually found—the fact that rehabilitation in Madhya Pradesh has been disastrous.[3] It's true that on a one-day visit, ministers cannot possibly come away with an exhaustive survey, but you don't need to spend more than a day in the Narmada valley to see that there is a massive problem on the ground. There is a huge disjuncture between the paperwork and the reality on the ground. What will be submitted to the court—what has always been submitted to the court—is more paperwork.

Two years ago, when I went to Harsud which was being submerged by the Narmada Sagar dam,[4] I also went to so-called New Harsud, which the government claimed was a fully functioning new city. There was absolutely nothing there—no houses, no water, no toilets, no sewage. Just a few neon street lights and a huge expanse of land. But officials produced photographs taken at night with star filters making it look like Paris!

At the last hearing on the seventeenth of April, the logical thing for the Supreme Court to do would have been to say, 'Stop

'There's a Fury Building Up ...' first appeared in Tehelka.

construction of the dam. We know there's a problem, let's assess the problem before we go ahead.' Instead it did the opposite and the problem has been magnified. Every metre the dam goes up, an additional 1,500 families come under the threat of submergence. This interim order is inconsistent with its own October 2000 and March 2005 Narmada judgements as well as the Narmada Water Dispute Tribunal Award, which state in no uncertain terms that displaced people must be resettled six months before submergence.[5]

Water for Gujarat is obviously an urgent issue. How do we reconcile these polarities?

The urgency is a bit of a red herring. Gujarat has managed to irrigate only 10 per cent of the land it could have irrigated and provides only a fraction of the drinking water that it could have provided at the current dam height. This is because the canals and delivery systems are not in place. In other words, it has not been able to use the water at even the current dam height. This is an old story with the Narmada dams. The Bargi dam, completed in 1990 at huge cost to the public exchequer and to tens of thousands of displaced people, today irrigates less land than it submerged—because canals haven't been built. In the case of the Sardar Sarovar, in fact, raising the dam's height immediately is just hubris. It has no practical urgency. The fair thing to do would be to stop the construction of the dam and ask the Gujarat government to construct the canals and use the water it already has. That will buy time to do a decent job of rehabilitation.

If we could go back to the beginning of your involvement, why were you drawn to the Narmada issue? Why has this become such a powerful symbol?

Because I believe that it contains a microcosm of the universe. I think it contains a profound argument about everything—power, powerlessness, deceit, greed, politics, ethics, rights and entitlements. For example, is it right to divert rivers and grow water-intensive crops like sugar cane and wheat in a desert ecology? Look at the disaster the Indira Gandhi canal is wreaking in Rajasthan. To me, understanding the Narmada issue is the key to understanding how the world works. The beauty of the argument is that it isn't human-centric. It's also about things that most political ideologies leave out. Vital issues—rivers, estuaries, earth, mountains, deserts, crops, forests, fish. And about human things that most environmental ideologies leave out. It touches a raw nerve, so you have people who know very little about it, people who admit that they know very little and don't care to find out, coming out with passionate opinions.

The battle in the Narmada valley has raised radical questions about the top-heavy model of development India has opted for. But it also raises very specific questions about specific dams. And to my mind, though much of the noise now is centred on the issue of displacement and resettlement, the really vital questions that have not been answered are the ones that question the benefits of dams. Huge irrigation schemes that end up causing waterlogging, salinization and eventual desertification have historically been among the major reasons for the collapse of societies, beginning with the Mesopotamian civilization. I recommend Jared Diamond's wonderful book *Collapse* to all those who wish to take a slightly longer, and less panicked, view of 'development'.[6] India already has thousands of acres of waterlogged land. We've already destroyed most of our rivers. We have unsustainable cropping patterns and a huge crisis in our agricultural economy. Even vast parts of the command area of our favourite dam—the Bhakra—is waterlogged and in deep trouble.[7] So the real issue is not how ordinary farmers in Gujarat will benefit from the Sardar Sarovar, but how they will eventually suffer because of it.

That's controversial. Could you elaborate?

I have written at length about it in my essay 'The Greater Common Good'—but let me just raise a few simple points here.[8] The Sardar Sarovar was built on the promise that it was going to take water to the drought-prone areas of Kutch and Saurashtra. That's the emotive, frenzied, political point that is made all the time. Because of the huge propaganda machine around it, year after year this dam has soaked up almost 95 per cent of Gujarat's irrigation budget at the expense of other, more effective, more local schemes. Gujarat has among the largest number of high dams of any state in India and continues to have such an acute water problem! If you look at the Gujarat government's own plans for the Sardar Sarovar, you'll see that Kutch and Saurashtra lie at the end of the canal. Even if everything goes brilliantly, supernaturally, if the big cities, big industry, golf courses, sugar mills and water parks do not siphon water off beforehand, if the river has as much water as the project engineers say it has (which it doesn't), and if it can achieve an irrigation efficiency of 60 per cent (when no dam in India has achieved more than 40 per cent), even then, the project is designed to irrigate only 2 per cent of the cultivable area of Kutch and 9 per cent of Saurashtra. The loot of canal water has already begun.

Recently, the real stakeholders were indiscreet enough to put their photographs in the huge, full-page advertisements that appeared in all the national dailies supporting the dam—religious leaders, politicians and big industrialists. Where were the farmers? The people of Kutch and Saurashtra? A group of people in Kutch have filed a petition in the Supreme Court complaining that the Gujarat government has reduced even that small allocation of water to Kutch and Saurashtra, in contravention of the Narmada Water Disputes Tribunal Award. The tragedy is that if they would only use more local, effective, rainwater-harvesting schemes, for less than 10 per cent of the cost of the Sardar Sarovar, every single village in Kutch and Saurashtra could have drinking water. The Sardar Sarovar has never made sense, ecologically or economically.

But in politics there's nothing as effective as a potential dam which promises paradise—it will soothe your sorrows, it will bring you breakfast in bed. The Sardar Sarovar has been the subject of frenzied political campaigning for every political party in Gujarat. And it's all propaganda. Look at the recent spectacle we witnessed. Narendra Modi claiming to speak on behalf of poor farmers and the corporate cartel, sitting on a symbolic hunger strike, a Gandhian satyagraha—and simultaneously issuing threats of violence. Incredibly, he went unchallenged by a single person in the UPA government. That's how deep the mainstream political consensus is.

I see your point about forcing a riverine ecology on a desert and the political lobbies at work. But what about electricity?

Recently, a group of international engineers has challenged the claims made by the Sardar Sarovar Narmada Nigam about power generation. So has Himanshu Thakkar, an engineer who has studied the Sardar Sarovar in some detail. I would like to make three points.

Having an installed capacity of 1450 megawatts means that the power generating machinery that has been installed is capable of producing 1450 megawatts of power. What is actually produced depends on actual water flows—which we know is much lower than what the Sardar Sarovar project was designed for.

Second, in a multi-purpose dam like the Sardar Sarovar, for the most part you can either use the water for irrigation or for power generation. In fact, as more and more water is used for irrigation, calculations show that the electricity from the riverbed powerhouse will be virtually zero. So to claim its benefits on both fronts simultaneously is dishonest.

Third, in power distribution, India has amongst the highest transmission and distribution losses in the world. Across the country, avoidable losses add up to more power than is generated by dozens of big dams. So before we go building more big dams and destroying communities, forests, rivers and ecosystems, maybe we could do something about how much electricity and water we waste and misuse. It would make a serious, radical difference. Minimizing waste would be revolutionary.

The NBA has been protesting for several years. Why do you think the protest reached such white heat this time?

Obviously because of the profile and commitment of Medha Patkar and the reputation of the NBA and the fact that the indefinite fast took place in Delhi. But I think it's also because displacement is becoming an urgent issue for millions—both in cities and in villages. The situation is out of control. Every single development project—whether it's an IT park in Bangalore or a steel plant in Kalinganagar or the Pollavaram dam—the first move is to take land from the poor. People are being displaced at gunpoint. Cities like Delhi and Bombay are becoming cities of bulldozers and police. The spectre of the shooting of adivasis in Kalinganagar in January—some of whose bodies were returned by the police mutilated, with their arms and breasts chopped off—all this hung over the protest at Jantar Mantar.[9] There is a fury building up across the country.

The whole argument against big dams has been submerged by the rising waters of the reservoir and narrowed down to the issue of rehabilitation. But even this vital, though narrow, issue of rehabilitation which should be pretty straightforward, contains a universe of its own—of deceit, lies and utter callousness. To pay lip service to rehabilitation is easy—even Narendra Modi does that. The real issue, as the Soz report points out, is that there is a world of difference between what's on paper and what's on the ground.

Could you draw a thumbnail sketch of what you mean by that? Talk about the issue of displacement and rehabilitation.

One of the major tricks that is played on the poor and on the public understanding of what's going on in these 'development' projects is that large numbers of the displaced do not even count as officially 'Project Affected'. Very few of the tribals whose land was acquired for the steel factory in Kalinganagar counted as Project Affected. Most were called 'encroachers', uprooted and told to buzz off. Those who did qualify were given Rs 35,000 for land that was sold for Rs 350,000 and whose market value was even higher. So you take from the poor, subsidize the rich, and then call it the Free Market.

In the case of the Sardar Sarovar, the tens of thousands who will be displaced by canal construction in Gujarat are not counted as

Project Affected. Those displaced by the sprawling Kevadia colony at the dam site and the compensatory 'afforestation' project don't count. Thousands of fisherfolk who lose their livelihood downstream of the dam don't count. Only those who are displaced by the reservoir count—and even there there's a problem. In Madhya Pradesh the poorest of the poor, the landless, mostly Dalits and adivasis who depend on the river for their livelihood—those who depend on seasonal cultivation on the riverbed, fisher-folk, sand-miners—are not counted as Project Affected. The whole discourse of land for land leaves these people out.

There's another problem: when communities are uprooted and given illegal cash compensation, the cash is given only to the men. Many have no idea how to deal with cash and drink it away or go on spending sprees. Automatically the women are disempowered. Just because it is being made to appear as though it's all inevitable, as though there's no solution, should we forget that there ever was a problem? Should we leave the poorest and most vulnerable out of the 'cost–benefit' analysis—and allow the myth of big dams to go on and on unchallenged?

As for those who are lucky enough to be counted as Project Affected, we know now they are being displaced without rehabilitation in utter violation of the Narmada Water Disputes Tribunal Award and the Supreme Court's own verdicts, all of which specify that displaced families must be given land for land. The Madhya Pradesh government is trying to force people to accept what it calls SRP—Special Rehabilitation Package—which is cash compensation.[10] That's illegal. The technique is to show hundreds of families the same plot of uncultivable land and when they refuse to take it, force cash compensation on them.

The Sardar Sarovar rehabilitation policy was cynically used to create middle-class consensus and make the NBA sound unreasonable. And now that the dam is more or less built, we have public figures like B.G. Verghese who campaigned for the dam and tom-tommed the promise of rehabilitation now openly saying land for land is not possible but that construction should still continue.[11] A columnist went so far as to say that rejecting cash compensation amounted to high treason! We are currently being promised that the Sardar Sarovar R&R policy will be used by the River-Linking scheme—more disastrous than hundreds of Sardar Sarovars—in which lakhs, perhaps millions of people will be displaced. It's an excellent plan to have a noble-sounding policy on paper. It confuses the opposition.

The NBA and you are often seen to be intrinsically anti-development. As people who are opposed to the forces sweeping across the globe. How do you react to that?

With acute boredom. Of course we're opposed to the forces sweeping across the world! Of course we're opposed to this kind of development! We spend our waking hours pointing out that it's not development, it's destruction. It's not democratic, it's not equitable, it's not sustainable. We're anti-destruction. That's what we keep repeating in everything we say and do. Whether we're effective in our opposition, whether we're doomed, whether we'll win or lose is a different matter.

Given the relentlessness of the onslaught of globalization, would you say your views paint you into a small corner?

I'd say our views paint us out of the small corner—the small, rich, glittering, influential corner. The corner with 'the voice'. The corner that owns the guns and bombs and money and the media. I'd say our views cast us onto a vast, choppy, dark, dangerous ocean where most of the world's people float precariously. And from having drifted there a while, I'd say the mood is turning ugly. Go to Kalinganagar, Raygada, Chhattisgarh—you'll see there's something akin to civil war brewing there. The adivasis of Kalinganagar have blocked the main highway to Paradip Port since January. There are districts in Chattisgarh which the Maoists control and the administration can't reach. I'm not saying that there will be a beautiful political revolution when the poor take over the state, I'm saying we could, as a society, be convulsed with all kinds of violence. Criminal, lumpen, political, mercenary—the kind that has broken out across so much of Africa.

So it really is in the enlightened self-interest of those jitterbugging in the glittering corner to sit up and pay heed.

Another strong criticism of you and the NBA is that you oppose a particular world view, but present no alternative vision. Is there an alternative vision? Is it important to have one?

There is an alternative vision. But it isn't some grand Stalinist scheme that can be articulated in three sentences—no more than the 'model' of this existing world can be described in three sentences. You asked this question about an alternative very sweetly. It is usually asked in a sneering, combative way. Let me explain the way I look at it. The world we live in right now is an enormous accretion of an almost infinite number of decisions that have been made: economic, ecological, social, political, pedagogical, ideological. For each of those decisions that was made, there was an alternative. For every high dam that is being built there is an alternative. Maybe no dam, maybe a less high dam. For every corporate contract that is signed there is an alternative. There is an alternative to the Indo–US nuclear deal,[12] there is an alternative to the Indo–US Knowledge Initiative in Agricultural Research,[13] there is an alternative to GM foods. There is an alternative to the Armed Forces (Special Powers) Act.[14] There is an alternative to the draconian Land Acquisition Act.[15] The fundamental issue is that 'a country is not a corporation', as Paul Krugman says.[16] It cannot be run like one. All policy cannot be guided by commercial interests and motivated by profit. Citizens are not employees to be hired and fired, governments are not employers. Newspapers and TV channels are not supposed to be boardroom bulletins. Corporations like Monsanto and Wal-Mart are not supposed to shape India's policies. But signing over resources like forests and rivers and minerals to giant corporations in the name of 'efficiency' and GDP growth only increases the efficiency of the terrible exploitation of the majority and the indecent accumulation of wealth by a minority—leading to the yawning divide between the rich and the poor and the kind of social conflict we're seeing.

The keystone of the alternative world would be that nothing can justify the violation of the fundamental rights of citizens. That comes first. The growth rate comes second. Otherwise democracy has no meaning. You cannot resort to algebra. You cannot say I'm taking away the livelihood of 200,000 to enhance the livelihood of 2 million. Imagine what would happen if the government were to take the wealth of 200,000 of India's richest people and redistribute it amongst 2 million of India's poorest? We would hear a lot about socialist appropriation and the death of democracy. Why should taking from the rich be called appropriation and taking from the poor be called development? This kind of development, as I've been saying again and again, is really pushing India to the edge of civil war spearheaded by the Maoists who now control huge swathes of land in India which they have declared 'liberated'.

There is a huge consolidation of these Maoist groups. Prime Minister Manmohan Singh says that they've become India's biggest internal security threat. What's your view on this?

I am sure the Maoists view the PM's statement as a compliment. In a recent article in the *Indian Express*, Ajit Doval, a former director of the Intelligence Bureau, argued that doctrinally, Maoists must be treated as terrorists. Poverty is being conflated with terrorism. The Indian government has learned nothing. It has tried the military solution in Kashmir, in Manipur, in Nagaland. It has got nowhere. Now it's ready to turn its army on its own people, like a maddened tiger eating its own limbs. Though here in the big cities we call ourselves a democracy, all kinds of illiberal ordinances have been passed, and in the countryside, thousands have been imprisoned, civil liberties are a distant dream. Villages are being evacuated and turned into police camps. The Chhattisgarh government is fuelling the situation by arming poor villagers to fight the Maoists. I don't know why they can't seem to understand that there can be no military solution to poverty. Or maybe I'm being stupid—maybe they're trying to eliminate the poor, not poverty.

On top of everything else that has happened over the years, now multinational companies have turned their greedy eyes on the wealth of natural resources in these states. Mountains, rivers and forests are being plundered—it's like the gold rush. And presiding over it are our own economic hit-men in the country's top jobs. These men are staunch disciples of the Washington Consensus. They have no imagination outside of it. They're at the helm of a no-holds-barred looting spree.

Who would have thought ten years ago that Kathmandu would be under siege? Who knows, ten years down the line, it might be Delhi that's under siege. Things are certainly moving in that direction. Something has to give. We cannot go on living this lie. And now that we've seen how contemptuously the government has treated a non-violent movement like the NBA, which of us can in good faith tell people how to fight their battles? Because whatever their strategies, they're up against the same behemoth.

Kanu Sanyal, one of the founders of the Naxalbari uprising, has distanced himself from much of the movement today saying that it has become extortionist, without ideology, predatory on the very poor it seeks to protect.

I'm sure Mahatma Gandhi would say the same of the Congress Party today. Every armed struggle will have its share of thugs and extortionists, along for the ride only for personal gain. That cadre exists in the Northeast, among the militants in Kashmir and, I'm sure, among the Maoists too. It also exists in the armed forces—every occupying army has its share of looters and rapists. But the Maoist phenomenon has arisen because people have had the doors of the liberal, democratic institutions slammed in their faces. To dismiss them all as extortionists and freeloaders is not just deeply apolitical, it's extremely unjust.

After all, the so-called non-violent world that claims to disagree with the current government policies and has broken out in a rash of NGOs peddling everything from peace to birth control also has its share of freeloaders and racketeers. The highly paid 'development jet set' that earns its living off poverty and conflict and misery. Many of them are as counterproductive to the cause of justice as the freeloaders and extortionists on the edge of armed struggles.

The real problem, as we've seen, is that whether a struggle is violent or not, the government's reaction is instinctively repressive. The military solution has not worked in Kashmir or Manipur or Nagaland. It will not work in mainland India. It may not be that the masses will rise in disciplined revolutionary fervour. It may be that we will become a society convulsed with violence—political, criminal and mercenary. But the fact remains that the problem is social injustice, the solution social justice. Not bullets, not bulldozers, not prisons.

‘You take from the poor, subsidize the rich, and then call it the Free Market.’

'People are fully aware that to take to arms is to call down upon yourself the myriad forms of the violence of the Indian state. The minute armed struggle becomes a strategy, your whole world shrinks and the colours fade to black and white. But when people decide to take that step because every other option has ended in despair, should we condemn them? We are living in times when to be ineffective is to support the status quo (which no doubt suits some of us). And being effective comes at a terrible price. I find it hard to condemn people who are prepared to pay that price.'

CHOOSING OUR WEAPONS

IN CONVERSATION WITH SHOMA CHAUDHURY, MARCH 2007.

There is an atmosphere of growing violence across the country. How do you read the signs? In what context should it be read?

You don't have to be a genius to read the signs. We have a growing middle class, reared on a diet of radical consumerism and aggressive greed. Unlike industrializing western countries, which had colonies from which to plunder resources and generate slave labour to feed this process, we have to colonize ourselves, our own nether parts. We've begun to eat our own limbs. The greed that is being generated—and marketed as a value interchangeable with nationalism—can only be sated by grabbing land, water and resources from the vulnerable. What we're witnessing is the most successful secessionist struggle ever waged in independent India—the secession of the middle and upper classes from the rest of the country. It's a vertical secession, not a lateral one. They're fighting for the right to merge with the world's elite somewhere up there in the stratosphere. They've managed to commandeer the resources, the coal, the minerals, the bauxite, the water and electricity. Now they want the land to make more cars, more bombs, more mines—supertoys for the new supercitizens of the new superpower. So it's outright war, and people on both sides are choosing their weapons. The government and the corporations reach for structural adjustment, the World Bank, the ADB, FDI, friendly court orders, friendly policy-makers, help from the 'friendly' corporate media and a police force that will ram all this down people's throats. Those who want to resist this

---

'Choosing Our Weapons' first appeared in Tehelka.

process have, until now, reached for dharnas, hunger strikes, satyagraha, the courts and what they thought was friendly media. But now more and more are reaching for guns. Will the violence grow? If the 'growth rate' and the Sensex are going to be the only barometers the government uses to measure progress and the well-being of people, then of course it will. How do I read the signs? It isn't hard to read sky-writing. What it says up there, in big letters, is this: the shit has hit the fan, folks.

You once remarked that though you may not resort to violence yourself, you think it has become immoral to condemn it, given the circumstances in the country. Can you elaborate on this view?

I'd be a liability as a guerrilla! I doubt I used the word 'immoral'—morality is an elusive business, as changeable as the weather. What I feel is this: non-violent movements have knocked at the door of every democratic institution in this country for decades and have been spurned and humiliated. Look at the Bhopal gas victims, the Narmada Bachao Andolan. The NBA had a lot going for it—high-profile leadership, media coverage, more resources than any other mass movement. What went wrong? People are bound to want to re-think strategy. When Sonia Gandhi begins to promote satyagraha at the World Economic Forum in Davos, it's time for us to sit up and think. For example, is mass civil disobedience possible within the structure of a democratic nation state? Is it possible in the age of disinformation and corporate-controlled mass media? Are hunger strikes umbilically linked to celebrity politics? Would anybody care if the people of Nangla Machhi or Bhatti mines went on a hunger strike? Irom Sharmila has been on a hunger strike for six years.[1] That should be a lesson to many of us. I've always felt that it's ironic that hunger strikes are used as a political weapon in a land where most people go hungry anyway. We are in a different time and place now. Up against a different, more complex adversary. We've entered the era of NGOs—or should I say the era of paltu shers—in which mass action can be a treacherous business. We have demonstrations which are funded, we have sponsored dharnas and social forums which make militant postures but never follow up on what they preach. We have all kinds of 'virtual' resistance. Meetings against SEZs sponsored by the biggest promoters of SEZs. Awards and grants for environmental activism and community action given by corporations responsible for devastating whole ecosystems. Vedanta, a company mining bauxite in the forests of Orissa, wants to start a university. The Tatas have two charitable trusts that directly and indirectly fund activists and mass movements across the country. Could that be why Singur has drawn so much less flak than Nandigram? Of course the Tatas and Birlas funded Gandhi too—maybe he was our first NGO. But now we have NGOs who make a lot of noise, write a lot of reports, but whom the sarkar is more than comfortable with. How do we make sense of all this? The place is crawling with professional diffusers of real political action. 'Virtual' resistance has become something of a liability.

There was a time when mass movements looked to the courts for justice. The courts have rained down a series of judgements that are so unjust, so insulting to the poor in the language they use, they take your breath away. A recent Supreme Court judgement, allowing the Vasant Kunj Mall to resume construction though it didn't have the requisite clearances, said in so many words that the question of corporations indulging in malpractice does not arise! In the era of corporate globalization, corporate land-grab, in the era of Enron and Monsanto, Halliburton and Bechtel, that's a loaded thing to say. It exposes the ideological heart of the most powerful institution in this country. The judiciary, along with the corporate press, is now seen as the lynchpin of the neoliberal project.

In a climate like this, when people feel that they are being worn down, exhausted by these interminable 'democratic' processes, only to be eventually humiliated, what are they supposed to do? Of course it isn't as though the only options are binary—violence versus non-violence. There are political parties that believe in armed struggle but only as one part of their overall political strategy. Political workers in these struggles have been dealt with brutally, killed, beaten, imprisoned under false charges. People are fully aware that to take to arms is to call down upon yourself the myriad forms of the violence of the Indian state. The minute armed struggle becomes a strategy, your whole world shrinks and the colours fade to black and white. But when people decide to take that step because every other option has ended in despair, should we condemn them? Does anyone believe that if the people of Nandigram had held a dharna and sung songs, the West Bengal government would have backed down? We are living in times when to be ineffective is to support the status quo (which no doubt suits some of us). And being effective comes at a terrible price. I find it hard to condemn people who are prepared to pay that price.

You have been travelling a lot on the ground—can you give us a sense of the trouble spots you have been to? Can you outline a few of the combat lines in these places?

Huge question—what can I say? The military occupation of Kashmir, neo-fascism in Gujarat, civil war in Chhattisgarh, mines raping Orissa, the submergence of hundreds of villages in the Narmada valley, people living on the edge of absolute starvation, the devastation of forest land, the Bhopal victims living to see the West Bengal government re-wooing Union Carbide—now calling itself Dow Chemicals—in Nandigram. I haven't been recently to Andhra Pradesh, Karnataka, Maharashtra, but we know about the almost hundred thousand farmers who have killed themselves. We know about the fake encounters and the terrible repression in Andhra Pradesh. Each of these places has its own particular history, economy, ecology. None is amenable to easy analysis. And yet there is connecting tissue, there are huge international cultural and economic pressures being brought to bear on them. How can I not mention the Hindutva project, spreading its poison subcutaneously, waiting to erupt once again? I'd say the biggest indictment of all is that we are still a country, a culture, a society which continues to nurture and practise the notion of untouchability. While our economists number-crunch and boast about the growth rate, a million people—human scavengers—earn their living carrying several kilos of other people's shit on their heads every day. And if they didn't carry shit on their heads they would starve to death. Some fucking superpower this.

How does one view the recent state and police violence in Bengal?

No different from police and state violence anywhere else—including the issue of hypocrisy and doublespeak so perfected by all political parties including the mainstream Left. Are communist bullets different from capitalist ones? Odd things are happening. It snowed in Saudi Arabia. Owls are out in broad daylight. The Chinese government tabled a bill sanctioning the right to private property. I don't know if all of this has to do with climate change. The Chinese communists are turning out to be the biggest capitalists of the twenty-first century. Why should we expect our own Parliamentary Left to be any different? Nandigram and Singur are clear signals. It makes you wonder—is the last stop of every revolution advanced capitalism? Think about it—the French Revolution, the Russian Revolution, the Chinese Revolution, the Vietnam War, the anti-apartheid struggle, the supposedly Gandhian freedom struggle in India … what's the last station they all pull in at? Is this the end of imagination?

The Maoist attack in Bijapur—the death of fifty-five policemen.[2] Are the rebels only the flip side of the state?

How can the rebels be the flip side of the state? Would anybody say that those who fought against apartheid—however brutal their methods—were the flip side of the state? What about those who fought the French in Algeria? Or those who fought the Nazis? Or those who fought colonial regimes? Or those who are fighting the US occupation of Iraq? Are they the flip side of the state? This facile new report-driven 'human rights' discourse, this meaningless condemnation game that we are all forced to play, makes politicians of us all and leaches the real politics out of everything. However pristine we would like to be, however hard we polish our halos, the tragedy is that we have run out of pristine choices. There is a civil war in Chhattisgarh sponsored, created, by the Chhattisgarh government, which is publicly pursuing the Bush doctrine: if you're not with us, you are with the terrorists. The lynchpin of this war, apart from the formal security forces, is the Salva Judum—a government-backed militia of ordinary people forced to take up arms, forced to become SPOs (special police officers). The Indian state has tried this in Kashmir, in Manipur, in Nagaland. Tens of thousands have been killed, hundreds of thousands tortured, thousands have disappeared. Any Banana Republic would be proud of this record. Now the government wants to import these failed strategies into the heartland. Thousands of adivasis have been forcibly moved off their mineral-rich lands into police camps. Hundreds of villages have been forcibly evacuated. Those lands, rich in iron ore, are being eyed by corporations like the Tatas and Essar. MOUs have been signed, but no one knows what they say. Land acquisition has begun. This kind of thing happened in countries like Colombia—one of the most devastated countries in the world. While everybody's eyes are fixed on the spiralling violence between government-backed militias and guerrilla squads, multinational corporations quietly make off with the mineral wealth. That's the little piece of theatre being scripted for us in Chhattisgarh.

Of course it's horrible that fifty-five policemen were killed. But they're as much the victims of government policy as anybody else. For the government and the corporations they're just cannon fodder—there's plenty more where they came from. Crocodile tears will be shed, prim TV anchors will hector us for a while and then more supplies of fodder will be arranged. For the Maoist guerrillas, the police and SPOs they killed were the armed personnel of the Indian state, the main, hands-on perpetrators of repression, torture, custodial killings, false encounters. They're not innocent civilians—if such a thing exists—by any stretch of imagination.

I have no doubt that the Maoists can be agents of terror and coercion too. I have no doubt they have committed unspeakable atrocities. I have no doubt they cannot lay claim to undisputed support from local people—but who can? Still, no guerrilla army can survive without local support. That's a logistical impossibility. And the support for Maoists is growing, not diminishing. That says something. People have no choice but to align themselves on the side of whoever they think is less worse.

But to equate a resistance movement fighting against enormous injustice with the government which enforces that injustice is absurd. The government has slammed the door in the face of every attempt at non-violent resistance. When people take to arms, there is going to be all kinds of violence—revolutionary, lumpen and outright criminal. The government is responsible for the monstrous situations it creates.

'Naxals', 'Maoists', 'outsiders': these are terms being very loosely used these days.

'Outsiders' is a generic accusation used in the early stages of repression by governments who have begun to believe their own publicity and can't imagine that their own people have risen up against them. That's the stage the CPM is at now in Bengal, though some would say repression in Bengal is not new, it has only moved into higher gear. In any case, what's an outsider? Who decides the borders? Are they village boundaries? Tehsil? Block? District? State? Is narrow regional and ethnic politics the new communist mantra? About Naxals and Maoists—well ... India is about to become a police state in which everybody who disagrees with what's going on risks being called a terrorist. Islamic terrorists have to be Islamic—so that's not good enough to cover most of us. They need a bigger catchment area. So leaving the definition loose, undefined, is effective strategy, because the time is not far off when we'll all be called Maoists or Naxalites, terrorists or terrorist sympathizers, and shut down by people who don't really know or care who Maoists or Naxalites are. In villages, of course, that has begun—thousands of people are being held in jails across the country, loosely charged with being terrorists trying to overthrow the state. Who are the real Naxalites and Maoists? I'm not an authority on the subject, but

A tribal holds a gun at a meeting with the Maoists in the forests of Chhattisgarh. AP Photo/Mustafa Quraishi.

here's a very rudimentary potted history.

The Communist Party of India, the CPI, was formed in 1925. The CPI (M), or what we now call the CPM—the Communist Party Marxist—split from the CPI in 1964 and formed a separate party. Both, of course, were parliamentary political parties. In 1967, the CPM, along with a splinter group of the Congress, came to power in West Bengal. At the time there was massive unrest among the peasantry starving in the countryside. Local CPM leaders—Kanu Sanyal and Charu Mazumdar—led a peasant uprising in the district of Naxalbari which is where the term Naxalites comes from. In 1969, the government fell and the Congress came back to power under Siddhartha Shankar Ray. The Naxalite uprising was mercilessly crushed—Mahasweta Devi has written powerfully about this time. In 1969, the CPI (ML)—Marxist-Leninist—split from the CPM. A few years later, around 1971, the CPI (ML) devolved into several parties: the CPM-ML (Liberation), largely centred in Bihar; the CPM-ML (New Democracy), functioning for the most part out of Andhra Pradesh and Bihar; the CPM-ML (Class Struggle) mainly in Bengal. These parties have been generically baptized 'Naxalites'. They see themselves as Marxist-Leninist, not strictly speaking Maoist. They believe in elections, mass action and—when absolutely pushed to the wall or attacked—armed struggle. The MCC—the Maoist Communist Centre, at the time mostly operating in Bihar, was formed in 1968. The PW, People's War, operational for the most part in Andhra Pradesh, was formed in 1980. Recently, in 2004, the MCC and the PW merged to form the CPI (Maoist). They believe in outright armed struggle and the overthrowing of the state. They don't participate in elections. This is the party that is fighting the guerrilla war in Bihar, Andhra Pradesh, Chhattisgarh and Jharkhand.

The Indian state and media largely view the Maoists as an 'internal security' threat. Is this the way to look at them?

I'm sure the Maoists would be flattered to be viewed in this way.

The Maoists want to bring down the state. Given the

autocratic ideology they take their inspiration from, what alternative would they set up? Wouldn't their regime be an exploitative, autocratic, violent one as well? Isn't their action already exploitative of ordinary people? Do they really have the support of ordinary people?

I think it's important for us to acknowledge that both Mao and Stalin are dubious heroes with murderous pasts. Tens of millions of people were killed under their regimes. Apart from what happened in China and the Soviet Union, Pol Pot, with the support of the Chinese Communist Party (while the west looked discreetly away), wiped out 2 million people in Cambodia and brought millions of people to the brink of extinction from disease and starvation. Can we pretend that China's Cultural Revolution didn't happen? Or that millions of people in the Soviet Union and Eastern Europe were not victims of labour camps, torture chambers, the network of spies and informers, the secret police? The history of these regimes is just as dark as the history of western imperialism, except for the fact that they had a shorter lifespan. We cannot condemn the occupation of Iraq, Palestine and Kashmir while we remain silent about Tibet and Chechnya. I would imagine that for the Maoists, the Naxalites, as well as the mainstream Left, being honest about the past is important to strengthen people's faith in the future. One hopes the past will not be repeated, but denying that it ever happened doesn't help inspire confidence ... Nevertheless, the Maoists in Nepal have waged a brave and successful struggle against the monarchy. Right now, in India, the Maoists and the various Marxist-Leninist groups are leading the fight against immense injustice here. They are fighting not just the state, but feudal landlords and their armed militias. They are the only people who are making a dent. And I admire that. It may well be that when they come to power, they will, as you say, be brutal, unjust and autocratic, or even worse than the present government. Maybe, but I'm not prepared to assume that in advance. If they are, we'll have to fight them too. And most likely someone like myself will be the first person they'll string up from the nearest tree—but right now, it is important to acknowledge that they are bearing the brunt of being at the forefront of resistance. Many of us are in a position where we are beginning to align ourselves on the side of those who we know have no place for us in their religious or ideological imagination. It's true that everybody changes radically when they come to power—look at Mandela's ANC. Corrupt, capitalist, bowing to the IMF, driving the poor out of their homes—honouring Suharto, the killer of hundreds of thousands of Indonesian communists, with South Africa's highest civilian award. Who would have thought it could happen? But does this mean South Africans should have backed away from the struggle against apartheid? Or that they should regret it now? Does it mean Algeria should have remained a French colony, that Kashmiris, Iraqis and Palestinians should accept military occupation? That people whose dignity is being assaulted should give up the fight because they can't find saints to lead them into battle?

Is there a communication breakdown in our society?

Yes.

'I've always felt that it's ironic that hunger strikes are used as a political weapon in a land where most people go hungry anyway.'

Arundhati Roy and Medha Patkar in a demonstration protesting the damming of the Narmada. Photo courtesy Anandabazar Picture Archives.

‘Every time there is a pogrom or a terrorist strike, people are sure there is no justice to be had. The courts, the media, the police—everyone is colluding in the process, everyone has become communalized.’

THE TERROR PUZZLE

In conversation with Shoma Chaudhury, September 2008.

What explains the rise in terror attacks which are not related to specific political struggles like those in Kashmir, the Northeast or Punjab? What has shifted in India?

It is clear that there is a manifesto of hatred we all have to deal with now. The manifesto announced in the BJP conclave last week was a litany of hatred. The Congress began a kind of divisive politics way back; the BJP is willing to take it further in a much more malignant way. Harvesting communal and caste votes is a part of our modernity, not our past, and it will be our future unless we do something. But we can't only blame politicians. There is a much more systemic problem. Every time there is a pogrom or a terrorist strike, people are sure there is no justice to be had. The courts, the media, the police—everyone is colluding in the process, everyone has become communalized. There is a complete breakdown of institutions that make a democracy; everyone is on their own. So people start taking the law into their own hands—ranging from lynching to 'terror attacks'.

Much of the debate on tackling terror is centred on India being a soft or a hard state. Is that a solution?

POTA,[1] TADA,[2] the Chattisgarh Public Security Act[3]—none of these are meant for nailing terrorists and do not have a good record of doing so. They are only useful for polarizing society further, criminalizing democratic space and silencing those who ask questions of the state.

'The Terror Puzzle' first appeared in Tehelka.

With elections nearing, there is a charged political climate in which the attacks are taking place. How do you read this?

I was struck by an interview [Congress leader] Digvijay Singh recently gave *Tehelka*.[4] It is the first time that a leading political leader has said that we don't know who these terrorists are, and given the timing of the attacks, who stands to gain. The wrong people are being picked up and even when the proof is furnished, no one wants to know who the real perpetrators are. Or if they do know, they are covering up.

Take the Indian Mujahideen. Is it a front for an existing terrorist group or a figment of the imagination of counter-insurgency operations? The point is, a situation has been created where, if it did exist, it wouldn't surprise. You are consistently putting out the message that be it Sikhs or, now, the Christians in Orissa—people cannot expect justice. The most dangerous thing in all this is that the BJP is trying to forge a Hindu-majority vote and is radicalizing the minorities—it is only in India that one can deem 200 million people a minority. This can certainly destroy the country. This is not just a danger to India, it is a danger to the whole world. You are radicalizing an entire generation who feel and know that there is no recourse. Some will put their heads down and suffer; all will not. The thing about terrorism is that it just wants to destroy; it wants to take something down. It is not revolutionary politics. Ask the security forces in Kashmir—it takes 700,000 people to hold such a small valley down, how are you going to do that to an entire country?

But much of what's going on in the immediate context has to do with elections. I assume the Congress will flounder and weakly arrive at the same conclusions as the BJP. Even by its own standards, the BJP is moving from a benign force to an era of malignancy. And we will have to face the consequences of this not just in India but internationally. There is a fire in the ducts. We have to come at it in a more systemic way.

How should one respond to SIMI? *Tehelka* has done a very

tricky investigation which proves that the government's existing case against SIMI does not hold water and many innocent Muslims have been victimized in its name.[5] Yet they are obviously a highly conservative and fundamentalist Islamist organization.

The rhetoric of SIMI should be seen and treated in the same continuum as the Bajrang Dal's. But no matter how much you dislike their ideology, you cannot substitute building evidence with lazy bludgeoning. I don't think mere outlawing works either. Once again, the cornerstone is justice. If the Bajrang Dal, VHP or SIMI knew that they were up against a justice and police system that was professional and unbiased, they would hesitate before doing something that involves violence. That's how societies are sustained. But we are creating a situation where one set of people know that even if they rape and burn people alive, and even if there is enough evidence that they have done so, they will walk free. And another set of people know that they have no hope of justice. The result of this may not be revolution, but there definitely will be a destruction of everything you took for granted. Because a radicalized minority may not be able to elect a government or effect a revolution, but it can certainly destroy a country and be a threat to the whole world.

There is a legitimate frustration with state agencies for not being able to preempt attacks or find the culprits. What do you think are the problems they face?

The heart of the matter is, there seems to be no real desire to get to the bottom of things. Time and again, it has been proved that a lot of lies are being told to us. After the parliament attack case, half a million soldiers were moved to the border, 800 soldiers died in that mobilization, we were at the brink of a nuclear war—all of that based on a clot of lies. Now, there's *Tehelka*'s SIMI investigation. Yet, every time, those who expose the lies are deemed anti-national and are blocked, but no attempt is made to nail the right guys, or disprove the lie. This lack of curiosity on the state's part to unearth who the real perpetrators are sets off a whole lot of thoughts. Why is it so impossible to conclusively prove who the Indian Mujahideen is? All we have are unexamined theories. Perhaps, the state doesn't really want to get to the bottom of these things.

'You are radicalizing an entire generation who feel and know that there is no recourse. Some will put their heads down and suffer; all will not. The thing about terrorism is that it just wants to destroy; it wants to take something down. It is not revolutionary politics.

'By most standards, I probably qualify for being an anti-national. I don't have a nationalistic bone in my body. It's just not my instinct. Yet it's inconceivable for me to not be here, because it contains everything that I love.'

TEN YEARS ON ...

IN CONVERSATION WITH SHOMA CHAUDHURY, MARCH 2008.

It's been ten years now. Looking back, what did the Booker do to you?

It's a little difficult for me to say because the Booker is conflated with so much else. From the moment I finished the manuscript, everything took off at such a trajectory—the Booker was just a part of it. I suppose it formalized it all, in a way. It was simultaneously a release and a burden. On the one hand, the artificiality got to me. It was almost as if I was supposed to turn into a boy scout and go home with the big prize and show it to Mummy. On the other hand, 'Booker Prize winner' became my middle name. Now I don't think about it much.

But didn't it open up your world and forge new platforms?

Do you think so? I don't know how much of that was the Booker and how much *The God of Small Things*. In my mind, they're very separate. What's interesting to me is that after ten years of a very intense political journey, my political instincts are the same as they were in *The God of Small Things*. And that has to do with what the book was grappling within itself. The Booker is an Anglo-centric prize, it means something in the English-speaking world, but *The God of Small Things* exists in forty languages. India, of course, has become such a success-oriented and prize-thirsty culture, in so many advertisements and in everyone's dreams everyone's always winning a prize, and so, it mattered here, enormously, to the middle class.

'Ten Years On ...' first appeared in Tehelka.

But I feel vaguely humiliated in having to discuss a prize in more depth than my own book.

Yes, the real magic carpet was the book. So, across continents, what did people respond to?

It is remarkable. It was exactly the opposite of what nuclear weapons do; how they divide people and countries and set them against each other. It vaulted over so many cultures. In Estonia, my translator said, 'You know, this was my childhood too.' In America, this bank of cool women editors would say with a drawl, 'You know, we've all got aunts like Baby Kochamma [mimicking].' People tell me they've read out passages at their weddings ... One of the sweetest things happened while I was sitting at home one day. This little man came up the stairs like some tropical Santa Claus with a lot of presents and said, 'Mai Eagle flasks se aya hoon.' And he had all these Eagle products, Flask of the Week, Mug of the Month and this brochure with all the parts in the *God of Small Things* where Eagle flasks are mentioned [laughs]! I was particularly amused because I remember when I wrote: 'Esthappen and Rahel walked across the airport car park with their Eagle flasks bumping around their hips. The twins knew the eagles watched the world by day and flew around their flasks at night ...'—for some reason it delighted me. I waltzed around the room for hours because I was so happy at thinking this thought. I was sure no one would notice it; it would mean nothing to the world, but it made me happy and that was enough. And now, here was this little man!

There have been many unusual receptions like that. Even today I get letters that just turn my heart. Someone wrote to me from the former Yugoslavia talking about the NATO bombing and said, 'My hair turned white during the horror and then I read your book and it helped me through the war ...' Things like that. Sometimes it's not the novel, sometimes it's the political writing. But it's all something for people to have; it's not meant for anything else. But my work is for people to have and to hold and to read and go to sleep at night; it's for people to be with themselves. Very often, I get taken aback by people who come and start telling me the most intimate things about their lives. It throws me because I don't know them. But it's to do with the writing. They feel they know you. It's different from being a star; it's very, very deep. Very, very wonderful. And it's not about me, but about writing itself and ideas and stories. As a writer, the clay you work with is so intimate ...

It spawns a million relationships with itself ...

Yes, and till today it fills me with delight because oddly enough, however I might appear to people, I did grow up in a little village like the one in the book and the fact that that story has such a universal resonance means a lot to me. Some people resonate to the political stuff, the caste politics, the Naxalism; others fix on the children's world; some resonate to all of it. And I love that. But I always used to say, I wish I could've been paid back in meals or movie tickets or something because the thing that complicated my life very deeply—far more than the Booker prize—was the commercial success of the book. That made me have to deal with something I never anticipated or sought, and being as political as I am, it was very difficult.

But didn't it free you too?

Of course, part of the reason I can write and think the way I do is because I don't really have to earn my keep any more. Even my political writing has certainly been informed or has emerged from that—that sense that I can be a mobile republic. But you have to be very careful about being that free—because everybody isn't, and you have to understand that. I do try and understand that I have a freedom that isn't available to other people. I see it as a very delicate thing, because it can make you arrogant or stupid or disconnected. If you see things politically though, you run less of a risk. I think it was very important that *The God of Small Things* came out in '97, and soon after that, in '98, there were the nuclear tests. So that whole trajectory coincided with something dark that began here.

The two together put me on a path that I didn't entirely control. You would imagine that if you had written a book that won a big prize and earned a lot of money that you'd be in control of your life, but I'm still very ambiguous about what I've done. I can't settle on it in any way.

Because the flight was so stupendous, was there any point when you lost your bearings or were pulled out of yourself?

I was lucky on several counts. I wasn't a teenager when it happened. I had been through quite a lot. So I wasn't willing to blush when everyone was clapping. I was already sceptical and embarrassed and ambiguous about it. I never walked out and embraced it. Sometimes I wish I had …

… More frothily enjoyed it.

Yes [laughing]. I was always prickly about it, always looking at it sideways and laterally … [pauses]. No, it devastated my life in many ways, which was not nice. I am somebody who doesn't—I don't come from the bosom of some stable family, I didn't have any stability. All I had were relationships I have forged myself, in many of which I was the waif, the most vulnerable person. And suddenly, I was loaded with all of this and it just changes your equation. On top of this came the fact that I never really had a choice of not coming out and saying the things I said politically because the nuclear tests happened. And as I've said a million times—to not say something is as political as to say something. But the moment you do that, you are in another universe, you are spinning away. I remember having a dream once—this hand coming and picking me out of the water and holding me up and saying, 'You can have anything that you want, what do you want?' And me saying, 'Just let me go, I don't want to be this.' Because you are scared of everything moving around you. Everything. Every intimate relationship. Yet because those relationships were forged in art and politics and so on, they are all relationships with wise people.

Everybody in my life had to deal with all this, not just me. And we did manage. All my old friends are still my friends. I was shot out of a cannon but I came and landed right back here. It's not like I wanted to live in LA.

At the same time, a whole new universe of friends and deep relationships have been formed. But it took a lot out of me. It took a lot of balancing. To suddenly be that public and that scrutinized, you have to be that much harder on yourself. And the more political you are, the more difficult it is. You have to search inside yourself for your own levels of what is acceptable, not live by other people's ideas.

Also, there was this other interesting combination of being a writer and—what does a writer do? A writer hones his or her language, makes it as clear and private and individual as possible. And then you look around and see what's happening to millions of people. You find yourself in the heart of the crowd, saying things that millions of people are saying and it's not private and individual any more. How do you hold those two things down? These are very fundamental questions. This is why so many writers are frightened of political engagement. They feel it is a risk, and it *is* a risk, and yet I would rather do it than not.

But sometimes it's a big struggle. There's always something happening, something that needs intervening in, and I run the risk of becoming someone more responsible than I ought to be. Before I wrote on the Parliament attack, I had literally sworn to myself, told myself a hundred times to pull back and work on something else.[3] But as I watched the news and the glee with which people were talking about the rope that would be used to hang Mohammed Afzal, and how much it weighed, and where it came from, I felt nauseous. I thought, I know all this is a lie, the whole case is fabricated, I'd been following it for a while—they'll hang him and if I don't write now I'll never be able to live with myself. John Berger once said to me, something is gathering in our world, something dark, but you have to find a way to get off the tiger. I keep saying I will, but I have failed to do that. It's a very big dilemma for me. Very, very big dilemma. I know that urgent intervention is important. So is the other thing. Perhaps more so. How do you handle it? I am at a loss to know.

Speaking of loss, did you outgrow any key relationships?

No. I am a loyalist. Some of the most profound conversations I've had have to do with the fact that if you grow and burst out of the confines of whatever was prepared for you and yet none of those things were superficial, none of those affections were superficial, how do you find a way of holding on to that and yet free yourself? To me, that's a very fundamental thing, because it's very easy to just walk away from everything.

But I struggled to find ways. I said, why does it have to be so conventional? Why must we be so consumerist even about our relationships [laughs]? I could've gone anywhere—I'm not totally unhedonistic, but I would like to look for it here, I would like to look for happiness—in whatever brief moments that it comes to anybody—I would like it to be here. It's important to recognize what the sources of happiness are. Even politically when I write, I think it's very important to place yourself in the picture, even if it makes you uncomfortable and to know that there isn't anything that's pristine about anybody. People who act most pristine are the most suspect.

What did *The God of Small Things* mean for you personally? What did you take pleasure in?

You know, when you're writing fiction, the world is different because you, sort of, come home with sentences like other people come home with shopping [laughs]. The process of writing is the process of sharpening your thought and that's the only thing that makes me really happy, regardless of what effect it has or what people think about it. And because writing is the same as thinking, everything in your body settles when you write. Eventually it's about something settling inside yourself. I am a person who's always slightly fearful of what might happen because, I think, when you have an unsafe childhood you never really settle, no matter how old you get. So for me, there are some things—like the four years when I wrote *The God of Small Things*, structured it, honed it, polished it—nobody can take that privilege away from me, no matter what happens now, nobody can say those four years didn't happen. Or that that book wasn't written. So for a long time, I didn't feel the need to come back home with sentences. But now again I feel that. I feel life has been lived for ten years at some reckless, breakneck, rock-star speed, in terms of experiences and stimulus and understanding and looking at something till your eyeballs hurt and internalizing that politics and living enough to write again.

Is the 'lived life' important in writing fiction? Is it important to process the personal?

If we didn't, it would be tragic. But I am not talking about gratuitous confession. The kind of writing I would respect is not about gratuitous individualization where each person is special and we all wear baby T-shirts saying, 'I'm Someone Special'. I think if you can see the world through a person, if you can see that there isn't anybody who is really not a product of their history and culture and who is not in the cross-hairs of many big guns that are booming—I would respect a writer who can see that, a writer who can scale from the personal to the other stuff, the epic. Every book doesn't have to be about everything. The point is, can you take a risk? When I wrote *The God of Small Things*, I didn't think it would make sense to anybody, but whether it makes sense to 300 people or six million people, it was still the same book.

Did it release you from some of the demons of your childhood?

The first time my brother read it, he said, 'What happened to all the monsters? Why are they missing?' So it wasn't really about my childhood, I haven't really written about that—maybe sometime one will. The idea wasn't to be therapeutic. For me, it was more important to see each person has got this trajectory behind him or her—that there's history at work, politics at work, and yet there's tenderness and it's totally personal.

There was such a detailed sense of place in *The God of Small Things*. Do you still think of it as home?

There is a very particular sense of place in the book, but it is imbued with dread. I don't think that can ever change. Someone remarked to me that everyone in the book is somehow homeless, spewed out from somewhere else. That sort of dysfunctionality is very much part of my make-up.

Is there a very different you that's writing the new novel?

I wonder in the new fiction what will change and what will stay. I don't want to write *The God of Small Things* again [laughs]. But I'm not one of those people who has radically changed. I function on instinct and that doesn't change. I suppose the sense of loss is relocated. It's not the village I grew up in and was terrorized by. That sense of dislocation has been relocated to another place [laughs]. There's such a polarization and hardening of things in the world around. There are other languages in my head now. It is not the English-speaking world I move in all that much any more, even though I do think it's necessary to engage with it and not lose that feeling of continuing to journey between these worlds. Less and less of us are doing that. But I'm uncomfortable talking about the new book in any specific way.

Last question. About sense of place: is it people who keep you here, or for all your being a 'mobile republic', does something really connect you to India?

By most standards, I probably qualify for being an anti-national. I don't have a nationalistic bone in my body. It's just not my instinct. Yet it's inconceivable for me to not be here, because it contains everything that I love. And it's not to do with flags or constitutions or any of that. But if I go away for even one week when I come back and see some shabby Zee TV show in the immigration lounge and the mouldering ceiling, I just feel so happy. It's just so many things—the quality of light, the raggedness, the food, the language, the jokes, everything—it's not even external. I'm just a full desi—a full-time desi in that way. I just feel, where else can I be? Where else can I interpret the darkness and all its layers? There are all the coded jokes and the whole sense of history ... It's not like one is looking to buy a slick new life in a supermarket.

NOTES

SCIMITARS IN THE SUN

1. See 'The Supreme Court Judgements', online at <http://www.narmada.org/sardar-sarovar/sc.ruling/index.html#judgements>.
2. See Bharat Dogra, 'Private Hydro Project on Narmada River Halted', *Asia Water Wire*, online at <http://www.asiawaterwire.net/node/359>. See also, 'A Temple Too Far', *New Internationalist*, online at <http://www.newint.org/issue336/temple.htm>.
3. L.C. Jain, *Dam Vs Drinking Water*, 2001, Parisar, New Delhi.
4. See Ramaswamy Iyer, 'Narmada Project: The Points at Issue', *The Hindu*, 13 April 2006, online at <http://www.hindu.com/2006/04/13/stories/2006041304250800.htm>.
5. For full text of the Narmada Water Disputes Tribunal Award, visit <http://www.sscac.gov.in/NWDT.pdf>.
6. R. Rangachari et al, *Large Dams: India's Experience*, 2000, a WCD case study prepared as an input to the World Commission on Dams, Cape Town, online at <http://www.dams.org/docs/kbase/studies/csinmain.pdf>.
7. See Virender Kumar, 'Gujarat War Cry: Panel on World Be Damned', *Indian Express*, 11 September 1998. Online at <http://www.indianexpress.com/res/web/pIe/ie/daily/19980911/25450034.html>.
8. See World Commission on Dams, *Dams and Development: A New Framework for Decision-Making*, 2000, Earthscan Publications Ltd, London and Sterling, Virginia. For full text of the report visit <http://www.dams.org//docs/report/wcdreport.pdf>.
9. Arundhati Roy, *The God of Small Things*, 2002, Penguin Books India, New Delhi.
10. Arundhati Roy, 'The End of Imagination', *The Algebra of Infinite Justice*, 2002, Penguin Books India, New Delhi.
11. See Ramachandra Guha, 'The Arun Shourie of the Left', *The Hindu*, 26 November 2000, online at <http://www.hindu.com/2000/11/26/stories/13260411.htm>.

12. See Chittaroopa Palit, 'The Historian as Gatekeeper', *Frontline*, Volume 17, Issue 26, 23 December 2000–05 January 2001, online at <http://www.frontlineonnet.com/fl1726/17261160.htm>.
13. Ramachandra Guha, *Savaging the Civilized: Verrier Elwin, His Tribals, and India*, 1999, University of Chicago Press, Chicago.
14. Madhav Gadgil and Ramachandra Guha, *This Fissured Land: An Ecological History of India*, 1992, University of California Press, Berkeley.
15. Madhav Gadgil and Ramachandra Guha, *Ecology and Equity: The Use and Abuse of Nature in Contemporary India*, 1995, Routledge, London.
16. Patrick McCully, *Silenced Rivers: The Ecology and Politics of Large Dams*, 1996, Zed Books, London.
17. See Arundhati Roy, 'The Greater Common Good', *The Algebra of Infinite Justice*, 2002, Penguin Books India, New Delhi, p. 136.
18. See Arundhati Roy, 'Power Politics', *The Algebra of Infinite Justice*, 2002, Penguin Books India, New Delhi p. 143.
19. See Ramachandra Guha, 'Perils of Extremism', *The Hindu*, 17 December 2000, online at <http://www.hindu.com/2000/12/17/stories/1317061b.htm>.
20. Rahul Ram, *Muddy Waters: A Critical Assessment of the Benefits of the Sardar Sarovar Project*, 1993, Kalpavriksh, Pune.
21. Arundhati Roy, 'The End of Imagination', *The Algebra of Infinite Justice*, 2002, Penguin Books India, New Delhi.
22. See Arundhati Roy, 'The Cost of Living', *Frontline*, Volume 17, Issue 03, 5–8 February 2000, online at <http://www.flonnet.com/fl1703/17030640.htm>.
23. See Ramachandra Guha, 'Perils of Extremism', *The Hindu*, 17 December 2000, online at <http://www.hindu.com/2000/12/17/stories/1317061b.htm>.
24. Arundhati Roy, *The God of Small Things*, 2002, Penguin Books India, New Delhi, p. 306.

THE COLONIZATION OF KNOWLEDGE

1. Nirmal Ghosh, 'Indian Caste Killings Put Rule of Law to Test', *The Straits Times* (Singapore), 10 August 2001, p. 13.
2. Arundhati Roy, *Power Politics*, 2nd ed., 2001, South End Press, Cambridge.
3. The Communist Party of India came to power in Kerala in 1957.
4. 'The Reproduction Function', *The Economist,* 8 January 1977, p. 72.

5. Arundhati Roy, *The God of Small Things*, 2002, Penguin Books India, New Delhi.
6. The essays were published in 1993 and 1994 in the now-defunct *Sunday*.
7. Abhay Mehta, *Power Play: A Study of the Enron Project*, 2000, Orient Longman, Hyderabad, p. 3.
8. See Arundhati Roy, 'Power Politics: The Reincarnation of Rumpelstiltskin', in *Power Politics*, 2nd ed., pp. 35–86, an updated version of an essay originally published in *Outlook*, 27 November 2000. See also Arundhati Roy, *The Cost of Living*, 1999, Flamingo.
9. 'India: Historians Flay Bid to Communalise History', *The Hindu*, 7 November 2001, online at <http://www.hinduonnet.com/2001/11/07/stories/02070008.htm>.
10. Arundhati Roy, *The God of Small Things*, 2002, Penguin Books India, New Delhi.
11. Arundhati Roy, 'The Greater Common Good', in *The Cost of Living*, 1999, Flamingo.
12. See The Friends of River Narmada, 'The Sardar Sarovar Dam: A Brief Introduction', <http://www.narmada.org/ sardarsarovar. html>; 'Sardar Sarovar Project—Denial of Rights!' <http://www.narmada.org/sardar-sarovar/rr.feb 2002. html>; and 'Who Pays? Who Profits? A Short Guide to the Sardar Sarovar Project', <http://www.narmada.org/sardar-sarovar/faq/whopays.htm>.
13. Bradford Morse et al., *Sardar Sarovar: The Report of the Independent Review*, 1992, Resource Futures International, Ottawa. See also Robert Marquand, 'Indian Dam Protests Evoke Gandhi', *Christian Science Monitor*, 5 August 1999, p. 1.
14. C.V.J. Sharma, ed., *Modern Temples of India: Selected Speeches of Jawaharlal Nehru at Irrigation and Power Projects*, 1989, Central Board of Irrigation and Power, Delhi, pp. 40–49.
15. R. Rangachari et al, *Large Dams: India's Experience*, 2000, a WCD Case study prepared as an input to the World Commission on Dams, online at <http://www.dams.org/docs/kbase/studies/csinmain.pdf>.
16. World Commission on Dams, *Dams and Development: A New Framework for Decision-Making*, Earthscan Publications Ltd, London and Sterling, Virginia. For full text of the report visit <http://www.dams.org//docs/report/wcdreport.pdf>.
17. Arundhati Roy, *The Cost of Living*, 1999, Flamingo, p. 8.
18. In 2001, according to United Nations statistics, 72.1 per cent of

India's population was rural and India ranked 127th in the Human Development Index. United Nations Development Program (UNDP), *Human Development Indicators 2003*, Table 5 (Demographic Trends): Urban Population (as % of Total), <http://www.undp.org/hdr2003/indicator/indic_41_1_1.html>.

19. Arundhati Roy, 'The End of Imagination', in *The Cost of Living*, 1999, Flamingo.
20. Jason Burke, 'Kashmir Feels Heat of Summer War', *The Observer*, 6 June 1999, p. 29.
21. Jonathan Braude, 'Little Hitler Calls Shots', *South China Morning Post*, 13 November 1995, p. 19; Peter Popham, 'Why Indian Nationalists Would Love to Massacre St. Valentine's Day', *The Independent*, 14 February 2002, p. 16; and Peter Popham, 'Valentine's Day Sullies Hindu Ways', *The Independent*, 13 February 2001, p. 14.
22. Arundhati Roy, *Power Politics*, 2nd ed., 2001, South End Press, Cambridge, pp. 2–3.
23. Christopher Thomas, 'Villages of the Dammed', *The Times*, 11 May 1991.
24. For more details, see Arundhati Roy, 'Democracy: Who Is She When She Is at Home', in *War Talk*, 2003, South End Press, Cambridge, pp. 17–44.

TERROR AND THE MADDENED KING

1. Simon Holden, 'Booker Winner Faces Morality Case in India', Press Association Limited, 15 October 1997.
2. Aradhana Seth, *DAM/AGE: A Film with Arundhati Roy*, 2003, First Run/Icarus Films, New York. Originally produced for the BBC 4, London, and aired April 2002.
3. Arundhati Roy, 'Come September', in *War Talk*, 2003, South End Press, Cambridge, p. 46.
4. Michael Moore, *Bowling for Columbine*, 2003, Metro-Goldwyn-Mayer, New York.
5. Arundhati Roy, *War Talk*, 2003, South End Press, p. 52.
6. Arundhati Roy, *War Talk*, 2003, South End Press, p. 49.
7. Claudio Alvares, 'The Bhopal Gas Disaster: Fresh Outrage', *Third World Resurgence* 143–44 (July-August 2002), pp. 12–13. See also Sabrina Jones, 'Survivors Pressure Dow on Bhopal Aftermath', *Washington Post*, 7 May 2002, p. E6.

8. 'MP Govt. Misused Relief Funds', *The Statesman*, 22 February 2001.
9. Arundhati Roy, *Power Politics*, 2003, South End Press, Cambridge, p. 138.
10. The White House, *The National Security Strategy of the United States of America*, The White House, Washington DC, 17 September 2002, online at <http://www.whitehouse.gov/nsc/nss.html>. Madeleine Albright quoted in Noam Chomsky, 'US Iraq Policy: Motives and Consequences', in *Iraq Under Siege: The Deadly Impact of Sanctions and War*, 2002, 2nd ed., South End Press, Cambridge, p. 72.
11. Cited in Noam Chomsky, *Hegemony or Survival: America's Quest for Global Dominance*, 2003, Metropolitan, New York, p. 190.
12. Churchill quoted in Editorial, 'Scurrying Toward Bethlehem', *New Left Review*, 2nd series (July/August 2001), p. 9, n. 5.
13. Arundhati Roy, *Power Politics*, 2nd ed., 2001, South End Press, Cambridge, p. 145.

DEVELOPMENT NATIONALISM

1. Noam Chomsky, *For Reasons of State*, updated ed., Introduction by Arundhati Roy, 2003, New Press, New York.
2. Dan Morrison, 'India's "Patriot Act" Comes Under Scrutiny', *Christian Science Monitor*, 30 October 2003, p. 7. See also Akshaya Mukul, '12-Year-Old Boy Arrested under POTA', *The Economic Times of India*, 21 February 2003. See also Teesta Setalvad, 'Do We Need Another TADA?' *The Times of India*, 23 July 2000.
3. Nirmal Ghosh, 'New Delhi Mall Shootout: Police Credibility On Line', *The Straits Times*, 9 November 2002. See also Agence France-Presse, 'Pakistan Says Indian Mall Clash Fake, Refuses to Collect Bodies', 11 November 2002.
4. On 29 October 2003, Geelani was freed, after nearly two years in jail, when a New Delhi appeals court overturned his conviction. See Edward Luce, 'Indian Court Quashes Academic's Terror Conviction', *Financial Times*, 30 October 2003, p. 13. See also Morrison, 'India's "Patriot Act" Comes Under Scrutiny', *Christian Science Monitor*, 30 October 2003, p. 7. Amnesty International, 'India: Open Letter to Law Minister about the Trial of Abdul Rehman Geelani and Three Others', 8 July 2002 (AI Index: ASA 20/011/2002 (Public), News Service No: 116), online at http://web.amnesty.org/library/index/ENGASA200112002>.

5. Hina Kausar Alam and P. Balu, 'J&K [Jammu and Kashmir] Fudges DNA Samples to Cover Up Killings', *The Times of India*, 7 March 2002.
6. Amy Waldman, 'A Web Site in India that Revealed Graft Becomes a Target', *New York Times*, 13 February 2003, p. A5. See also Celia W. Dugger, 'Bribery Scandal Engrosses TV Viewers in India', *New York Times*, 24 March 2001, p. A3.
7. Luke Harding, 'Act of Desecration which Changed the Face of Indian Politics', *Guardian*, 1 March 2002, p. 19; John F. Burns, 'A Decade After Massacre, Some Sikhs Find Justice', *New York Times*, 16 September 1996, p. A4.
8. Arundhati Roy, *War Talk*, 2003, South End Press, Cambridge, pp. 17–44.
9. Agence France-Presse, 'India, Enron Deny Payoff Charges Over Axed Project', 7 August 1995.
10. Arundhati Roy, *Power Politics*, 2nd ed., 2001, South End Press, Cambridge, p. 138.
11. Arundhati Roy, *The Cost of Living*, pp. 50–51; Usha Ramanathan, 'Along the Narmada...', Report of Public Hearings (*Jan Sunvayi*) from the Narmada Valley, 13–15 July 2002, online at <www.narmada.org/sardar-sarovar/jan.sunvayi.report.pdf>; Christopher Kremmer, 'The Flood of Outrage', *Sydney Morning Herald*, 4 September 1999, p. 6.
12. World Commission on Dams, *Dams and Development: A New Framework for Decision-Making*, 2000, Earthscan Publications Ltd, London and Sterling, Virginia. Stewart Fleming, 'Damning of the World's Dam-Builders', *Evening Standard*, 16 November 2000, p. 45; Phil Williams and Patrick McCully, 'Lies, Damn Lies', *Guardian*, 22 November 2000, p. 8; Phil Williams, 'Poor Are Sold Down the River', *Manchester Guardian Weekly*, 13 December 2000, p. 26.
13. Sanjay Kak, *Words on Water*, 2002.
14 George Eliot, *Felix Holt, the Radical*, 1980, OUP, New York, p. 58.
15. 'Speed Up Linking of Major Rivers: Supreme Court Tells Government', *Times of India*, 1 November 2002. See also Medha Patkar and L.S. Aravinda, 'Interlinking Mirages', *The Hindu*, 3 December 2002; Manoj Mitta, 'The River Sutra', *Indian Express*, 1 March 2003.
16. Atal Behari Vajpayee quoted in Celia W. Dugger, 'India Reacts With Anger to a Speech by Pakistani', *New York Times*, 7 February 2002, p. A9.
17. Amy Waldman, 'New Government in Kashmir Brings Hope for Peace', *New York Times*, 3 November 2002.

18. 'Nobel laureate Amartya Sen may think that health and education are the reasons why India has lagged behind in development in the past 50 years, but I think it is because of defence,' said L.K. Advani. See 'Quote of the Week, Other Voices', *India Today*, 17 June 2002, p. 13.
19. 'VHP Calls Advani a Pseudo-Secularist', *The Hindu*, 20 November 2002.
20. Raj Chengappa and Malini Goyal, 'Housekeepers to the World', *India Today*, 18 November 2002, online at <http://www.india-today.com/itoday/20021118/cover.shtml>.
21. Noam Chomsky, *Hegemony or Survival: America's Quest for Global Dominance*, 2003, Metropolitan, New York, p. 225–32.
22. Arundhati Roy, *Power Politics*, 2nd ed., 2001, South End Press, Cambridge, p. 30.
23. Frederick Douglass, 'The Significance of Emancipation in the West Indies', in *The Frederick Douglass Papers, Series One: Speeches, Debates, and Interviews, Volume 3: 1855–63*, ed. John W. Blassingamem, 1985, Yale University Press, New Haven, p. 204.
24. Muhammed Iqbal, *Bang-i-Dara* (1924), in *Kulliyat-e-Iqbal*, 1975, Aligarh Book Depot, India, p. 278. Translated by David Barsamian.
25. Prayas (Initiatives in Health, Energy, Learning and Parenthood), Pune, India, <http://www.prayaspune.org/>. See Rasika Dhavse, 'Determined Efforts, Definite Direction', November 2002, Indiatogether.org, online at <http://www.indiatogether.org/stories/2002/rdl102.htm>.
26. Martin Luther King, Jr., 'Beyond Vietnam', 4 April 1967. In Martin Luther King, Jr., Martin Luther King Papers Project at Stanford University, Stanford, California, online at <http://www. stanford.edu/group/King/publications/speeches/Beyond_Vietnam.pdf>.
27. Martin Luther King, Jr., 'Letter from Birmingham Jail', 16 April 1963. In Martin Luther King, Jr., Martin Luther King Papers Project at Stanford University, Stanford, California, online at <http://www.stanford.edu/group/King/popular_requests/frequentdocs/>.
28. 'US Treasury Secretary Rubs It In: Reform, Reform and Reform', *Indian Express*, 22 November 2002.
29. Lee Walczak and Richard S. Dunham, 'Corporate Crime: Why It's Not Sticking to Republicans', *Business Week*, 7 October 2002, p. 57.
30. Howard Zinn, *Terrorism and War*, ed. Anthony Arnove, 2002, Seven Stories Press, New York, p. 55.

31. See Ashutosh Varshney, 'Doomed from Within,' *Newseek*, 18 March 2002, p. 29. See also Maria Misra, 'Religious Bigotry Is Poisoning Indian Democracy', *Financial Times*, 4 March 2003, p. 19.
32. Ben H. Bagdikian, *The Media Monopoly*, 6th ed., 2000, Beacon Press, Boston.
33. See Bhaskar Roy, 'Censor Board Bombards Peace Film', *The Times of India*, 23 June 2002.
34. Noam Chomsky, *9-11*, ed. Greg Ruggiero, 2001, Seven Stories Press, New York.
35. Thomas Babington Macaulay, 'Minute of 2 February 1835 on Indian Education', *Prose and Poetry*, ed. G.M. Young, 1952, Harvard University Press, Cambridge, pp. 721–29.
36. *The New Yorker*, 23 and 30 June 1997.
37. See Arundhati Roy, 'The Cost of Living', *Frontline*, Volume 17, Issue 03, 5–8 February 2000, online at <http://www.flonnet.com/fl1703/17030640.htm>.
38. Rashme Sehgal, 'Female Foeticide Leaves Haryanvi Grooms Abegging', *The Times of India*, 10 November 2002.
39. Nargis is quoted in Salman Rushdie, 'India's Courts Flounder as Dam Pressure Builds', *Guardian*, 11 August 2001, p. 14.

GLOBALIZATION OF DISSENT

1. 'Stray Incidents Take Gujarat Toll to 544', *The Times of India*, 5 March 2002.
2. 'Chinese Steel Firm Buys 50,000 Tonnes of World Trade Center Scrap', Agence France-Presse, 23 January 2002. See 'WTC Scrap at Gujarat Port Awaits Toxicity Test', *Indian Express*, 17 April 2002. See also L.H. Naqvi, 'Workers Exposed to Toxic Ship Scrap', *Tribune*, 2 June 2003, online at <http://www.tribuneindia.com/2003/20030602/biz. htm#l>. Rinku Pegu, 'WTC Wreckage for India: Exporting Toxins', 1 February 2002, Tehelka.com, online at <http://www.tehelka.com/channels/currentaffairs/2002/feb/1/printabl/ca20102wtcpr.htm>.
3. See, for example, Niall Ferguson, 'Welcome the New Imperialism', *Guardian*, 31 October 2001, p. 20, and Niall Ferguson, *Empire: The Rise and Demise of the British World Order and the Lesson for Global Power*, 2003, Basic Books, New York.
4. Thomas L. Friedman, 'Bored With Baghdad—Already', *New York*

Times, 18 May 2003, p. 4: 13.

5. Arundhati Roy, *War Talk*, 2003, South End Press, Cambridge, p. 111.
6. Andrew H. Card quoted in Elisabeth Bumiller, 'Bush Aides Set Strategy to Sell Policy on Iraq', *New York Times*, 7 September 2002, p. Al. See Arundhati Roy, *War Talk*, 2003, South End Press, Cambridge, p. 66.
7. Paul Wolfowitz quoted in Walter Pincus, 'Syria Warned Again Not to "Meddle" in Iraq', *Washington Post*, 11 April 2003, p. A37.
8. Arundhati Roy, interview by Anthony Arnove, 'The Outline of the Beast', *Socialist Worker*, 13 April 2003, pp. 6–7, online at <http://www.socialistworker.org/2003-1/449/449_06_ArundhatiRoy.shtml>.
9. Elizabeth Becker, 'Feeding Frenzy Underway, as Companies from All Over Seek a Piece of the Action', *New York Times*, 21 May 2003.
10. Nicholas Kristof, 'Bigotry in Islam—and Here', *New York Times*, 9 July 2002, p. A21. Jerry Falwell, interviewed by Bob Simon, *60 Minutes II*, 6 October 2002.
11. Sanjeev Miglani, 'Opposition Keeps Up Heat on Government Over Riots', Reuters, 16 April 2002.
12. Michael Ledeen quoted in Jonah Goldberg, 'Baghdad Delenda Est, Part Two: Get On With It', *National Review*, 23 April 2002, online at <http://www.nationalreview.com/goldberg/goldberg042302.asp>.
13. Arundhati Roy, Press Conference sponsored by the Center for Economic and Social Rights, New York, 12 May 2003. See also Roy, 'Instant-Mix Imperial Democracy (Buy One, Get One Free)', New York, 13 May 2003, online at <http://www.cesr.org/arundhatiroytranscript>.
14. The White House, *The National Security Strategy of the United States of America,* Section VIII, 'Develop Agendas for Cooperative Action with the Other Main Centers of Global Power', <http://www.whitehouse.gov/nsc/nss.html>.

SEIZE THE TIME!

1. 'A System Suffocating the Majority', *International Socialist Review*, Issue 36, July–August 2004, online at <http://www.isreview.org/issues/36/roy.shtml>.
2. The US presidential election was held on 2 November 2004. George W. Bush, the candidate from the Republican Party defeated Democratic candidate John Kerry. The main issues on which the

election was fought were Bush's war on terrorism and the invasion of Iraq in 2003.

3. Arundhati Roy, 'Public Power in the Age of Empire', *Frontline*, Volume 21, Issue 21, 9–22 October 2004, online at <http://www.hinduonnet.com/fline/fl2121/stories/20041022008300400.htm>.
4. Barbara Starr and Elise Labott, 'U.S. Calls off Search for Iraqi WMDs', CNN.com, 12 January 2005, online at <http://www.cnn.com/2005/US/01/12/wmd.search/>. See also, Sidney Blumenthal, 'Bush Knew Saddam Had No Weapons of Mass Destruction', salon.com, online at <http://www.salon.com/opinion/blumenthal/2007/09/06/bush_wmd/index.html>.
5. Luiz Inácio Lula da Silva, born on 27 October 1945, is the current president of Brazil, and a founding member of the Workers' Party (Partido dos Trabalhadores). Lula was elected to the post on 27 October 2002 with 61 per cent of the votes, and took office on 1 January 2003. On 29 October 2006, Lula was re-elected with more than 60 per cent of the votes.
6. Michael Ignatieff, 'The Burden', *New York Times* magazine, 5 January 2003.
7. Salman Rushdie, 'Anti-Americanism Has Taken the World by Storm', *Guardian*, 6 February 2002, online at <http://www.guardian.co.uk/afghanistan/comment/story/0,645579,00.html>.
8. Arundhati Roy, 'Do Turkeys Enjoy Thanksgiving?' in *An Ordinary Person's Guide to Empire*, 2006, Penguin Books India, New Delhi, p. 193.
9. Arundhati Roy, 'Terror and the Maddened King', in *The Checkbook and the Cruise Missile: Conversations with Arundhati Roy*, 2004, South End Press, Cambridge.
10. Ibid.
11. Pratap Chatterjee, 'Water Wars', CorpWatch.org, 1 May 2003, online at <http://www.corpwatch.org/article.php?id=6670>.
12. The Armed Forces (Special Powers) Act, 1958; Act 28 of 1958, 11 September 1958, online at <http://www.satp.org/satporgtp/countries/india/document/actandordinances/armed_forces_special_power_act_1958.htm>. See also, 'Armed Forces (Special Powers) Act: A Study in National Security Tyranny', South Asia Human Rights Documentation Centre, online at <http://www.hrdc.net/sahrdc/resources/armed_forces.htm>.
13. For more on the Terrorist and Disruptive Activities (Prevention) Act

(TADA), see <http://www.satp.org/satporgtp/countries/india/document/actandordinances/TADA.HTM>.

14. For full text of the USA Patriot Act see <http://epic.org/privacy/terrorism/hr3162.html>.
15. For full text of the Prevention of Terrorism Act, 2002, see <http://www.satp.org/satporgtp/countries/india/document/actandordinances/POTA.htm#7>.
16. Arundhati Roy, *An Ordinary Person's Guide to Empire*, 2006, Penguin Books India, New Delhi.
17. Michael Francis Moore is an American author and Academy Award-winning director and producer of three of the top five highest-grossing documentaries of all time: *Fahrenheit 9/11*, *Sicko*, and *Bowling for Columbine*. He was named one of the world's 100 most influential people by *Time* magazine in 2005.
18. Jehane Noujaim, *Control Room*, 2004. See, 'Director Interview', BBC, 5 August 2004, online at <http://www.bbc.co.uk/bbcfour/documentaries/storyville/jehane-noujaim.shtml>.
19. Arundhati Roy, 'The Algebra of Infinite Justice', in *The Algebra of Infinite Justice*, 2002, Penguin Books India, New Delhi, p. 217.
20. Kathy Kelly is an American peace activist and three-time Nobel Peace Prize nominee.
21. Voices in the Wilderness was founded in 1996 and has campaigned to end economic and military warfare against the Iraqi people. It has organized over seventy delegations to Iraq in deliberate violation of UN economic sanctions and US law. For more on Voices in the Wilderness visit <http://vitw.org/>.
22. A women's organization in Afghanistan that promotes women's rights and secular democracy, the Revolutionary Association of the Women of Afghanistan (RAWA) was founded in Kabul in 1977 by Meena Keshwar Kamal, a student activist who was assassinated in 1987 for her involvement in politics. For more on the RAWA and its activities visit <http://www.rawa.org/index.php>.
23. Arundhati Roy, *War Talk*, 2003, South End Press, Cambridge.

THE OUTLINE OF THE BEAST

1. See Denis J. Halliday, 'UN Sanctions Against Iraq Only Serve US Ambition', *Irish Times*, 11 August 2000.
2. See Samuel P. Huntington, *The Clash of Civilizations and the Remaking of World Order*, 1997, Touchstone, New York.

3. See Michael Ignatieff, 'The American Empire (Get Used to It)', *New York Times* magazine, 5 January 2003.
4. On 15 February 2003 there were coordinated protests against the imminent invasion of Iraq in approximately 800 cities around the world. According to BBC News, between 6 and 10 million people took part in protests in up to sixty countries over two days. Opposition to the war was highest in the Middle East, although protests there were relatively small. Mainland China was the only major region not to see any protests.

THE WAR THAT NEVER ENDS

1. See, 'Iran "Biggest Threat to Mid-East"', 31 July 2003, BBC News, online at <http://news.bbc.co.uk/2/hi/middle_east/6923430.stm>.
2. See, 'Iraq Work Helps Halliburton', 29 October 2003, www.cnnmoney.com, online at <http://money.cnn.com/2003/10/29/news/companies/halliburton_earns/index.htm>.
3. See David R. Segal and Mary W. Segal, 'Army Recruitment Goals Endangered as Percent of African-American Enlistees Declines', Population Reference Bureau, online at <http://www.prb.org/Articles/2005/ArmyRecruitmentGoalsEndangeredasPercentofAfricanAmericanEnlisteesDeclines.aspx>.
4. See, Ian Traynor, 'The Privatization of War', *Guardian*, 10 December 2003. See also, Antonia Juhasz, 'Bush's Other Iraq Invasion', 22 August 2005, online at <http://www.alternet.org/waroniraq/24307/>.
5. See Veterans against the Iraq War, online at <http://www.vaiw.org/vet/index.php>.

INDEPENDENCE DAY SPECIAL

1. See P.R. Brahmananda, 'The Poverty Controversy', *The Hindu Business Line*, 1 November 2000, online at <http://www.thehindubusinessline.com/2000/11/01/stories/040120ac.htm>.
2. The National Rural Employment Guarantee Act (NREGA) was enacted on 25 August 2005 by the United Progressive Alliance government. NREGA provides a legal guarantee for one hundred days of employment, at the statutory minimum wage, in every financial year to adult members of any rural household willing to do

unskilled manual work. For more details on NREGA see <http://nrega.nic.in/>.

3. For full text of the speech see, 'In Acceptance of an Honorary Degree from Oxford University on 8 July, 2005', *The Hindu*, online at <http://www.hinduonnet.com/thehindu/nic/0046/pmspeech.htm>.
4. See Chandrabhan Prasad, *Dalit Diary: 1999-2003, Reflections on Apartheid in India*, 2004, Navayana Publishing, Pondicherry.
5. See National Campaign on Dalit Human Rights (NCDHR) Resolution, 'Discrimination Based on Work and Descent', 2004, online at <http://www.dalits.org/Discrimination_work_descent.htm>.
6. See Naveen Jaganathan, 'The Gurgaon Riots', *Counterpunch*, 30 July 2005.
7. See Rehan Ansari, 'The News of a Kidnapping', *Chowk*, 18 May 1999.
8. Dahr Jamail, 'What Have We Done', 6 August 2005, Antiwar.com, online at <http://www.antiwar.com/jamail/?articleid=6893.
9. Arundhati Roy, *The God of Small Things*, 2002, Penguin Books India, New Delhi.

THE QUESTION OF VIOLENCE

1. See Tarun J. Tejpal, 'Sleaze, Senseless Greed and Dirty Heroes', 13 March 2004, Tehelka.com, online at <http://tehelka.com/home/20041009/operation/tarun.htm>. See also Avinash Dutt, 'Catching Up with Jaya Jaitly', 20 January 2007, Tehelka.com, online at <http://www.tehelka.com/story_main25.asp?filename=Ne012007Catching_up.asp>.
2. Shaad Ali, *Bunty aur Babli*, 2005.
3. See Shripad Dharmadhikary, 'Arundhati Roy Donates Booker Prize Amount to the Narmada Bachao Andolan', Narmada Bachao Andolan Press Release, 26 June 1999, online at <http://www.narmada.org/nba-press-releases/june-1999/booker.html>.
4. See Sydney Peace Foundation at <http://www.spf.arts.usyd.edu.au/index.shtml>. See also, Arundhati Roy, 'Sydney Peace Prize Lecture', 2004, online at <http://www.smh.com.au/news/Opinion/Roys-full-speech/2004/11/04/1099362264349.html>.

I HOPE KASHMIR WILL BE IN ALL THE BOOKS I WRITE ...

1. In 2005, a major earthquake measuring 7.6 to 7.7 on the Richter scale

hit Jammu and Kashmir, Pakistan and parts of Afghanistan. The epicentre was Pakistan-administered Kashmir. The total official death toll, including Afghanistan, Pakistan-administered Kashmir and the areas controlled by India was pegged at 74,600.

2. Arundhati Roy, *The Algebra of Infinite Justice*, 2002, Penguin Books India, New Delhi.
3. For text of the letter see, 'Arundhati Roy Refuses Sahitya Akademi Award', South End Press, 13 January 2006, online at <http://www.southendpress.org/news/news4>.
4. For full text of the Nuremberg principles see, 'International Humanitarian Law: Treaties and Documents', online at <http://www.icrc.org/ihl.nsf/FULL/390?OpenDocument>.
5. Arundhati Roy, *An Ordinary Person's Guide to Empire*, 2006, Penguin Books India, New Delhi.
6. *The Checkbook and the Cruise Missile: Conversations with Arundhati Roy*, 2004, South End Press, Cambridge.

THERE'S A FURY BUILDING UP ...

1. In this interview, Arundhati Roy updates her essay on the Narmada issue, 'The Greater Common Good', published in 1999 in *Frontline* which was also published in *The Algebra of Infinite Justice*, Revised and Updated Edition, 2002, Penguin Books India, New Delhi.
2. Writ Petition 319 of 1994 argued that the Sardar Sarovar Project violated the fundamental rights of those affected by the project, and that the project was not viable on social, environmental, technical (including seismic and hydrological), financial or economic grounds. The petition asked for a comprehensive review of the project, pending which construction on the project should cease. On 18 October 2000, a three-judge bench of the Supreme Court, comprising Justice A.S. Anand, Justice S.P. Bharucha and Justice B.N. Kirpal, delivered its final verdict on the writ, saying that the construction of the Sardar Sarovar dam be completed as 'expeditiously' as possible. For more details see Arundhati Roy, 'Postscript' to the essay 'The Greater Common Good', in *The Algebra of Infinite Justice*, Revised and Updated Edition, 2002, Penguin Books India, New Delhi, p. 138.
3. For text of report see <http://www.hinduonnet.com/2006/04/17/stories/2006041705231100.htm>.

4. See Arundhati Roy, 'The Road to Harsud', in *An Ordinary Person's Guide to Empire*, 2006, Penguin Books India, New Delhi, p. 241.
5. For full text of the recommendation of the Narmada Water Dispute Tribunal Award see <http://narmada.aidindia.org/docs/nwdt.final.award.pdf>.
6. Jared Diamond, *Collapse*, Viking Penguin, 2005, Penguin Group (USA) Inc., New York.
7. Shripad Dharmadhikary, *Unravelling Bhakra: Assessing the Temple of Resurgent India*, 2005, Manthan Adhyayan Kendra, Madhya Pradesh.
8. Arundhati Roy, *The Algebra of Infinite Justice*, Revised and Updated Edition, 2002, Penguin Books India, New Delhi.
9. For report on the incident, visit <http://www.amnesty.org/es/alfresco_asset/1722a3fa-a341-11dc-8d74-6f45f39984e5/nws21006 2007en.html>.
10. See Narmada Bachao Andolan, 2002, online at <http://www.narmada.org/nba-press-releases/april-2002/mp.maanpackage.html>. See also Gargi Parsai, 'Madhya Pradesh's Rehabilitation Claims Exposed', 17 April 2006, online at <http://www.hinduonnet.com/2006/04/17/stories/2006041719720100.htm>.
11. See 'The Greening of Gujarat: Unsung Miracle of Sardar Sarovar', *Indian Express*, 30 July 1997, online at <http://www.indianexpress.com/res/web/pIe/ie/daily/19970730/21150193.html>.
12. For key points of the Indo–US nuclear deal, see <http://www.financialexpress.com/news/Highlights-of-IndoUS-nuclear-deal/208405/>.
13. See, Indo-US Knowledge Initiative on Agricultural Research and Education: Draft Indian Proposal, online at <http://www.csrees.usda.gov/nea/international/pdfs/india_proposal.pdf>. See also, Kavitha Kuruganti, 'The Indo-US Knowledge Initiative on Agriculture: An Overview', Centre for Sustainable Agriculture, online at <http://www.csa-india.org/kiaworkshop/KIA_TOTAL/KIA_ PAPERS/2.KIA-an%20overview-kkuruganti.pdf>.
14. See The Armed Forces (Special Powers) Act, 1958; Act 28 of 1958, 11 September 1958, online at <http://www.satp.org/satporgtp/countries/india/document/actandordinances/armed_forces_special_power_act_1958.htm>. See also, 'Armed Forces (Special Powers) Act: A Study in National Security Tyranny', South Asia Human Rights Documentation Centre, online at <http://www.hrdc.net/sahrdc/resources/armed_forces.htm>.

15. See 'Land Acquisition Act, 1984', Government of India, Ministry of Law and Justice, online at <http://dolr.nic.in/hyperlink/acq.htm>.
16. See Paul Krugman, 'A Country Is Not a Company', *Harvard Business Review*, 1996.

CHOOSING OUR WEAPONS

1. See Kavita Joshi, 'Irom's Iron in the Soul', *Tehelka*, 25 March 2005, online at <http://www.tehelka.com/story_main17.asp?filename=Cr032506_Iroms_iron.asp>. See also Shoma Chaudhury, 'The Unlikely Outlaw', *Tehelka*, 9 December 2006, online at <http://www.tehelka.com/story_main23.asp?filename=Ne120906The_unlikely_CS.asp>.
2. See, 'Maoists Attack Toll Rises to 55', 16 March 2007, BBC News, online at <http://news.bbc.co.uk/2/hi/south_asia/6456989.stm>.

THE TERROR PUZZLE

1. For full text of the Prevention of Terrorism Act, 2002, see <http://www.satp.org/satporgtp/countries/india/document/actandordinances/POTA.htm#7>.
2. For more on the Terrorist and Disruptive Activities (Prevention) Act (TADA), see <http://www.satp.org/satporgtp/countries/india/document/actandordinances/TADA.HTM>.
3. For an unofficial translation of the text of the Chhattisgarh Public Security Act, see <http://www.cgnet.in/Med/cgact/document_view>.
4. See Digvijay Singh's interview with Neha Dixit, *Tehelka Magazine*, Volume 5, Issue 53, 23 August 2008. Online at <http://www.tehelka.com/story_main40.asp?filename= Ne230808Incoldblood.asp>.
5. See Ajit Sahi, 'The Kafka Project', *Tehelka Magazine*, Volume 5, Issue 32, 16 August 2008. Online at <http://www.tehelka.com/story_main40.asp?filename=Ne160808thekafka_project.asp>.

NOTES ON THE INTERVIEWERS

S. Anand is the publisher of the imprint Navayana. As a journalist he has worked for *The Hindu*, *Outlook* and *Tehelka*.

Anthony Arnove is the author of *Iraq: The Logic of Withdrawal*, published by Metropolitan Books and the American Empire Project. He is also the editor of the critically acclaimed *Iraq Under Siege: The Deadly Impact of Sanctions and War* (South End Press), *Terrorism and War*, a collection of post–9/11 interviews with Howard Zinn published by Seven Stories Press and, with Howard Zinn, *Voices of a People's History of the United States* (Seven Stories), a primary-source companion to Zinn's *A People's History of the United States*. His latest book, forthcoming from Penguin India, is *The Essential Chomsky*. Arnove lives in Brooklyn, New York, and is on the editorial board of the *International Socialist Review* and of Haymarket Books.

David Barsamian is the founder and director of Alternative Radio, www.alternativeradio.org, the independent weekly series based in Boulder, Colorado. He is a radio producer, journalist, author and lecturer. He has been working in radio since 1978. His interviews and articles appear regularly in *The Progressive* and *Z Magazine*.

His latest books are *Targeting Iran* and *What We Say Goes: Conversations on U.S. Power in a Changing World* with Noam Chomsky, *Speaking of Empire and Resistance: Conversations with Tariq Ali* and *Original Zinn: Conversations on History and Politics* with Howard Zinn. His earlier books include *The Checkbook and the Cruise Missile* with Arundhati Roy, *Imperial Ambitions* with Noam Chomsky, *Eqbal Ahmad: Confronting Empire* and *The Decline and Fall of Public Broadcasting*.

Barsamian lectures on US foreign policy, corporate power, the media and propaganda all over the world. He was awarded the Media Education Award by Friends of Community Media for outstanding work as a progressive media voice. The Institute for

Alternative Journalism named him one of its Top Ten Media Heroes. He is the winner of the ACLU's Upton Sinclair Award for independent journalism, the Rocky Mountain Peace and Justice Award and the Cultural Freedom Fellowship from the Lannan Foundation. In December 2007 he delivered the prestigious Eqbal Ahmad lectures in Pakistan in Karachi, Islamabad and Lahore.

Shoma Chaudhury is a founder-member and editor with *Tehelka*.

N. Ram is the editor-in-chief of *The Hindu*. He also heads the other publications of The Hindu Group such as *Frontline*, *The Hindu Business Line* and *Sportstar*. Ram has been awarded the Padma Bhushan.

P.G. Rasool writes, in Urdu, a weekly column on current affairs in *Kashmir Uzma (Greater Kashmir)*, published from Srinagar. He has also written *Kashmir 1947* (Urdu).

Amit Sengupta is the editor-in-charge of *Hardnews*. He was, earlier, editor, commentary and analysis, at *Tehelka*.

INDEX